Herodian Messiah

Case For Jesus As Grandson of Herod

Second Edition

Joseph Raymond

St. Louis, Missouri, USA

Tower Grove Publishing
St. Louis, MO USA

Herodian Messiah
Case For Jesus As Grandson Of Herod

ISBN - 10:   0615355080
ISBN - 13:   9780615355085

Other Books by Joseph Raymond

Chicken Farmer, An American Fable
(Fiction 2008)

Grandson of Herod, Iesvs Nazarenvs Rex Ivdaeorvm
(Tower Grove Publishing 2012)

About the Author

Joseph Raymond was raised in a devout Roman Catholic family in St. Louis, MO USA and educated in Catholic schools. He received degrees from two Jesuit universities graduating law school in 1986. Thereafter, he served as a Department of Justice lawyer in Washington, DC but later left the practice of law to found an internet company. In 1988, he began a spiritual journey of study and reflection largely focused upon the origins of Christianity. Once started, the journey is never complete. In January of 2012, Joseph Raymond gave an on-camera interview to Karga Seven Pictures in Los Angeles regarding theories contained in *Herodian Messiah* for an upcoming documentary to air on the Discovery Channel later in 2012.

Acknowledgement

I wish to thank my old friend Jan Van Puffelen for his encouragement to pursue the self-study of religious history. He also conducted early debates with me on the theory of Jesus as a Hasmonean member of the House of Herod.

JJR

Family Tree of Herod The Great

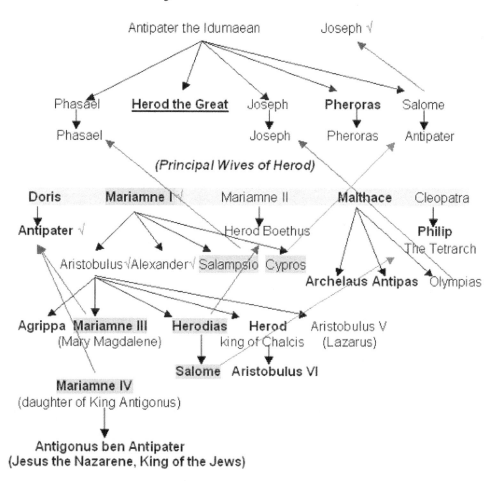

Antipater the Idumaean   Joseph √

Phasael   **Herod the Great**   Joseph   **Pheroras**   Salome

Phasael   Joseph   Pheroras   Antipater

(Principal Wives of Herod)

Doris   **Mariamne I**   Mariamne II   **Malthace**   Cleopatra

Antipater √   Herod Boethus   **Philip**
                                                            The Tetrarch

Aristobulus √ Alexander √ Salampsio Cypros

                                     Archelaus Antipas Olympias

Agrippa **Mariamne III**   **Herodias**   **Herod**   Aristobulus V
(Mary Magdalene)   king of Chalcis   (Lazarus)

                                Salome Aristobulus VI

Mariamne IV
(daughter of King Antigonus)

Antigonus ben Antipater
(Jesus the Nazarene, King of the Jews)

    Hasmonean Princess   √ Executed by Herod
⟵ First marriage of selected Herodian females.
Bold denotes kings / tetrarchs and queens.

Contents

Introduction

The received Christian tradition asserts that 2000 years ago a carpenter's son of uncertain education and parentage accompanied by a small band of scruffy fishermen burst onto the sacred grounds of the Temple complex in Jerusalem claiming to be both a righteous teacher and king of the Jews. Surely, upon hearing this proclamation, the chief priests would have erupted in laughter taking the carpenter's son for an insane person. But the chief priests didn't laugh at Jesus, nor did the members of the Sanhedrin, nor the high priest, nor Herod Antipas, nor even the Roman prefect of Judea (Pontius Pilate). They all treated him as a serious and real threat to their power. Why? The Bible does not present Jesus as a military commander (unless one considers a dozen fishermen with swords under their cloaks to be a military force). The logical source of Jesus' perceived threat to the Roman and Jewish authorities must have been his royal bloodline, so unique and high standing that Pilate regarded Jesus as a rightful king.

> Pilate therefore said to him, "So you are a king?" Jesus answered, "You say correctly that I am a king. For this reason I have been born, and for this reason I have come into the world, that I should testify to the truth." * * * [Pilate] went out again to the Jews, and said to them, "I find no guilt in him."[1] [Emphasis added.]

The obvious conclusion to be drawn from this Gospel passage is that Jesus claimed to be a king and Pilate agreed he was a legitimate

---

[1] *John* 18:37; See also *Luke* 23:3-4 (emphasis added).

Jewish king. Moreover, Pilate recorded on a board nailed to the cross the following words--"Iesvs Nazarenvs Rex Ivdaeorvm"[2], which translates as **Jesus Nazarene King Jews**. How could it be that a carpenter's son raised in a tiny village of Galilee came to be regarded by the Roman prefect as a true Jewish king?

Orthodox Christianity responds with the claim that Jesus was a descendant of King David allegedly making him of royal blood.[3] This fact (even if true) would not have held much value for advancing the political career of Jesus when placed in context of the historical fortunes of the House of David in the first century of Common Era. At that time, a descendant of David had not sat on the Jewish throne for over 600 years. The entire extended Jewish royal family was deported to Babylon by the invading Chaldeans in 586 BCE. The Davidic princes stayed in Babylon never returning to Jerusalem even though the Persians overthrew the Chaldean dynasty fifty years later and their king (Cyrus the Great) granted permission to the Jews to return home. The Persians appointed a royal descendant of King David to the office of Exilarch as ruler over the exiled Jewish community and allowed them to populate their own towns. The Jews essentially formed an autonomous region inside Babylon where the Davidic royal family settled in as potentates. History records but a very small number of Jews said to descend from David returning from Babylonian captivity and taking up positions of authority in Jerusalem. None of these individuals made claims upon the Jewish throne; however, Davidic princes did serve in the Sanhedrin as president. Rabbi Hillel the Elder who lived during the time of Herod is such an example.

Also, being a descendant of King David didn't place you in an exclusive club in first century Judea. Jewish kings adopted the custom of eastern monarchs keeping numerous wives and even more concubines. King Solomon (son and successor of David)

---

[2] See also *John* 19:21-22 where the chief priests attempt to dissuade Pilate from identifying Jesus as the king of the Jews in the message placed onto the cross. Pilate refused to change the inscription.

[3] See Romans 1:3: "Concerning his Son Jesus Christ our Lord, which was made of the seed of David according to the flesh."

was said to have had 300 wives and 700 concubines. Jesus lived 1000 years after David, or 40 to 50 generations later. One can safely assume many thousands of Jews living in Palestine during the time of Jesus traced their ancestry back to King David. For a modern example, geneticists studying the DNA from present day Mongolia concluded that 8% of the males of the former Mongol empire trace their lineage back to Genghis Khan, a 13th century ruler. Eight percent of the males of this territory translates to 16 million men.[4] This degree of penetration of genes (no pun intended) occurred over a shorter time span than that which separated King David and Jesus. Descent from King David would not have been unusual during the time of Jesus. Further, the royal branch of the Davidic family tree resided in Babylon during the time of Jesus yet he was born in Judea.

Perhaps an example from the modern age gives us perspective on the notion that Jesus claimed the Jewish throne on the basis of descent from King David. A group of British historians asserted in the 2005 BBC program *Britain's Real Monarch* that strong proof exists for the contention that 15th century king Edward IV was illegitimate and, thus, the crown should have went to his younger brother George, Duke of Clarence. When the researchers followed the patrilineal line of descendent from the Duke of Clarence down 500 years to the present day, they determined that an Australian rice farmer named Michael Hastings was the true king of England. What chance do you think the rice farmer from the Aussie outback has of reclaiming the British throne? Carrying this example back in time to Jesus, try and imagine a carpenter's son from Galilee turning up in the Jewish capital claiming to be the descendant of a Davidic king who last ruled the Israel six hundred years in the past. The rice farmer at least possesses extant written birth records establishing his claim to royal ancestry. The parents of Jesus were portrayed in the New Testament as peasants. At a bare minimum one must accept the extreme difficultly the supporters of Jesus faced in authenticating a claim that he was of Davidic royal blood via an ancestor who lived

---

[4] Hillary Mayell, National Geographic News (Feb. 14. 2003).

in Jewish antiquity and, further, distinguishing his particular ancestry as more significant than the many thousands of Jews of the first century of the Common Era who likely traced their roots back to King David.

The kicker to this line of reasoning is that the Romans recognized only one man and his descendants as the legitimate royal family of the Jewish kingdom—the Herodians. On what basis would a Roman prefect recognize a descendant of David from the countryside of Galilee as a legitimate Jewish king? I submit it is an absurd assertion when placed in the context of Roman and Jewish history. Even more perplexing is the Sanhedrin's treatment of Jesus. The New Testament tells us the Sanhedrin convicted Jesus of the crime of blasphemy, a capital offense. Upon conviction, Jesus should have been taken to the courtyard outside the Hall of Hewn Stones and put to death.[5] The Bible records Stephen, a follower of Jesus, being condemned to death and summarily executed by the Sanhedrin in this fashion.[6] Further, Josephus records the Sanhedrin condemning and executing Jesus' own brother (James the Just).[7] However, in the case of Jesus, the chief priests appeared before Pilate proclaiming they lacked the authority to execute the prisoner and asked Pilate to put Jesus to death. Why?

The Bible offers one possible explanation for these seemingly inconsistent actions by the Sanhedrin —the case of Paul of Tarsus. He too was taken into custody by Jewish authorities at the Temple but Roman soldiers saved Paul during his trial in the Sanhedrin because he was "a Roman citizen by birth."[8] The

---

[5] "According to the *Mishnah Sanhedrin* 4.1 capital cases are to be held during the day and the verdict must also be reached during the day. * * * If the verdict was guilty they must wait until the next day [to execute the prisoner]." CSI: Gethsemane to Golgotha by Steve Rush (PublishAmerica, 2005) at page 25. It appears the Sanhedrin violated their own procedural rules in a rush to prosecute Jesus.

[6] *Acts* 7:57-59. In another Bible passage, the Pharisees bring a woman before Jesus who had been caught committing adultery and asked, "Now the laws of Moses command that she be stoned: but what say you?" John 8:5.

[7] Antiquities XX 9:1 (200).

[8] *Acts* 22:25 through 23:10.

soldiers then brought Paul for trial before Roman authorities. If Jesus was a Roman citizen that would explain why the Sanhedrin lacked authority to execute him and instead demanded Pontius Pilate carry out the deed. In Roman provinces,[9] the local tribunals of subject peoples lacked jurisdiction to administer criminal punishment against Roman citizens, especially in capital cases. This was an early form of diplomatic immunity. Roman citizens could only be executed by Roman tribunals and members of the royal family of a subject kingdom all received Roman citizenship. However, Roman citizens could not be executed by crucifixion under Roman law. So we are left with a conundrum--Roman citizenship would explain why the Sanhedrin lacked authority to execute Jesus but, if true, then Pilate lacked authority to crucify Jesus under Roman law.

The few scattered facts listed above mark the point where my journey investigating the identity of the historical Jesus began. This book presents a bold and, in some ways, shocking theory that Jesus was the grandson of both Herod the Great and King Antigonus (the last Hasmonean king). Although this premise has previously been proposed,[10] the case supporting the theory is original having been constructed through synthesis of Josephus, Philo, the canonical Bible, Roman histories, and apocryphal Jewish and Christian texts. The proof is acknowledged to be less than conclusive; however, the theory harmonizes what we know of Jesus. I submit it offers a stronger case for the identity of the historical Jesus than the accepted tradition of a carpenter's son from a small Galilean village called Nazareth.

---

[9] Judea was part of the Roman province of Syria.
[10] See King Jesus by Robert Graves (Farrar, Straus and Giroux 1946). Note: although Graves wrote a work of historical fiction claiming Jesus was the son of Antipater, eldest son of Herod, Graves declined to give the proof for this theory. See also The Marian Conspiracy by Graham Phillips (Pan Books 2000).

Chapter 1
Summary Argument

I approached this work as a lawyer constructs a legal brief. First collect the facts, next research the law, then analyze the law to the facts (with a healthy dose of returning to step one when the pieces of the jigsaw puzzle refuse to align). Procedural rules require legal briefs filed with appellate courts to include an opening section setting forth a concise summary of the party's case. Before launching into a detailed examination of the matter, below is a summary of the legs upon which the theory stands. Each of these points shall be properly footnoted with source material in the body of this work.

1. **The names of Hasmonean kings appear in the *Gospel of Luke*'s genealogy for Jesus.** Separate genealogies for Jesus given in the Gospels of *Matthew* and *Luke* are inconsistent; however, the Roman Catholic Church attempts to explain this inconsistency through the assertion that the genealogy given in *Luke* is actually that of Mary the mother of Jesus while *Matthew* records the ancestors of Joseph the carpenter. I accept this premise regarding *Luke*. The genealogy list found in *Luke* contains the name "Melchi" which is Hebrew for king. The generation during which "Melchi" would have lived corresponds to the Hasmonean dynasty (i.e., the only Jewish kings of this period were the Hasmoneans). Further, *Luke* gives the father of Melchi as Jannai, which corresponds to the name of a specific Hasmonean

king (Alexander Jannai). The list also contains the name Levi, the priestly tribe to which the Hasmonean kings belonged. Summarizing the *Luke* genealogy, an ancestor of Jesus named Jannai had a son named Melchi (king) and a grandson Levi (priest). Jannai was a rare Jewish name of the period and Luke's Jannai lived during the Hasmonean dynasty. The only kings from the tribe of Levi were the Hasmoneans and Jannai was the best-known king of this dynasty. The evidence strongly supports the conclusion that *Luke* lists Hasmonean king Alexander Jannai as an ancestor of Jesus. The Hasmoneans were members of the tribe of Levi, not Judah which was King David's tribe.

2. The Hebrew name of the the last Hasmonean king, Mattatayah Antigonus, also appears as "Matthat" on *Luke*'s list in the position of a close ancestor of Jesus. The identification of this individual as King Antigonus comes from the names of Matthat's immediate ancestors—Levi (priest), Melchi (king), and Jannai (King Alexander Jannai). Hasmoean king Mattatayah Antigonus was a grandson of King Alexander Jannai. Josephus identifies only one descendant of King Antigonus living until the last days of Herod the Great, a daughter who was married to crown prince Antipater ben Herod. I contend this daughter of Antigonus was the mother of Jesus.

3. Ancient tradition holds that Mary the mother of Jesus was from a priestly Levite family. The *Gospel of Luke* identifies Elizabeth as a "kinswoman" of Mary the mother of Jesus and, also, a "daughter of Aaron". This term means the daughter of a Kohen priest. The Kohanim were patrilineal descendants of Aaron[11] who controlled the Temple as the highest ranking Levitical priests. If Elizabeth was the daughter of a Kohen priest, in all probability her kinswoman Mary was as well given that Kohen priests tended to marry daughters of their Kohanim brethren. According to the Quran, Mary the mother of Jesus was a "sister of Aaron", also meaning the daughter of Kohanim. These two pieces of evidence

---

[11] Meaning a Kohen priest must trace his ancestry father to son all the way back to Aaron.

point to an ancient tradition that Mary was the daughter of a Kohen priest.

4. Jesus had no officially acknowledged biologic father. Any claim he possessed to royal blood must have come from his mother Mary. If Mary was the daughter of a Kohen priest, the only source of Jesus' claim to royal lineage rested upon descent from the Hasmonean kings. The Kohanim were not descendants of King David and their only link to Jewish royalty was via the Hasmonean dynasty.

5. The *Protoevangelium of James* describes the father of Mary as "exceedingly rich" and the mother of Mary wearing a head-band with a "mark of royalty". Mary assuredly grew up during Herod's reign and, in this period, only high-ranking Temple priests and Herodians were allowed to be exceedingly rich. The Hasmoneans were both rich (as elite Temple priests) and the royal family before Herod deposed them. Outside of Herod's family and political retainers, high ranking Temple priests were the only class of Jewish citizens who were rich. Only two families could have been considered <u>both</u> rich and royal during the reign of Herod--Herod's own family and the Hasmoneans—and only the Hasmoneans were both royal and priestly. Josephus tells us Herod killed off the Hasmoneans except for those Hasmoneans who were descendants of Herod. This leads us to the interesting case of Josephus himself. Jospehus claims to be both of Hasmonean royal blood and born into a family whose ancestors included "high priests". As no high priests were known to be members of Herod's family, my conclusion is that lesser ranking Hasmoneans within the Temple priesthood survived the purge of Herod. I argue that Mary the mother of Jesus was adopted into a Kohanim family of Hasmonean blood after the execution of her father, King Antigonus.

6. **The synoptic Gospels of *Mathew*, *Mark* and *Luke* each record Jesus saying to the Pharisees that the Christ (i.e., Jesus himself) is NOT a son of King David.** Therefore, the claim of Jesus to the Jewish throne was not made on the basis of descent from David. <u>See</u> *Matthew* 22:41-45, *Mark* 12:35-37, and *Luke* 20:41-44.

7. The *Book of Jubilees* and other texts from the Dead Sea Scrolls talk of two messiahs, one from Judah and the other from Levi. Another text of this milieu, the *Aramaic Levi Document*, goes a step further merging the two messiahs into one priest-king of the tribe of Levi. When Jesus claimed to be the messiah, he meant the priest-king messiah from Levi.

8. Jesus and his brother James shared the same mother, Mary. Early church historian Hegesippus stated that James entered the "Holy of Holies". Only the high priest could enter the holy of holies in the Temple. Prof. Robert Eisenman opines that James operated as an opposition high priest. All sacramental duties at the Temple above the lowest level were reserved for the Kohanim. The foregoing suggests James was a Kohen priest, which also means Joseph the carpenter (father of James the Just) was a Kohen priest as the status of Kohen only passed father to son.

Points 1-8 support the contention that Jesus descended from Hasmonean kings through his mother Mary. The more difficult leap is from the Hasmoneans to Herod. This proof is offered in points 9-14.

9. Herod infused his own family tree with Hasmonean blood. Josephus records Herod himself marrying the granddaughter of a Hasmonean king while his son Antipater married the daughter of the last Hasmonean king, Antigonus. Ironically, Marc Antony executed King Antigonus at the urging of (and most likely bribing by) Herod.

10. After Herod captured Jerusalem in 37 BCE, Josephus tells us Herod massacred the entire Hasmonean royal family except five individuals who became members of his family.[12] He later

---

[12] The five were Princess Mariamne bat Alexander (wife of Herod), Princess Alexandra bat Hyrcanus (mother of Mariamne), former high priest Hyrcanus II (grandfather of Mariamne), Aristobulus III (brother of Mariamne) and a daughter of King Antigonus who Josephus, inexplicably, fails to name. Josephus records Herod executing or murdering four of these five Hasmoneans. The unnamed daughter of King Antigonus survived to 4 BCE and then disappeared from the writings of Josephus. As explained later in this work, I conclude that the only Hasmonean of royal blood alive after 9 BCE not known to have been murdered by Herod (i.e., the daughter of Antigonus) was in fact Mary, the mother of Jesus.

executed four of the five remaining Hasmoneans who were then members of his family. The fate of the fifth Hasmonean royal was unaccounted for by Josephus (and I theorize she was the mother of Jesus).

11.   Therefore, any individual born of Hasmonean royal blood in the last few years before the start of the Common Era was in all probability a member of Herod's family although the case of Josephus indicates a lesser branch of the Hasmonean tree survived in the Temple priesthood outside of the family of Herod. However, the refusal of the Sanhedrin to execute Jesus after convicting him of a capital offense (claiming they lacked the authority to do so and demanding the Romans carry out the punishment) indicates Jesus held Roman citizenship.   All members of Herod's immediate family were Roman citizens. The foregoing suggests that Jesus was a Hasmonean member of Herod's family. The Talmud makes the connection to Herod in more direct terms stating, "Jesus the Nazarene ... was close to the government."[13]

12. Jesus was born of Hasmonean royal blood in 3 BCE. Josephus recorded Herod's eldest son Antipater marrying the only known daughter of Hasmonean king Antigonus to survive until the end of Herod's reign. Those named by *Luke* as ancestors of Jesus match, to a degree, the lineage of Antigonus. This supports the hypothesis that the only surviving daughter of Antigonus mentioned in Josephus was the mother of Jesus.

13. The individual I reason to have been Jesus' mother was recorded by Josephus as married to Herod's son at the time Jesus was likely conceived. Discounting the possibility that a bastard could have been viewed by the Roman and Jewish authorities as a legitimate king, the fact that the mother of Jesus was married to Herod's son Antipater until his death in late 4 BCE strongly indicates Jesus was the grandson of Herod. This explains why the chief priests of the Sanhedrin declared they lacked authority to execute Jesus (he was a Roman citizen) and, further, why Pontius Pilate concluded that Jesus was indeed a Jewish king (he was the

---

[13] Peter Schafer, <u>Jesus in the Talmud</u> (Princeton University Press 2007) at page 63, translating Babylonian Talmud, 43a.

only man then alive who was the grandson of two Jewish kings, Herod and Antigonus).

14. A theory with a moderate level of proof exists for the proposition that Antipater ben Herod, who I identify as the father of Jesus, descended from King David through the royal Idumean lineage of his mother Doris. She was born in Jerusalem although of Idumean royal blood. If true, this explains why Jesus allowed himself to be addressed as a "son of David" although Jesus never uttered those words.[14] Jesus could not publicly claim descendent from David through his father Antipater without revealing that Herod was his grandfather. The Jewish people's hatred for Herod required Jesus to remain silent upon the identity of his father. The Gospels present Jesus as allowing the people to suppose he was the son of Joseph the carpenter. In modern parlance, this would be termed political expediency.

Chapter 2 begins with an in depth look at the largest stumbling block to the theory—how could Jesus claim to be the messiah if he denied he was a descendant of David? Once clearing that hurdle, the book examines the evidence from *Luke's* ancestor list in Chapter 3, the cornerstone upon which the theory rests. Also presented are alternative views of other biblical figures building upon the Herodian-Hasmonean theme including Mary Magdalene, Paul of Tarsus, and further discussion of Antipater ben Herod (the father of Jesus).

---

[14] <u>See</u> Chapter 8.

Chapter 2
Jesus, Messiah of Levi

In 2007 while building my theory of Jesus as a mixed Herodian-Hasmonean prince, I ~~spammed~~ circulated via email the supporting evidence for my theory (as it then stood) to several randomly selected professors of religion from universities throughout the United States. Only one responded and asked to remain anonymous. She wasn't warm to the theory; however, she did give me one important piece of advice--my theory must explain how Jesus could be the messiah without being a descendant of King David. In her view, the entire theory was dead in the water until I convincingly cleared this hurdle. This chapter states the case for Jesus as messiah from the priestly tribe of Levi.

<u>Fall of the House of David</u>

David is thought to have ascended to the Jewish throne in the eleventh century BCE, although history lacks archeological evidence outside of the Bible to even support his existence. He was the youngest son of Jesse, a Judean shepherd. Although born of common blood, God directed the prophet Samuel to anoint David king.[15] According to Samuel, God promised the Jewish throne to "the seed" of David forever.[16] However, Yahweh is not

---

[15] 1 *Samuel* 16:1-13.
[16] 2 *Samuel* 7:12-13; another passage is thought to indicate that the Jewish king must also descend from David's son Solomon and not one of his numerous other sons. 1 *Chron* 28:5-7.

a God to make open-ended promises lacking qualifiers. Like any good lawyer, Yahweh provided himself an out in his contract with the House of David.

> The Lord hath sworn in truth unto David; he
> will not turn from it; of the fruit of thy body
> will I set upon thy throne. <u>If thy children will
> keep my covenant and my testimony</u> that I
> shall teach them, their children shall also sit
> upon thy throne for evermore."[17] [Emphasis
> added.]

The Davidic dynasty came crashing down when King Nebuchadnezzar II captured Jerusalem in 597 BC taking Jewish king Jeconiah and the entire extended royal family to captivity in Babylon and, later adding insult to injury, destroyed the Temple. Jeconiah descended from David and sat upon his throne; therefore, the only conclusion for the Jewish people to draw from this turn of events was that David's descendants broke the covenant with God. By failing to keep the covenant, God allowed the Chaldeans to sack Jerusalem, carry the Davidic king and his extended family off into captivity, and destroy the Temple.

If there be any doubt that Yahweh viewed the covenant with David breached, one need read no further than the curse of Jeconiah proclaimed by the prophet Jeremiah.

> "As surely as I live," declares the
> Lord, "even if you, Jeconiah[18] son of
> Jehoiachin king of Judah, were a signet ring
> on my right hand, I would still pull you off.
> I will hand you over to those who seek your
> life, those you fear—to Nebuchadnezzar king
> of Babylon and to the Babylonians. I will hurl
> you and the mother who gave you birth into
> another country, where neither of you were
> born, and there you both will die. You will
> never come back to the land you long to

---

[17] *Psalm* 132:11-12.

[18] Some Bible translations use the name Jehoiachin, which is an alternate for Jeconiah.

return to."

Is this man Jehoiachin a despised, broken pot, an object no one wants? Why will he and his children be hurled out, cast into a land they do not know O land, land, land, hear the word of the Lord! This is what the Lord says: "Record this man as if childless, a man who will not prosper in his lifetime, for none of his offspring will prosper, none will sit on the throne of David or rule anymore in Judah.[19] [Emphasis added.]

Clearly Jeconiah and his descendants were mud under Jewish law, which is odd given that the *Gospel of Matthew* names Jesus a descendant of the accursed Jeconiah. See *Matthew* 1:12. For this reason, Jesus' alleged genealogy given in *Matthew* is illegitimate for a claimant to the Jewish throne under Jewish scripture. The Roman Catholic Church asserts *Matthew's* genealogy is that of Joseph the carpenter, the step-father of Jesus. I view it as highly suspect.

King Jeconiah strikes me as something of a biblical fall guy. He ascended to the throne at age 18 while the Chaldean army besieged Jerusalem. His reign lasted all of three months before his capture and exile to Babylon. What could the kid have done in 3 months to deserve Jeremiah's wicked curse upon he, his mother, and all his descendants? Jeconiah seems to have been made to pay for his father's sins. His father, King Jehoiakim, gained the throne as a puppet to Pharaoh Necho II of Egypt after pharaoh deposed and killed Jehoiachin's older brother. Jehoiachin heavily taxed the Jewish people in order to pay tribute to pharaoh and burned a scroll containing the prophecies of Jeremiah because they criticized the king.[20] Another ancestor, King Manasseh, reinstated pagan worship in the Temple[21] and built altars to pagan gods in Judea.[22] The point to be gained from this discussion is that the royal line

---

[19] Jeremiah 22:24-30 (New International Version).
[20] *Jeremiah* 36:1-32.
[21] *2 Kings* 21.
[22] *2 Chronicles* 33:1-10.

from David had fallen out of favor with God by the sixth century BCE. Further, the curse of Jeconiah explains why the royal descendants of David residing in Babylon never returned to Israel to reclaim the Jewish throne.

Until Shiloh Comes

Although open to interpretation, a passage from *Genesis* lends credence to the position that the Jewish throne does not eternally belong to the descendants of King David. It reads, "The scepter shall not depart from Judah, nor the ruler's staff from between his feet, until Shiloh comes: And unto him shall the obedience of the people be."[23] The Talmud interprets this reference to Shiloh to mean the Messiah.[24] Substituting Messiah for Shiloh renders the phrase, "The scepter shall not depart from Judah ... until the Messiah comes, and unto him shall the obedience of the people be." David was of the tribe of Judah. If the scepter passed out of the hands of Judah when the Messiah came, then the Messiah was not to come from the tribe of Judah. Consider further that Shiloh was a city located in the traditional homeland of the tribe of Ephraim[25] and, therefore, outside of the territory of Judah. It's difficult to conger a reading of this line from *Genesis* that equates Shiloh with Judah.

Moving past the issue of whether or not the House of David perpetually retained divine right to the throne of Israel, what other tribe possessed scriptural support for a claim upon the Jewish throne? If not Judah, then whom?

Sectarian Jewish Belief In Two Messiahs

Mashiach is the Hebrew word translated into English as messiah. It means "anointed one" denoting one chosen by God. The prophet Samuel anointed David with oil as king of Judah at the direction of God.[26] This is why Jesus was anointed with costly oil before he entered Jerusalem to claim the throne. The act of

---

[23] *Genesis* 49:10 (American Standard Version).
[24] Sanhedrin 98b.
[25] Shiloh was also the original location of the Arc of the Covenant.
[26] 1 *Samuel* 16:1-13.

anointment signified the messiah and king. The Jewish concept of messiah in the time of Jesus grows nebulous beyond reference to an anointed king. "While messianic doctrine varied in detail from sect to sect, it generally represented a desire for a king who was appointed directly by God to perform supernatural wonders for the Jews. He was to remove from them oppression and injustice, defeat all forces of evil, and usher in the true reign of God."[27]

Josephus identified three major Jewish sects existing in the first century CE: the Sadducees, Pharisees, and Essenes. Modern Rabbinic Judaism grew out of the Pharisee movement. In examining the historical Jesus, prime importance should be given to his own testimony. The Gospels lay bare the antipathy Jesus held for the Pharisee movement. The below-quoted words of Jesus directed to the Pharisees as recorded in *Matthew* dispel any ambiguity on the subject.

> Therefore you are witnesses against yourselves that you are sons of those who murdered the prophets. Fill up, then, the measure of your fathers' guilt. Serpents, brood of vipers! How can you escape the condemnation of hell?[28]

The Sadducees were aligned with the Herodians and the occupying Romans. Sadducee doctrine conservatively centered upon the Pentateuch (first five books of the Old Testament) and departed even further from the teachings of Jesus than the Pharisees. For instance, the Sadducees denied the existence of an afterlife.

As discussed in Chapter 8, I view the Jewish reform movement established by Jesus as a synthesis of Essene and Therapeutae doctrine. The Therapeutae were a community of ascetic monks based in Egypt as described in the works of Philo of Alexandria. Saving a discussion of this topic for later in this work, suffice it to say the teachings of Jesus fall outside the canon of Pharisee / Rabbinic Judaism. On this basis, we direct our search for an alternative concept of Messiah to pre-Christian, non-

---

[27] The Jews in the Time of Jesus by Stephen M. Wylen (Paulist Press 1996) at page 25.
[28] *Matthew* 23:31-33.

canonical Jewish texts with special emphasis on the Dead Sea Scrolls.

The Book of Jubilees

The *Book of Jubilees* is an apocryphal Jewish work predating Herod's reign that forms an important key for understanding the particular theology used by the Hasmoneans to justify their position on the Jewish throne as priests of the tribe of Levi. "The prevailing opinion today in *Jubilees* scholarship * * * dates the composition of the book to 161-140 BCE."[29] I use the word apocryphal to describe *Jubilees* because it is not part of modern day Jewish or Christian canon. However, fragments of fifteen copies of *Jubilees* were found among the *Dead Sea Scrolls* at Qumran. The work obviously held importance for the community that assembled the scrolls at Qumran in antiquity. A "major eschatological passage in *Jubilees* * * * warn[s] against contact with Gentiles and their ways, lest you be destroyed."[30] See Chapter 8 herein for a discussion of the teaching of James the Just on this issue. The "ideas of the Book of Jubilees (and, therefore, one infers, some form of the text itself) was known to Paul and to the authors of Luke and Acts, James, Hebrews, and 2 Peter."[31]

Jubilees rewrote much of the first five books of the Jewish Bible adding in additional material and characters. It gives a prominent role to the patriarch Jacob. Of particular note for our purposes is *Jubilees* treatment of Jacob's sons Levi and Judah, who are given precedence over his other sons. Judah was the progenitor of King David's tribe and Levi of the priestly tribe by the same name. According to *Jubilees* Jacob took only Levi and Judah to visit his father Isaac while he lay on his deathbed, although Jacob had twelve sons. Levi held his grandfather's right hand and Judah the left while their grandfather Isaac gave them his

---

[29] The Book of Jubilees: Rewritten Bible, Redaction, Ideology and Theology By Michael Segal (BRILL 2007) at page 36.
[30] The Eschatology of the Book of Jubilees by Gene L. Davenport (Brill Academic Publishers 1997) at page 32. See *Jubilees* Chapters 22 and 23.
[31] Surpassing Wonder: The Invention of the Bible and the Talmuds by Donald Harman Akenson (University Of Chicago Press 2001) at page 146.

blessing. He blessed Levi first thusly, "shall the seed of thy sons be for glory and greatness and holiness, and may [God] make them great unto all the ages. And they shall be judges and princes, and chiefs of all the seed of the sons of Jacob."[32] Note that Isaac blessed Levi first and made him "chief and judge" over all Jacob's sons, which implicitly included Judah. Isaac then gave Judah the following blessing, "Then shall the Gentiles fear before thy face. ... And when thou sit on the throne of honor of thy righteousness, there shall be great peace for all the seed of the sons of the beloved."[33] In *Jubilees*, Judah's descendants sat on a throne but Levi's held all real power. In the *Jubilees* formulation, Levi stood first among the sons of Jacob.

Dead Sea Scrolls and Two Messiahs

Several other apocryphal works go further than *Jubilees* speaking of the salvation of the Lord springing from Levi and Judah.[34] Texts among the *Dead Sea Scrolls* reference two messiahs. The *Rule of the Community* and the *Damascus Document* reference the coming of "the messiahs of Aaron and Israel."[35] Aaron was a descendant of Levi. The term "Israel" is thought to refer to Judah. Note that Aaron (Levi) was listed ahead of Israel (Judah) in each instance where these phrases were used in the Dead Sea Scrolls. The Hasmoneans, as descendants of Levi, claimed they fulfilled the prophecies found in these messianic texts. The primacy of Levi in these scriptures formed the foundation for legitimatization of Hasmonean rule yet did not go so far as proclaiming Levi king.

That final step to Levi's kingship was taken by the *Aramaic Levi Document* (ALD).

According to ALD, Levi is a pious and even prophetic figure, a person beloved by God

---

[32] *Jubilees*, 31:14-15 (emphasis added).
[33] *Jubilees*, 31:18-20.
[34] See *Testament of Dan*, *Testament of Naphtali*, and *Testament of Joseph*; See also Jewish Writings of the Second Temple Period by Michael Stone (Fortress Press 1984) at page 338.
[35] See Qumran-Messianism: Studies on the Messianic Expectations in the Dead Sea Scrolls By James H. Charlesworth, et alia (Mohr Siebeck 1998).

and the recipient of two divine visions. "We have magnified you over everyone," an angelic speaker says to him at the conclusion of the second. In addition to being installed as a priest, Levi is also portrayed as a sage and champion of wisdom. Indeed, he says to his children that they will be "chiefs and judges and ... and servants ... <u>even priests and kings</u> ... your kingdom will be ... and will have no end forever ... and will not depart from you until all ... ." (4Q213, frag. 2, 10-18).[36]

The notation "4Q213" is a Dead Sea Scroll identifying number meaning Qumran Cave 4, Text 213. Scholars debate whether ALD was written before or after *Jubilees* but all agree it is pre-Christian. Fragments of ALD were also found in the Cairo Genzia indicating that this text had a wider following than an obscure desert sect.[37]

In summation, the two messiah formula placed Levi above Judah (David's tribe). ALD elevates Levi's descendants to the Jewish throne as the lone messiah. Although a sectarian view out of the mainstream, the concept of two messiahs with one coming from the tribe of Levi clearly existed in the Jewish world during the time of Jesus. Further, one ancient Jewish text pre-dating Jesus (ALD) declares a single messiah and king from the tribe of Levi. Authority for a king from the tribe of Levi is found not just in obscure texts but, also, in the historical record of the Jewish people in the person of the Hasmonean kings. Thus, the concept of a messianic king from the tribe of Levi was established in both Jewish religious writing and history by the time Jesus launched his public campaign.

<u>Hasmonean Kings, Tribe of Levi</u>

When Israel lay low oppressed by the successors to

---

[36] <u>The Ladder of Jacob</u> by James L. Kugel (Princeton University Press 2006) at page 153, emphasis added.

[37] <u>Reworking the Bible: Apocryphal and Related Texts at Qumran</u> by Lawrence H. Schiffman (Brill Academic Pub, 2005) at p. 177-78, edited by Esther G. Chazon, Devorah Dimant and Ruth A. Clements.

Alexander the Great (known as the Seleucid Empire) in the second century BCE, it was not the descendants of King David who came to rescue the nation but Kohanim priests from the tribe of Levi— i.e., the Maccabees a/k/a the Hasmoneans. These Jewish priests expelled the Greeks from the holy land through protracted guerilla warfare. After their victory against the Seleucid army, the Hasmoneans entered Jerusalem in triumph and ritually cleansed the Temple as a precursor to reestablishing traditional Jewish worship according to the laws of Moses. This cleansing and rededication of the Temple by the Hasmoneans is celebrated today by the major Jewish holiday of Hanukkah. One view of Jesus' actions in expelling the money-changers from the Temple is that it constituted a cleansing of corrupting practices not unlike the deeds of his Hasmonean forbearers. The Hasmoneans first ruled as high priest but eventually elevated their leader to king presiding over an expanded Israel for 100 years before their dynasty fell to Herod and the Romans. The Hasmonean priests were, however, not descendants of David. The Hasmonean military accomplishments and enforcement of Jewish law (i.e., expelling a foreign oppressor and cleansing the Temple) are what all Jews expected from a messiah. Against this biblical and historic backdrop, I submit the Jews of the first century of the Common Era did not restrain their concept of a messiah and king exclusively to the House of David.

Jesus Says He Is NOT A Son of David

Those with a Christian upbringing are taught in Bible class that Jesus descended from King David, a claim resting chiefly on the letters of Paul.[38] However, careful examination of the NT Gospels reveals Jesus, in his own words, rebuking the suggestion that he is a son of David, see *Matthew* 22:41-45, *Mark* 12:35-37, and *Luke* 20:41-44. Jesus relies upon *Psalm* 110 in these parallel passages to support the position that the Christ (i.e., the Messiah) is not the son of King David. All three Gospels record the words of Jesus in nearly identical fashion. Here is *Luke*'s formulation.

---

[38] Paul of Tarsus claims Jesus descended bodily from King David. *Romans* 1:3 and 2 *Timothy* 2:8.

> Then Jesus said to them, "How is it that they
> say the Christ is the Son of David? David
> himself declares in the Book of Psalms: 'The
> Lord said to my Lord, sit at my right hand
> until I make your enemies a footstool for
> your feet.' David calls him 'Lord.' How then
> can he be his son?"[39]

Obviously, Jesus refers to himself in the third person as "the Christ". The confusion in this passage centers upon reference to two different lords. The *Book of Psalms* is a collection of wisdom sayings allegedly authored by King David. Psalm 110 starts with, "The Lord says to my Lord." The initial "Lord" is clearly God. Who then is the second lord? It's not David; he's narrating and addresses the individual as "my Lord". The salient point made by Jesus in quoting Psalm 110 is that David is NOT the second lord but is subservient to this individual. Who then is this person?

There is only one logical conclusion to be drawn from reading the quoted language from *Luke* together with Psalm 110--Jesus identifies the second lord in Psalm 110 as the Messiah. Further, Jesus equates himself with this individual. It's the only way to make sense of what Jesus is saying. Let's now rephrase *Luke* 20 using this interpretation.

> Then Jesus said to them, "How is it that they
> say the Messiah is the son of David? David
> himself declares in the *Book of Psalms*: 'God
> said to my Lord (the Messiah), sit at my right
> hand until I make your enemies a footstool
> for your feet.' David addresses the Messiah
> as 'my Lord'. Thus, the Messiah is not a son
> of David."

Carrying this logic through, the bottom line is that Jesus proclaims that the Messiah does NOT descend from David. This implicitly means Jesus identifies himself as the messiah of Levi and not of Judah. It is the only messiah known to Jewish scripture other than the messiah of Judah. This fits neatly into the tradition of *Jubilees*,

---

[39] New International Version.

Aramaic Levi, and other texts from the *Dead Sea Scrolls* that proclaim Levi to be the messiah and superior to Judah (David). This argument is not a novel invention by Jesus. It was first used by the Hasmonean kings, who were his forefathers.

A phrase found in verse 4 of Psalm 110 lends further weight to the conclusion that the second lord referred to in verse 1 of Psalm 110 is the messiah of Levi. In verse 4, God tells the second lord, "Thou art a **priest forever according to the order of Melchizedek**."[40] Emphasis added. Melchizedek was a shadowy figure appearing only twice in the Old Testament, once each in Genesis and Psalms. The unique quality of Melchizedek is that he was both a king and a priest. David was not a priest. The descendants of Levi, on the other hand, were proclaimed in *Aramaic Levi* to be both kings and priests just like Melchizedek. The *Book of Jubilees* goes further in connecting Levi and Melchizedek.

Genesis states that Melchizedek was a "priest of God Most High".[41] The term "God Most High" is only used in the Old Testament texts of *Genesis*, *Psalms*, and *Daniel*. Melchizedek is the only individual described in Jewish Rabbinic canon as a priest of the "Most High God." However, the *Book of Jubilees* (a book outside the Jewish canon) relates a dream of Levi at Bethel. "Levi dreamed that they had ordained and made him the **priest of the Most High God**."[42] Emphasis Added. Melchizedek and Levi are the only individuals recorded in pre-Christian orthodox or sectarian Jewish scripture as "priests of the Most High God." The second lord discussed in Psalm 110 who is identified as a priest of the order of Melchizedek is in fact the messiah of Levi, who the New Testament refers to as "the Christ".

Letter to the Hebrews

The theory that Jesus presented himself as the messiah of Levi holds together tightly if one only tests it against the Gospels

---

[40] Melchi is the Hebrew for king. Melchizedek literally translates as righteous king.
[41] *Genesis* 14:18.
[42] *Book of Jubilees*, Chapter 32.

of the New Testament. Those calling Jesus "son of David" in the NT Gospels are variously described as blind men, the crowd, children at the Temple, beggars, and angels. The same cannot be said for the *Letter to the Hebrews* also found in the New Testament. It directly assaults the argument painstakingly built in this chapter.

> If perfection could have been attained through the Levitical priesthood (for on the basis of it the law was given to the people), why was there still need for another priest to come—one in the order of Melchizedek, not in the order of Aaron? For when there is a change of the priesthood, there must also be a change of the law. He of whom these things are said belonged to a different tribe, and no one from that tribe has ever served at the altar. <u>For it is clear that our Lord descended from Judah,</u> and in regard to that tribe Moses said nothing about priests.
>
> And what we have said is even more clear if another priest like Melchizedek appears, one who has become a priest not on the basis of a regulation as to his ancestry but on the basis of the power of an indestructible life. For it is declared: "You are a priest forever, in the order of Melchizedek."[43] [Emphasis added.]

Hebrews is easy to dismiss as an authoritative work in my view. First, no one knows who authored this document. Most agree it was not authored by Paul. His letters begin with "Paul, a bond-servant to Christ Jesus." Second, the line of reasoning contained in the quoted passage is faulty. Let's break it down.

Melchizedek lived in the time of Abraham. Levi came along several generations later and Aaron was one of his descendants. The priesthood was reserved for descendants of Levi while the most sacred duties at the Temple were reserved for a

---

[43] *Hebrews* 7:11-17 (New International Version).

further subgroup of Levi, the sons of Aaron (known as Kohanim). The author of *Hebrews* suggests that in order for Jesus to overturn the laws of Moses, that a new priesthood must emerge outside of the priesthood established by Moses. Perhaps the author of *Hebrews* never read the *Gospel of Matthew*, which quotes Jesus thusly, "Think not that I am come to destroy the law, or the prophets: I am not come to destroy, but to fulfill."[44] Jesus interprets the laws of Moses but he never claims they are invalid or lack authority. As discussed in Chapter 8, Paul of Tarsus does make the outlandish claim that Jesus came to destroy Jewish law so one cannot discount his authorship of *Hebrews* on this ground alone.

Continuing the analysis of *Hebrews*, how is the "order of Melchizedek" a new priesthood if it existed in the ancient time of Abraham? The priesthood of Melchizedek was obviously very ancient and not a new innovation, strike two. The author of *Hebrews* then says the tribe of Judah never served at the altar under Mosaic Law yet, somehow, God chose the descendants of David from the tribe of Judah for his new priesthood naming them priests of the order of Melchizedek. One can only assume the author of *Hebrews* based this leap in conclusory reasoning on Psalm 110, the only passage used by the NT Gospels to connect Jesus with Melchizedek. Remember that Jesus referred to Psalm 110 while rebuking people for calling him a son of David. Further, Levi was a priest of the order of Melchizedek, not David. The author of *Hebrews* identification of the second lord in Psalm 110 as King David is not only a ludicrous construction of the words of this Psalm but contradicts the interpretation Jesus himself espoused for the passage. The entire twisted logic found in *Hebrews* regarding Melchizedek is necessitated by the assertion that Jesus was a priest and king yet still a descendant of David. If one instead accepts the position that Jesus was the descendant of Hasmonean kings, we immediately overcome the necessity for disavowing the Levitical priesthood as somehow invalidated by God in the person of Jesus Christ.[45]

---

[44] *Matthew* 5:17.

[45] One caveat on this point— Jesus lacks Kohanim priestly status under my theory as his father (Antipater) was not of Levi even though his mother was.

The first edition of this book ended the discussion of the above-quoted language from *Hebrews* at this point. My previous assumption had been that the author of *Hebrews* pulled the concept of a priestly line of Judah out of thin air with no prior textual support for such a claim. Since initial publication of this book, I became aware of an interesting reference in an apocryphal text known as *Testament of Levi* (TPL) that indeed speaks of a priesthood of Judah.

> And they [angels who spoke to Levi in a dream] said to me, Levi, thy seed shall be divided into three branches, for a sign of the glory of the Lord who is to come; and first shall he be that hath been faithful; no portion shall be greater than his. The second shall be in the priesthood. The third—a new name shall be called over Him, because He <u>shall arise as King from Judah, and shall establish a new priesthood, after the fashion of the Gentiles, to all the Gentiles.</u>[46] [Emphasis Added.]

Interesting similarities exist between this section from TPL and *Hebrews*; however, the individual who the angels prophesy to Levi as the "King of Judah" who shall establish a new priesthood is a descendant of Levi (presumably having married into the tribe of Judah). In TPL the descendants of Levi essentially take over leadership of Judah. This hybrid figure is a priest-king who starts a new priesthood relegated to gentile ministry. If one reads the entire passage in TPL containing the above-quoted language, it is clear this new priesthood does not supplant or do away with the Levitical priests but merely serves as an auxiliary priesthood meant for ministry to gentiles only. If *Hebrews* borrowed from TPL in arguing Jesus was the king of Judah who established a new

---

That disqualified Jesus from the Jewish priesthood; however, he could still have been a rabbi. There was no ancestral barrier to become a rabbi. This point would not disqualify Jesus from the office of Jewish king and messiah. In this office, he would have still been the ultimate authority over the Jewish people.
[46] *Testament of Levi* 8:14. See http://www.ccel.org/ccel/schaff/anf08.iii.v.html.

priesthood, then it implicitly means Jesus was also a priestly descendant of Levi.

Paul of Tarsus

Paul contends in two of his letters found in the New Testament that Jesus descended from King David. See *Romans* 1:3 and 2 *Timothy* 2:8. Paul also removed the possibility of arguing that he referred to adoption of Jesus by Joseph, who the *Gospel of Matthew* identifies as a descendant of David. In *Romans*, Paul declares Jesus "was born of a descendant of David according to the flesh."[47] Emphasis added.

It's tempting to try and downplay his words on the basis that Paul joined the Jesus movement after the crucifixion and, therefore, may have lacked direct knowledge of the ancestry of Jesus. This defense supposes Paul merely repeated what he had been told by others (i.e., hearsay). I devote an entire chapter in this book to Paul (see Chapter 7) and conclude Paul was himself a Herodian-Hasmonean, a cousin of Jesus. The New Testament tells us Paul was a Roman citizen by birth, an official of the Sanhedrin, and a leader of anti-Nazarene forces before his conversion. Setting aside my theory on Paul's ancestry, I find it hard to believe a person with those credentials didn't know exactly who Jesus was.

Christian doctrine maintains Jesus had no biologic father. My theory asserts the father of Jesus was Antipater ben Herod, the eldest son of Herod the Great.   If one accepts that Jesus had a biologic father, then one possible way to harmonize Paul's letters with the theory is if the biologic father of Jesus descended from King David. Then Paul's statement in his letters would be correct while, on the other hand, Jesus could also descend from Hasmonean kings through his mother. Chapters 2 and 3 of this book present a reasonable case that Mary was a Hasmonean princess. Chapter 9 makes the case for identifying the father of Jesus (Antipater ben Herod) as a descendant of David, although it is more speculative than the proof for Mary as a Hasmonean. This theory allows Paul's statement in *Romans* that Jesus descended

---

[47] *Romans* 1:3.

bodily from David to be true while also accommodating the contention that Jesus descended from Hasmonean kings. The only other option, as I see it, is that Paul lied about the identity of Jesus for reasons only known to him. Paul defected from the Roman-Herodian side of a religious battle to that of Jesus and his band of reformers. Defectors are inherently untrustworthy. An extreme minority view Paul as an agent provocateur who hijacked Christianity steering it away from the foundations laid by Jesus and his brother James the Just to something else.[48] One cannot dismiss this view out of hand for Paul's theology clearly clashed with that of James the Just, the successor of Jesus. Who knew the teaching of Jesus better, James the brother and successor of Jesus or a recent convert from the enemy camp? More on this issue in Chapters 7 and 8.

Conclusion

Jesus contests the suggestion that he is a "son of David"; therefore, his claim to be the messiah does not rest on descent from King David. Direct support for the concept of a messiah of Levi exists in pre-Christian, Jewish sectarian texts. The messiah of Levi doctrine is the only theologic avenue allowing Jesus to claim to be the messiah while denying he is a son of David. Not only was it used by Jesus but, also, the Hasmonean kings to justify their place on the Jewish throne. In the next chapter, I connect the dots between Jesus and the Hasmonean kings using the genealogy list found in the *Gospel of Luke*.

---

[48] See The Brother of Jesus and the Lost Teachings of Christianity by Jeffrey J. Bütz (Inner Traditions 2005). Jeffrey Butz is an adjunct professor of world religions at Penn State University. My wife is from Kenya, a former British colony. Most Kenyans of her generation have two first names: i.e., a proper British name and a Kenyan tribal name. So it was with the Hasmoneans—one Greek name, one Hebrew. The Hebrew name of King Antigonus was Mattatayah.[48]

Chapter 3
Luke's Genealogy

The Bible contains two separate and incompatible ancestor lists for Jesus—one each in *Matthew* and *Luke*. The Roman Catholic Church and a minority of scholars resolve the difference by concluding that the genealogy of *Luke* is actually that of Mary the mother of Jesus. Below is the ancestor list from *Luke* (chapter 3) opposite Hasmonean king Antigonus and his known ancestors (as recorded by Josephus). Why use Antigonus and not another Hasmonean king? Because Josephus records Antigonus' daughter as having been alive in 4 BCE[49] making here the only daughter or granddaughter of a Hasmonean king known to have lived during the last decade of the Common Era.

Luke Chapter 3	Hasmonean Kings
Heli	
Matthat ←	—— Mattatayah Antigonus
Levi	Aristobulus II
Melchi	—— Alexander Jannai
Jannai ←	John Hyrcanus I
Joseph	Simon Maccabee
Mattathias ←	—— Mattathias Maccabee

The identification of Mattatayah Antigonus as the second name on the list is rather self-evident in my opinion when put in context of the names found immediately thereafter on the list, i.e., Levi (priest) and Melchi (king). It may be argued that "Matthat" is

---

[49] <u>Antiquities</u> XVII 5:2 (92).

a Hebrew variant of Matthew or Matthias.[50] But five names down on the list, *Luke* completely writes out the name "Mattathias". This infers Matthat and Mattathias on the *Luke* list represent different although similar names. My wife is a native of Kenya, a former British colony. Most Kenyans of her generation have two first names: i.e., a proper British name and a Kenyan tribal name. So it was with the Hasmoneans—one Greek name, one Hebrew. The Hebrew name of King Antigonus was Mattatayah.[51]

After Matthat, the modern version of *Luke* lists Levi, Melchi, and Jannai. Levi was the patriarch of the Jewish priesthood. Thus, this name plays into the theory that Jesus presented himself as the Messiah of Levi and, I submit, was unlikely to have been used by anyone outside of the Jewish priesthood during the Second Temple period. The term Levite means priest. As previously stated, melchi is the Hebrew word for king. I am not aware of another instance where the word melchi was used as a Jewish name by a historical figure in the Second Temple period. The only Jewish kings known to history in the time period corresponding to the name Melchi on *Luke's* list (i.e., four generations or 80 plus years before Jesus) were the Hasmoneans. Jannai is a rare Jewish name. The only historical figures I uncovered with the name were Hasmonean king Alexander Jannai (103 BCE - 76 BCE) and a Rabbi Jannai from Sepphoris who lived in the second to third centuries CE (i.e., after the destruction of the Second Temple).[52] The *Luke* list names Jannai's son and grandson, respectively, as king (Melchi) and priest (Levi). Only the Hasmoneans were both priests and kings. I submit the name Jannai found in the ancestor list of *Luke* undoubtedly refers to Hasmonean king Alexander Jannai.

---

[50] The standard Hebrew equivalent of Matthew is Matitiyahu, not Matthat or Mattatayah.

[51] We know Antigonus, last king of Hasmonean dynasty, used the name Mattatayah because he struck coins during his reign and these coins are still in existence today. They contain a double-sided inscription: one side in Hebrew reads "Mattatayah the High Priest" and the reverse side in Greek, "King Antigonus".

[52] The Universal Jewish Encyclopedia by Isaak Landman (Varda Books 2009) at page 36.

For those who speculate that these were common names of the period potentially referring to another family than the Hasmonean kings, research exists supporting the position that these names (Levi, Melchi and Jannai) were all unusual names for the Second Temple period. The table below gives the frequency of occurrence of male names in the first century CE in Jerusalem.[53]

Name	Percentage
Simon	21%
Joseph	14%
Judah	10%
Yochanan (John)	10%
Eleazar	10%
Jesus	9%
Jonathan	6%
Matthew	5%
Hanina	3%
Yo-ezer	3%
Ishmael	2.2%
Menachem	2%
Jacob (James)	2%
Hanan	2%
Levi	0.2%
Isaac	0.2%
Gamaliel	0.2%
Hillel	0.2%

Levi comes in at 1/5th of one percent or 1 in 500 Jewish males. Melchi and Jannai don't even make the list, meaning they occur less than 1 in 500.

---

[53] The Brother of Jesus by Hershel Shanks and Ben Witherington (HarperOne 2004) at page 56. The table is based on data from Rachel Hachlili's article, "Names and Nicknames of Jews in Second Temple Times," published by the Israel Exploration Society in 1984 in volume 17 of Eretz-Israel.

One additional point exists worthy of mention concerning the name found after Heli on the *Luke* list. The *Gospel of Luke*, in the form we now have it, lists the ancestors of Jesus as Joseph, the son of Heli, son of Matthat, son of Levi, son of Melchi, et cetera. Eusebius (263 - 339 CE) was the Bishop of Caesarea in Samaria and author of the earliest history of the Roman Catholic Church now existent, a work called <u>Ecclesiastical History</u>. In this history, Eusebius quotes extensively from a letter by early church father Julius Africanus (160 – 240 CE).[54] Eusebius' quotation of Africanus is the only surviving fragment we have from this work of Africanus which attempted to explain why *Luke* and *Matthew* have different genealogy lists.[55] Therein, Julius Africanus quotes *Luke* as follows: "Joseph, the son of Heli, the son of Melchi." Remember the term "Melchi" means king. Writing at most two centuries after the time of Jesus Christ, Africanus named the individual in the position of Matthat as Melchi. As the ancestor lists of *Luke* and *Matthew* were the primary subject matter of Africanus' letter and, given the extensive nature of the analysis found in the letter, I do not believe the positioning of the name Melchi by Africanus was an accident. The stronger conclusion is that an early version of *Luke* in the possession of Julius Africanus listed "Melchi" (king) in the position of Matthat on the Jesus genealogy. My reasoned inference from these facts is that the names Melchi and Matthat apply to the same individual. Melchi Matthat from *Luke* 3 was King Mattatayah Antigonus, the last Hasmonean ruler executed by Marc Antony in 37 BCE.

The Heli Issue

Astute readers surely noted that I sidestepped discussion of the first name on the *Luke* list, Heli. Again, I accept the assertion of the Catholic Church that the ancestor list from *Luke* is that of Mary the mother of Jesus. I have presented evidence tending to show that this list contains the names of Hasmonean kings and,

---

[54] <u>Ecclesiastical History</u>, Book I, Chapter 7.
[55] See http://reedsportchristianchurch.com/christgenehist.html#epistle

further, that the name Matthat in said list refers to Mattatayah Antigonus, the last Hasmonean king. Who then can Heli be?

King Antigonus died in 37 BCE. According to Josephus, Herod executed his entire family. The only descendant of Antigonus recorded by Josephus as surviving Herod's takeover of the Jewish kingdom was his daughter who was the wife of Crown Prince Antipater. Considering her historical significance as the last living vessel of pure Hasmonean royal blood, it's shocking Josephus failed to give her name and, further, that he mentions her but once in his multivolume history of the Jews.

I date the birth of Jesus to 3 BCE, see the next chapter herein. If the daughter of King Antigonus was the mother of Jesus and Antigonus died in 37 BCE, Mary was at least 34 years of age at his birth. To still be of childbearing years in 3 BCE, Mary would have been a baby at the death of Antigonus. If so, it logically follows that Mary was adopted upon the execution of her father and mother (and aunts and uncles and close cousins) in 37 BCE. If an infant daughter of Antigonus survived Herod's massacre of her family, did any Hasmoneans further removed from the king exist who might have stepped up to adopt the child? The historian Josephus claims to be of a priestly family (including high priests) and, also, to himself be of Hasmonean blood. History does not record a high priest every being a descendent of Herod. The only Hasmoneans explicitly named by Josephus to have survived to the time of Jesus were members of Herod's family. How then could a Hasmonean born in the first century of the Common Era be Hasmonean yet not related to Herod? I infer from these facts that a line of lesser Hasmonean nobles who were Temple priests survived Herod's purge. Factions within the Temple priesthood collaborated with Herod so it's not inconceivable that he spared Temple priests despite their noble Hasmonean blood. It's the only mechanism by which Josephus, a self-described Kohanim priest, could have been born in 37 CE yet been a descendant of Hasmonean kings without the stain of Herod's blood. My conclusion is that one clan of Hasmonean priests supported Herod after he overthrew King Antigonus in 37 BCE and, thus, avoided execution.

As discussed in Chapter 4, the *Protevangelium of James* (a Christian apocryphal work) states that Mary was raised in the Temple. Women were only allowed into an outer courtyard of the Temple and all people left when the doors shut for the evening.[56] Thus, I do not take the words literally that she was raised in the Temple. Rather, the reasonable inference from the *Protevangelium of James* is that Mary was raised in the family of a Temple priest thereby closely connecting her childhood with the Temple. If Hasmonean priests survived Herod's takeover, they would have been Mary's only surviving relatives and the logical family to adopt her. Thus, I theorize Heli of *Luke* was a Temple priest (Kohanim) of lesser Hasmonean blood who survived Herod's purge. By "lesser", I mean not a son or grandson of a Hasmonean king.

The Catholic Church has long recognized Mary's father to have been Joachim. This name comes to us from the aforementioned *Protoevangelium of James*. There are two places in the Old Testament where the name Joakim (which I take as a variation of Joachim) is given as interchangeable for Eliakim.[57] Jehovah and Eli are alternative Hebrew names for God. Thus, the names Jehoiakim and Eliakim mean the same thing--one who God has raised up. Substituting Eliakim as a variant of Joachim, it is then a simple matter to make the following connection: Eliakim = Eli = Heli.[58] By this logic, Joachim is an equivalent name for Heli. Thus, a reasonable argument can be put forth that the *Protoevangelium of James* is consistent with *Luke* in the naming of Mary's father as Heli; however, I view Joakim / Heli as the adoptive father of Mary. This shall be discussed further in Chapter 4.

Hole In The *Luke* Argument

I find it intellectually dishonest presenting the *Luke* genealogy evidence without acknowledging a sizable hole in this proof. Problem: the genealogy list found in *Luke* names King

---

[56] Except for the Day of Atonement when the high priest spent the night in the holy of holies.

[57] 2 *Kings* 23:34 and 2 *Chronicles* 36:4.

[58] Prof. James D. Tabor, The Jesus Dynasty (Simon & Schuster 2006) at page 52.

David further down from the names I allege to be those of Hasmonean kings; however, we know from other sources that the Hasmoneans were not descendants of King David. This means one of two things: (a) I'm relying on a faulty piece of evidence (i.e., the *Luke* list contains errors) or (b) those really are not Hasmonean kings on the *Luke* list.

My view of the ancestor list found in *Luke* is that the author only knew the identity of three ancestors of Jesus: King Mattatayah Antigonus, King Alexander Jannai, and Mattathias Maccabee (patriarch of the Hasmonean clan). The rest was filler. That is why the author of *Luke* used the Hebrew term for king (melchi) as a name on the list. Melchi is an office, not a name. Likewise, Luke used the name of the patriarch of the priestly tribe of Levi to fill in another gap. Luke's mixing of Hasmonean kings within a genealogy that extends to King David does lessen the credibility of the evidence but I still find it of value.

Chapter 4
Mary, the Mother of Jesus
(Mariamne bat Antigonus)

Mary was the only acknowledged biologic parent of Jesus. As such, his claim to the Jewish throne must lie in her ancestry. The *Luke* genealogy indicates she was a Hasmonean princess. This chapter restates the evidence indicating Mary was the daughter of a Kohen priest of the tribe of Levi, presents her Hasmonean family tree, and examines her life in the broader context of Jewish history. Her story is not unlike the legend of Princes Anastasia of Russia, the youngest daughter of the last Russian czar thought to have survived the mass execution of her family. That legend proved false but I believe Mary the mother of Jesus was indeed the last surviving Hasmonean of high royal blood untainted by intermarriage with Herod.

<u>Mary as a Daughter of Aaron</u>

This topic has already been discussed so the evidence has been recapped in bullet point style below.

1. In the *Gospel of Luke*, Elizabeth was identified as a "kinswoman" of Mary the mother of Jesus and, also, as a "daughter of Aaron". This term means the daughter of a Kohen priest. The Kohanim were patrilineal descendants of Aaron[59] who controlled the Temple as the highest

---

[59] Meaning a Kohen priest must trace his ancestry father to son all the way back to Aaron.

ranking Levitical priests. If Elizabeth was the daughter of a Kohen priest, in all probability her kinswoman Mary was as well given that Kohen priests tended to marry daughters of their Kohanim brethren. According to the Quran, Mary the mother of Jesus was a "sister of Aaron", also meaning the daughter of Kohanim. These two pieces of evidence point to an ancient tradition that Mary was the daughter of a Kohen priest.

2. Jesus and his brother James shared the same mother, Mary. Early church historian Hegesippus stated that James entered the "Holy of Holies". Only the high priest could enter the holy of holies in the Temple. Prof. Robert Eisenman opines that James operated as an opposition high priest. All sacramental duties at the Temple above the lowest level were reserved for the Kohanim.

3. Mary's genealogy given in *Luke* contains the names of Hasmonean kings and, thus, she was the daughter of a Kohen priest of Hasmonean descent.

Mary stands as Jesus' only publicly acknowledged ancestral link to the Jewish throne yet her father was so inconsequential in the view of the authors of the NT Gospels that he was never mentioned? I submit Mary's father must have been of high Jewish nobility. Further, there is a long-standing tradition that she was of a Kohanim family. The Hasmoneans were the only Jewish clan from the first century BCE fitting that description (priestly nobility).

This leads to an interesting question, who suppressed information regarding the Hasmonean ancestry of Jesus? My frequent whipping boy in this book, the Roman Catholic Church, appears blameless in this regard. The Romans actively persecuted the young Nazarene movement in the early years after the death of Jesus. What we know today as the Roman Catholic Church did not emerge until the rule of the emperor Constantine in the early fourth century of the Common Era. The Gospels of the New Testament and letters of Paul of Tarsus largely painting Jesus as a "son of David" were written in the first century CE.

Who then attempted to wash the Hasmoneans out of the official biography of Jesus? I see only one party with motive and opportunity, the Romans. What motive would the Romans have had for recasting Jesus as a descendant of David and expunging his Hasmonean past? The Hasmoneans were Jewish nationalists and heroes to the Jewish people. The royal family of David was an ancient memory by the first century CE and never threatened Roman rule of Palestine. The Hasmoneans, on the other hand, in the person of Antigonus had formed an alliance with the Parthians (Rome's arch enemy) and captured the Jewish kingdom. Jesus and his brother James represented the last link to the bloodline of Antigonus. The Romans were masters at propaganda and it suited their political ends to recast Jesus as a carpenter's son from Galilee. I conclude their primary agents in this mission were Paul of Tarsus and Josephus. More on this topic later.

Mary's Royal Family Tree

This subchapter presents Mary's family tree under the theory that she was the daughter of Hasmonean king Mattatayah Antigonus. The dates in parenthesis are the dates of reign for a king or queen.

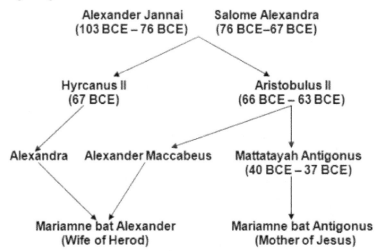

Mariamne is a Greek / Latin form of the Hebrew name Miryam used by Josephus. Miryam was the sister of Moses and Aaron.

Modern Christian Bibles render the Hebrew Miryam as Mary. Thus, the name Mariamne from Josephus is equivalent with our modern English name of Mary.

Notice that Jesus' mother was the first cousin of Herod's wife; however, Mary the mother of Jesus was of a higher royal rank. One's royal status was measured by the degree of separation from a king. Herod's wife was the granddaughter of a Jewish king yet Jesus' mother was the daughter of a king. Mariamne bat Antigonus was briefly mentioned in the histories of Josephus but omitting her first name. Josephus relates the execution of the entire family of Antigonus after Jerusalem fell in 37 BCE. Then, out of the blue while discussing events 33 years later, Josephus cryptically states that Herod's eldest son Antipater was married to a daughter of Antigonus.[60] That's his one and only mention of an important royal, the only living descendant of the last Hasmonean king. Further, Josephus never even gave us the name of Antigonus' daughter. I reason her name was Mariamne (Miryam) from the genealogy list contained in *Luke*. This unnamed daughter of King Antigonus clearly rated deeper discussion leading me to believe the omission was intentional.

Josephus was a Jewish nationalist leader during the revolt against Rome that commenced in 66 CE. In fact, he commanded the military district in Galilee. After surrendering to the Romans upon their defeat of his forces, Josephus defected to the enemy. He became so close to General Vespasian (later emperor) that Vespasian adopted Josephus into his family. Josephus wrote his histories in Rome financed by Vespasian's sons, the emperors Titus and Domitian. His pro-Roman bias is universally acknowledged. "The distorting lens of Josephus has slanted our vision for too long."[61] In my view, Josephus or his Roman editors intended to write Mary (daughter of Antigonus and mother of Jesus) completely out of his histories yet one brief reference slipped through.

---

[60] <u>Antiquities</u> XVII 5:2 (92).
[61] <u>Heritage and Hellenism: The Reinvention of Jewish Tradition</u> By Erich S. Gruen (University of California Press 2002) at page 70.

Queen Salome Alexandra

Hasmonean queen Salome Alexandra ruled in her own right after the death of her controversial second husband, Alexander Jannai. [62] As queen, she was not a mere figurehead. Salome Alexandra named the high priest and engineered a rapprochement with the Pharisees, bitter enemies of her husband King Jannai. She ruled the Jewish kingdom at a time when it was against Jewish law to teach the Torah to women. Hyrcanus II and Aristobulus II were her sons by Jannai. Mary the mother of Jesus was Salome's great granddaughter. She was the most powerful woman in Jewish history.

According to the Talmud, Salome Alexandra was the sister of the leading Pharisee Rabbi Shimon ben Shetach, which probably explains her switch in religious affiliation after the death of Jannai.[63] The rift between the Pharisees and Jannai came to a head during the Feast of Tabernacles. This is a week-long harvest festival that begins five days after Yom Kippur (the Day of Atonement). An ancient tradition during this period was the Water-Libation Ceremony, wherein the high priest offered sacrificial water to God by pouring it over the Temple alter. As the ceremony was not part of Mosaic Law, the ultraconservative Sadducees opposed it. The Water-Libation Ceremony was performed by the high priest each day during the Feast of Tabernacles. During the feast, Jannai raised the ceremonial pitcher and poured the water onto the ground instead of the altar thereby infuriating the Pharisee priests in attendance at the Temple. Predictably, they rioted. Jannai turned his soldiers loose on the rebellious priests and rabbis killing 6000. Outside of his internal war with the Pharisees, Jannai was known as a superior military leader. He expanded the Jewish Empire to a size beyond that ruled by kings David and Solomon. Queen Salome Alexandra brought peace and reconciliation to the Jewish nation. She made Rabbi Shetach, her brother, president of the Sanhedrin. That peace was

---

[62] See Josephus, the Bible, and History by Geldman (Yamamoto Shoten Publishing House 1988) at pages 135-140.
[63] Pirke Avot: A Modern Commentary on Jewish Ethics by Leonard S. Kravitz (Urj Press 1993) at page 7.

shattered upon her death when the Hasmoneans again warred against one another.[64]

The Hasmonean Civil War

Salome Alexandra died in 67 BCE naming Hyrcanus II (her eldest son by Jannai) successor to the Jewish throne. He already served as high priest and shared his mother's sympathetic view of the Pharisees. Hyrcanus reigned for only three months before being deposed by his younger brother, Aristobulus II, who seized Jerusalem with the backing of Parthian troops.

The Parthian Empire rose out of the ashes of the Persian Empire in the middle of the third century BCE by smashing the Greek successor's to Alexander the Great who previously ruled the near east. At its height, the borders of the Parthian Empire stretched east to China, south to India, north to Afghanistan, and west to Palestine. Zoroastrianism was the state religion of Parthia and its priests were known in the west as magi. After the Roman destruction of Carthage in 146 BC, Parthia became the only other superpower of the day to rival Roman world hegemony. Rome fought a series of wars against the Parthians generally tasting defeat before the advent of the Common Era. In 53 BCE at the battle of Carrhae, the Parthians annihilated 20,000 Roman legionnaires under Marcus Crassus.[65] Among the Roman dead were Crassus and his son Publius. I rate it as one of the three greatest defeats in the history of the Roman Empire.[66]

These two Hasmonean brothers (Hyrcanus and Aristobulus) briefly made peace after Aristobulus seized the throne

---

[64] Teaching Jewish History by Julia Phillips Berger and Sue Parker Gerson (A.R.E. Publishing, Inc. 2005) at page 64.

[65] Crassus was known for his extreme avarice. His memory gave rise to the modern English word "crass".

[66] The other two Roman defeats being the Battle of Cannae in 271 BCE and the Battle of the Teutoburg Forest in 9 CE. At Cannae, the Carthaginians under Hannibal killed more than 50,000 Roman soldiers while losing less than 7,000 of their own men. At the Teutoburg Forrest, Romans under Publius Varus were defeated by a German alliance led by Arminius. 15,000 Roman soldiers died in this battle including Varus. Publius Varus was governor of the Roman province of Syria (which included Palestine) at the birth of Jesus.

but it didn't hold. Hyrcanus, the weaker of the two brothers, fled Jerusalem and appealed to Rome for help. Roman general Pompey Magnus invaded the Jewish kingdom at the invitation of Hyrcanus capturing Jerusalem in 63 BCE. Instead of returning Hyrcanus to the Jewish throne, Pompey made him high priest with no real political power. The Romans installed Antipater the Idumean (father of Herod) as "regent" and de facto Roman client ruler in Jerusalem. Herod later became Roman governor of Galilee. In 49 BCE, Aristobulus and his elder son Alexander were both assassinated by unknown parties leaving Antigonus as King Aristobulus' only surviving son. One can only assume Antipater the Idumean initiated these assassinations. Antipater was himself poisoned shortly thereafter presumably orchestrated by Antigonus to avenge the deaths of his father and brother.

This brings us to the ascendance of Mary's father, Antigonus. Julius Caesar was assassinated in 44 BCE by a group of Roman senators headed by Marcus Junius Brutus. Thereafter Rome descended into civil war between the Caesar loyalists (led by Marc Antony) and the self-proclaimed defenders of the Republic who killed Caesar (Brutus, Cato, Cicero, et alia). Roman legions in the provinces were withdrawn to fight in the civil war. The Parthians took advantage of the Roman civil war by marching west against Roman territories all along their border with the Roman Empire, including Palestine. The Parthians allied themselves with Antigonus and other Jewish nationalists to oust the Romans from Palestine. Antigonus and his Parthian allies captured Jerusalem in 40 BCE proclaiming Antigonus king and high priest. Thus, the Hasmonean dynasty was briefly reborn as a Parthian client. Antigonus cut the ear off Hyrcanus II to disqualify his uncle from ever again serving as high priest and exiled him to Babylon.[67] Antigonus captured Antipater's eldest son Phasael when Jerusalem fell and he died in prison. Antipater's middle son Joseph also died in battle with the forces of Antigonus. Herod, then Roman governor of Galilee, nearly died himself escaping to the safety of

---

[67] The Kohen Gadol (high priest) had to be free from physical deformity in order to serve in the office.

Fortress Masada where he left his family (including his Hasmonean fiancé, Mariamne bat Alexander) besieged by Antigonus. Herod traveled overland to Egypt and then by ship to Rome. Despite arriving in Rome exhausted of funds and with very few men, the Romans declared Herod king of the Jewish territories in 40 BCE.

Herod Takes Jerusalem And Exterminates Family of Antigonus

In essence, the Hasmonean civil war ended when Pompey Magnus captured Jerusalem in 63 BCE. From that point forward, the weak Hyrcanus was nothing more than a Roman puppet with Antipater and his sons holding real power. The Romans ended the charade of keeping a Hasmonean ruler by naming Herod their client king. The war between Antigonus and Herod was a proxy battle waged between two superpowers, Rome and Parthia. After the murderers of Julius Caesar were vanquished, the Romans engaged the Parthians on a vast north-south front where the borders of the two empires met. Herod manned but one Roman allied axis in the larger conflict. Marc Antony campaigned to the north of Herod in the Syrian province and even requested Herod's assistance at one point. It was during Herod's absence from Judea while taking troops north to help Antony that his brother Joseph died in battle against Antigonus. Herod completed a herculean comeback by recapturing Jerusalem in 37 BCE with Roman assistance including General Sossius; however, the bulk of his manpower consisted of non-Roman troops that Herod recruited.

The Jews did not go down without a fight. The fall of Jerusalem to Herod and his Roman allies occurred after a five month siege. Once breaching the city walls, the attackers showed no mercy on the Jewish defenders. Josephus tells us "there was no pity taken of either infants or the aged, nor did they spare so much as the weaker sex."[68] Further, Herod "slew forty-five of the principal men of Antigonus' party" taken prisoner after the fighting.[69] Antigonus was captured alive and sent by Sossius to Marc Antony, then in Antioch. Herod paid a massive bribe and, in

---

[68] Antiquities XIV 16:2 (480).
[69] Antiquities XV 1:2 (6).

return, Antony beheaded Antigonus. Josephus even reports why Herod paid a large bribe for the prompt execution of Antigonus.

> Herod was afraid lest Antigonus should be kept in prison by Antony, and that when he was carried to Rome by him, he might get his case to be heard by the senate, and might demonstrate, as he [Antigonus] was himself of the royal blood, and Herod but a private man, that therefore [the Jewish kingdom] belonged to [Antigonus'] sons ... on account of the family they were.[70]

There it is plain as day—Herod feared Hasmonean royal blood in his quest to consolidate and retain his grip on the Jewish throne because of his common ancestry. The political danger Antigonus and his family posed to Herod was more than high born status as Hasmonean royalty. The Jewish people loved Antigonus for having kicked the Romans out of the holy land and reestablishing an independent Jewish kingdom. Josephus quotes the Roman historian Strabo on the subject of how the Jewish people felt about Antigonus and Herod.

> Antony seems to me to have been the very first [Roman] who beheaded a king, as supposing he could no other way bend the minds of the Jews so as to receive Herod * * * . For by no torments could [the Jews] be forced to call him king, so great a fondness they had for their former king [Antigonus].[71]

There can be little doubt that Herod ordered the extermination of the extended family of Antigonus after capturing Jerusalem. Beyond the killing described by Josephus when Jerusalem fell in 37 BCE, we have a curious incident that occurred roughly ten years later. Herod executed his brother-in-law Costobarus (then governor of Idumea) for harboring the "sons of

---

[70] <u>Antiquities</u> XIV 14:4 (489).
[71] <u>Antiquities</u> XV 1:2 (9-10).

Babas" who were Hasmonean supporters of Antigonus.[72] First, this incident shows that even ten years into his reign Herod feared the Hasmonean ghost and killed them when found. Secondly, Josephus notes at the end of his retelling of the sons of Babas incident that "now none at all [were] left to the kindred of Hyrcanus."[73] Josephus means by this comment that there were no longer any members of the Hasmonean royal family left. We know the statement is incorrect because 23 years later, at the trial of Antipater ben Herod, Josephus tells us that the daughter of Antigonus was there in the room as the wife of Antipater. The daughter of Antigonus was certainly a "kindred" of Hyrcanus. She was his grandniece. This incident backs up my contention that Josephus intended to write Mary the mother of Jesus (and daughter of Antigonus) out of his histories. Josephus records the sons of Babas incident as if Mary did not exist, when he knew full well of her existence.

Protoevangelium of James

Let us return briefly to the apocryphal work attributed to James, the brother of Jesus. The *Protoevangelium of James* names Mary's father as Joachim and describes him as "exceedingly rich and he offered his gifts twofold."[74] The only persons allowed to be "exceedingly rich" in first century BCE Palestine were relatives of the king or the upper crust of the Temple priesthood. A few paragraphs later, Anna the wife of Joachim is approached by her handmaid who suggests she put on her headband that "hath a mark of royalty."[75] Again, the only Jewish royalty of this period was the Hasmonean dynasty. The *Protoevangelium* records Mary's birth as a miraculous event along the lines of the birth of Isaac to an elderly Abraham. Joachim and Anna were apparently an older couple without children. Joachim went into the desert fasting for 40 days

---

[72] Antiquities XV 7:10 (259-266).
[73] Antiquities XV 7:10 (266).
[74] *Protoevangelium* I.1. See The Apocryphal New Testament: A Collection of Apocryphal Christian Literature in an English Translation, Translation by M.R. James, Edited by J.K. Elliott (Oxford University Press 1994) at page 48.
[75] *Protoevangelium* II.2.

and 40 nights praying for a child; Anna humbled herself at home also praying for a child. While Joachim was still in the desert, an angel appeared to him with the message, "behold thy wife Anna hath conceived."[76] Joachim could not have impregnated his wife while in the desert; therefore, Joachim was not the biologic father of Mary. Considering the appearance of angles and other miraculous events contained in the story, what makes more sense is that the *Protoevangelium* renders as a fable the facts of Mary's childhood. Perhaps the politically sensitive nature of her true identity required this approach.

The *Protoevangelium* further tells us that the child Mary was raised at the Temple until age twelve as her mother Anna dedicated her to God in honor of her miraculous birth. My interpretation of the story places it in the context of Mary as the infant daughter of a besieged king who was soon to die. Thus, I read the *Protoevangelium* as a veiled reference to the infant Mary hidden in the Temple complex with sympathetic priests for her own safety, probably priests related to the king. As a daughter of Antigonus, Herod surely ordered her execution so hiding her was the only way for the infant Mary to survive the slaughter.

Do we know Hasmonean priests survived the fall of Jerusalem in 37 BCE? I believe this can be inferred from Josephus' own ancestry. He stated in his Vitae that he was a descendant of the Hasmoneans and of high priests. The only Hasmoneans known to have survived Herod's capture of Jerusalem in 37 BCE were all married into Herod's family or killed. Josephus used quite harsh language in describing Herod's low ancestry.[77] I find it hard to believe Josephus' Hasmonean priestly roots passed through Herod. It makes more sense that a priestly Hasmonean line of lesser royal status survived the 37 BCE purge by publicly supporting Herod's new government. These same Hasmonean priests, while publicly supporting Herod, sheltered Mary out of a sense of family obligation.

---

[76] Ibid IV.2.

[77] Herod's father Antipater is described by Josephus as "of no more than a vulgar family and of no imminent extraction." Antiquities XIV 16:4 (491).

Identity of Joachim / Heli

A section in the preceding chapter discussed the connection between Joachim from the *Protoevangelium* and Heli found in *Luke*. If Mary was raised by a Hasmonean Temple priest who adopted her, we might be able to identify this priest in the writings of Josephus. I propose a speculative theory that Joachim / Heli was Joseph ben Ellemus, said by Josephus to have served as high priest for one day near the end of Herod's reign. Matthias ben Theophilus was high priest in 4 BCE and, according to Josephus, declared himself ritually unfit on the eve of the Day of Atonement. In such cases, the closest "kinsman" of the high priest served in his place. This person was Joseph ben Ellemus according to Josephus.[78] As the closest male relative to Theophilus, in all likelihood Ellemus was the brother of Theophilus. Theophilus is a Greek word meaning friendly with god. Ellemus is a Hebrew word meaning possessed of God. I conclude these words are rough equivalents and, thus, Theophilus (Greek) is the same name as Ellemus (Hebrew). The root word of Ellemus is Eli. Heli and Eli are equivalent names. Thus, Heli of *Luke*'s ancestor list could be Joseph ben Ellemus a/k/a Joseph ben Theophilus, Hasmonean Temple priest, and high priest for one day.

How do we know high priests Matthias ben Theophilus and Joseph ben Theophilus (Ellemus) were Hasmonean? We don't. It's conjecture on top of conjecture. Josephus claimed to be the descendant of Hasmonean kings and high priests yet failed to detail the basis for that claim. I believe the Theophilus line of high priests were his ancestors yet Josephus shrouded this connection in his writings. See Chapter 10 for a further discussion of this topic.

Anna The Prophetess

After the birth of Jesus, the *Gospel of Luke* records Mary going to the Temple to present Jesus (her first-born son) and make the required sacrifices after her 40-day purification period. During

---

[78] Antiquities XVII 6:4.

this trip to the Temple, *Luke* also relates an encounter with a prophetess.

> And there was a prophetess, **Anna** the daughter of Phanuel, of the tribe of Ashe. She was advanced in years * * *. And she never left the Temple, serving night and day with fasting and prayer.[79]

The Jewish Tanach records seven female prophetesses from the period of the judges, a period that ended well before the birth of Jesus. Although there was precedence for a Jewish prophetess, to my knowledge none existed in first century BCE. Further, she is said by *Luke* to have served in the Temple. Women and children were only allowed inside the outer courtyard during daylight hours so this seems quite odd. The *Protoevangelium* indicates Mary was adopted by a woman named "Anna" and raised in the Temple. I conclude the two Anna's named in the *Protoevangelium* and *Gospel of Luke* were one in the same person. Anna was the daughter of a Kohen priest, also the wife of a Kohen priest named Joachim or Heli and the adoptive mother of Mary.

Zoroastrian Priests Attend Birth of Jesus

The *Gospel of Matthew* relates the appearance of magi "from the east" at the stable where Jesus was allegedly born. The magi were priests of the Zoroastrian religion, the official state religion of the Parthian empire. A version of Zoroastrianism was prevalent among the lower ranks of the Roman legions (i.e., Mithraism); however, one can safely assume the magi who visited Mary at the birth of Jesus were not Roman legionnaires. Rome was allied with the Herodians who tried to kill Jesus. Further, *Matthew* identifies the magi as coming from the east of Palestine. Rome lay to the west of Palestine, Parthia to the east. Why then would Zoroastrian priests appear at the birth of a baby in Judea to venerate the child as a newborn king? One logical explanation is that these magi acted as ambassadors from the Parthian Empire welcoming the birth of the successor to the Hasmonean dynasty. Only one

---

[79] Luke 2:36-37.

branch of the Hasmonean clan allied itself with the Parthians, that of Aristobulus II and his youngest son Antigonus. The appearance of Zoroastrian priests at the birth chamber of the baby Jesus offering gifts is yet another verification of the identity of Jesus as a descendant of King Antigonus.

Last Stand At Hyrcania & The Copper Scroll

Two pieces of seemingly disconnected information, one from modern archeology and the other from Josephus, may help us explain how Princess Mary bat Antigonus became separated from her royal mother ending up hiding in the Temple under the protection of priests. These clues also may shed light on the enduring mystery of the treasure described in the Copper Scroll. In 2007, Israeli archeologists found an ancient tunnel in Jerusalem beneath the old city's main road. The tunnel's described purpose was water drainage; however, it stood up to three meters in height. "Archeologists think the tunnel [is one kilometer long and] leads [from the Temple mount] to the Kidron River, which empties into the Dead Sea."[80] This was much more than a standard water drainage canal. At three meters in height (i.e., about ten feet), the tunnel might have been large enough for a horse to walk through. The Wadi Kidron mentioned by an Israeli archeologist in the above quote passes very close to an ancient Hasmonean fortress called Hyrcania before emptying into the Dead Sea.

Other than the execution of the king by Marc Antony, Josephus does not relate the fates of any other members of Antigonus' royal family. Yet we find the following curious reference in Jewish Wars.

> Now when the war about Actium was begun, Herod prepared to come to the assistance of Antony, as being already freed from his troubles in Judea, **and having gained Hyrcania, which was a place that was**

---

[80] "Ancient tunnel discovered in Jerusalem", Jerusalem Post (September 9, 2007).

held by Antigonus' sister.[81]   [Emphasis added.]

The Battle of Actium (lost by Antony and Cleopatra to Octavian) occurred in 31 BCE. The only conclusion to be drawn from this brief statement from Josephus is that members of the royal family of Antigonus escaped the fall of Jerusalem but were trapped by Herod at Hyrcania. They survived there for six years before being executed by Herod. Notice also that King Antigonus put a woman in charge of this party (his sister), very unusual for Jewish culture of the period. If they lasted six years inside the fortress, one must assume a large military force accompanied this party to Hyrcania.

Piecing this information together, one reasonably concludes Antigonus sent the women and children of his family out of Jerusalem through the tunnels to the Wadi Kidron which they followed to Fortress Hyrcania. Why was Princess Mary left behind in the Temple? I infer she was too young for horseback. The women and children most likely made a mad, night-time dash through the Roman lines out of the city. Also, the *Protoevangelium* tells us Joachim and Anna miraculously received an infant daughter in Jerusalem. Rather than a miracle, it was the king requesting the couple to care for his infant daughter after evacuating all the other women of his family out of the city. On this basis, I date the birth of Mary to no more than a few months before the fall of Jerusalem in 37 BCE.

I have long suspected that the Copper Scroll found among the Dead Sea Scrolls at Qumran is in fact a Hasmonean treasure map listing the hiding places for assets tucked away by Antigonus during his war with Herod. Qumran lies a short distance northeast from Hyrcania. Two places mentioned in the Copper Scroll as holding buried treasure are Hyrcania (a Hasmonean fortress) and Jericho (the site of the most important Hasmonean palace outside of Jerusalem).[82] One can almost draw a direct line from Jericho to

---

[81] Jewish Wars I 19:1 (364).

[82] The first item on the Copper Scroll treasure list was described as, "In the fortress which is in the Vale of Achor, forty cubits under the steps entering to the east: a money chest and its contents, of a weight of seventeen talents." Scholar John Allegro believed this fortress was Hyrcania and excavated in

Qumran to Hyrcania running from the Jordan River along the banks of the Dead Sea. The theory goes that Antigonus' sister escaped to Hyrcania with not only the women and children of the royal family but, also, the Temple treasury. Before they were trapped by Roman soldiers inside the fortress, she disbursed the treasure into hiding places around the Dead Sea then stashed a copy of the map in Cave 3 at Qumran. The size and value of the treasure described in the Copper Scroll is staggering, almost beyond belief.

> When the weights of the treasures itemized in the Copper Scrolls are totaled, we come to the following:
>> Gold – 1285 Talents
>> Silver – 666 Talents
>> Gold and Silver – 17 Talents
>> Gold and silver vessels – 600 Talents
>> Mixed precious metals – 2,088 Talents
>
> Items with unspecified weights are as follows:
>> Gold ingots – 165
>> Silver bars – 7
>> Gold and Silver vessels – 609
>
> In Biblical Talent terms the sheer weight of the gold and silver is enormous. One talent is estimated to be about 76 lb or 34.47 kg. The Copper Scroll seems to be referring to precious metals worth around $2 billion at current prices, but whose intrinsic historic value would be many times this figure![83]

Hyrcania looking for the 17 talents. He discovered underground chambers at Hyrcania but no treasure. The Copper Scroll mentions Jericho by name in several places.

[83] "Unfolding the Secrets of the Copper Scroll of Qumran" by Robert Feathers, New Dawn Magazine No. 80 (September-October 2003); Chris Mitchel of Christian World News puts the current value of the Copper Scroll treasure at $3 billion. See "The Mystery of the Copper Scroll", cbn.com, September 27, 2009.

The above-quoted article was written in 2003; however, the price of gold has since more than doubled, meaning the Copper Scroll treasure (if found intact) would currently be valued far in excess of $2 billion US.

Scholars agree that the most likely source of such a vast hoard of precious metals was the Temple treasury. Let us return to Jerusalem in 37 BCE as the city fell to Herod. Josephus tells the story twice, once in <u>Antiquities</u> and again in <u>Jewish Wars</u>. As with the detail of Antigonus' sister holding out at Hyrcania for six years, we glean additional information from the account found in <u>Jewish Wars</u>. In <u>Antiquities</u>, Josephus records Herod agreeing to pay the soldiers from his own pocket in return for not looting Jerusalem yet he himself looted all the homes of the wealthy men of Antigonus' party and, presumably, the Hasmonean palace. After paying off the soldiers and General Sossius, Herod gave the rest to Antony as a bribe for executing Antigonus.

> Herod ... carried off all the royal ornaments, and spoiled the wealthy men of what they had gotten; and when, by these means, he had gotten together a great quantity of silver and gold, he <u>gave it all to Antony</u>, and his friends that were about him.[84] [Emphasis added.]

<u>Jewish Wars</u> adds one additional nugget of information. Herod "slew [the men of Antigonus' party]; and, **as his money ran low**, he turned all the ornaments he had into money."[85] Emphasis added.

If Herod captured the Temple treasury, surely his money would not have "run low" requiring him to melt down all the looted fixtures and ornaments made of precious metals in order to pay Antony. The Copper Scroll describes a treasure worth in excess of $2 billion US in today's currency. Antigonus was high priest as well as king. Therefore, he controlled the Temple treasury. These facts reinforce the conclusion that Herod never

---

[84] <u>Antiquities</u> XV 1:2 (5).
[85] <u>Jewish Wars</u> I 18:4 (358).

got his hands on the vast wealth of the Temple treasury after Jerusalem fell, or at least not in 37 BCE.

After Octavian defeated Marc Antony and Cleopatra at Actium in 31 BCE, Herod sailed to Rhodes to pledge his support to the new ruler and deliver another massive bribe. Herod sided with the wrong side in this Roman civil war and could have very easily lost his throne because of it. The tribute paid by Herod was so satisfactory to Octavian that not only did he confirm Herod in his position as Jewish king but added a few extra cities for good measure. Far from being broke, Herod thereafter embarked on a massive building campaign. Scholars record that Herod experienced mild financial problems early in his kingship but his financial situation improved later in his reign.

> In the early years of his kingship, his financial situation seems to have been steadily improving. He reluctantly paid tribute to Cleopatra ... and began the construction of Sebaste a few years later. But the outlook was still precarious [for Herod], since when a famine struck Judea shortly afterward, he had to liquidate his personal art collection and purchase grain from Petronius, the prefect of Egypt. ... By 20 BC, Herod was able to reduce taxes by one-third, even though construction of Caesarea had just begun and that of the Temple at Jerusalem was about to start. Josephus specifically noted that the Temple was built at Herod's own expense.[86]

The Judean famine occurred in 27 BCE during which time Herod sold off his art work to buy grain yet by 20 BCE Herod was so well off that he cut taxes by 1/3rd while building the city of Caesarea and the magnificent Jewish Temple at Jerusalem. Caesarea, the grandest city in Herod's kingdom outside of

---

[86] The Building Program of Herod the Great by Duane W. Roller (University of California Press 1998) at pages 120-121.

Jerusalem, possessed the look of a Roman metropolis--magnificent aqueduct bringing fresh water to the city from Mount Carmel, hippodrome seating 38,000 spectators, amphitheater seating 4500, baths, fountains, and a deep water harbor on the Mediterranean. The port of Caesarea, called Sebastos, contained the first artificial harbor in the world. It equaled the size of Piraeus in Athens with anchorage for 100 ships. The construction projects of the Jerusalem Temple and the city of Caesarea were on a Titanic scale, some of the largest projects undertaken in the ancient world, yet Herod cut taxes while undertaking these projects.

The obvious inference from these facts is that Herod found a new and significant source of wealth outside of tax revenue allowing for a tax cut in 20 BCE. My conclusion is that Herod's men found most or all of the Temple treasure described in the Copper Scroll sometime between 27 and 20 BCE.[87]

Dating The Death of Herod

The *Gospel of Matthew* presents Herod as still alive at the birth of Jesus. See story of the Magi appearing in Jerusalem[88] and the infamous Slaughter of the Innocents.[89] Thus, the date of Herod's death is generally accepted to have been the latest date for the birth of Jesus and it is where we start our analysis on this subject. According to Josephus, Herod died five days after executing his son Antipater.[90] Consequently, evidence aiding in dating the death of one directly relates to the date of death of the other. Antipater, the father of Jesus, became crown prince after Herod executed his Hasmonean sons (Aristobulus and Alexander) in 7 BCE. Thereafter, Antipater stood first in line of succession to

---

[87] The Copper Scroll text is written in an ancient form of Hebrew apparently no longer used by the Jewish priests in 37 BCE. On this basis, scholars date the creation of the Copper Scroll to an earlier period. But one must keep in mind that the Copper Scroll is a treasure map, not a standard religious text. Treasure maps are often written in code. Might not the priests Antigonus assigned to document the location of the buried treasure use an old script known to but a handful of elderly priests? One cannot discount the possibility.

[88] *Matthew* 2:1-7.

[89] *Matthew* 2:13-23.

[90] Antiquities, XVII 8:1.

Herod's throne. An extensive discussion of the strange relationship between Herod and his son Antipater appears in Chapter 9 so I'll refrain from further commenting on that topic for now.

In reviewing the theories of many authors and scholars on the date of Herod's death, they don't seem to read Josephus as a whole but, rather, fixate on one specific fact. The most popular event zeroed in on by theorists is Josephus' statement that Herod died at some point after a lunar eclipse visible in Palestine.[91] The most popular lunar eclipses championed by scholars occurred in 5 BCE, 4 BCE and 1 BCE. But cracking the puzzle is not so easy. One must plumb the whole of the record to put the facts in proper historical context. Another significant event recorded by Josephus relevant to dating the deaths of Herod and Antipater is that Herod died 34 years after the execution of his nemeses Antigonus and 37 years after being named king of the Jews by the Roman senate.

We have now placed our foot into the morass. The first obstacle to any theory on Herod's date of death is the conflict between two key pieces of evidence. Marc Antony executed King Antigonus in 37 BCE. Subtracting 34 years gives us a date of 3 BCE; however, there was no lunar eclipse visible in Palestine in 3 BCE. The closest eclipse occurred in September of 4 BCE. One may ask, is that a big deal? In early drafts of this book, I took the attitude that no, it was not a big deal. Josephus says 34 years after the death of Antigonus so I went with 3 BCE. It was only later when filling out the details of my timeline located at the end of this book that this minor discrepancy began to trouble me. Several facts from Josephus and other sources cast doubt on 3 BCE. The doubts gnawed at me drawing blood. I spent weeks puzzling over the issue chewing on it like a dog with a bone. Finally, I sent my wife to stay with her sisters and barricaded myself in the house for four straight days doing nothing but churning my brain on the deaths of Herod and Antipater. After several lost nights of sleep, light appeared at the end of the tunnel. Like Jesus, I emerged from the tomb alive. There are facts tending to push the date of

---

[91] Antiquities, XVII 6:4.

Herod's death both earlier and later than 3 BCE. I'll address the two groups of facts separately.

Arguments Supporting Herod's Death in 1 BCE
The alternate date most popular on the later side of 3 BCE is 1 BCE for the following reasons.

1. The lunar eclipse in 1 BCE was total in Palestine whereas the 4 BCE eclipse was partial.[92] This is the only lunar eclipse mentioned in the whole of the writings of Josephus. Why would Josephus take special note of a relatively minor lunar eclipse in 4 BCE?

2. Emperor Augustus reduced the troop strength of the Roman legions during the period 7-2 BCE. A major Jewish revolt broke out against Herod's successor, Herod Archelaus, close in time to his accession to the throne. The revolt was so large that it took three Roman legions to stamp it out. If the revolt against Archelaus broke out in 3 BCE, how could Caesar still be drawing down troops?

3. The Jewish revolt against Herod Archelaus ended in 1 BCE, which chronologically matches up with the 1 BCE lunar eclipse and the end of Caesar's troop draw down.

Of these points, the eclipse argument gives me the least pause for thought. There were two total lunar eclipses in 5 BCE. There is nothing unique about the nature of the 1 BCE eclipse making it a more worthy candidate than the 5 BCE eclipse. As discussed in more detail later in this chapter, the extent of an eclipse or other celestial phenomenon has little import for use by priests to claim god was for or against any contemporary action in my view. The priests which laud or condemn an event so they to the skies for something to confirm their desired result.

Thus, I start with the premise that the 5, 4, and 1 BCE eclipses are all equally viable candidates for the one mentioned in

---

[92] See *The Chronology of the Reign of Herod the Great* by W.E. Filmer, The Journal of Theological Studies 1966 XVII(2):283-298 (Oxford Press) and *Chronological, Nativity, and Religious Studies* by David W. Beyer published in <u>Chronos, Kairos, Christos II</u> (Mercer University Press (1998) at page 88.

Josephus. The other evidence for dating Herod's death carries greater weight than the eclipse in my view. One such clue comes from Antiquities where Josephus relates that Herod removed Matthias ben Theophilus as high priest for failing to stop two rabbis for inciting a Jewish crowd to pull down a golden eagle Herod erected on the Temple gate.[93] This high priest is universally agreed to have left office in 4 or 5 BCE. To move his high priesthood forward by three additional years to 1 BCE means one has to monkey with the accepted terms in office of four other high priests to make the timeline work.

The alleged troop draw down by Caesar from 7 to 2 BCE takes more effort to address. The only place I found this event recorded was an article by David W. Meyers published in Chronos, Kairos, Christos II.[94] Nowhere else in my research did I find such a claim. Meyers cites not source material but an academic, Ronald Syme, for authority on this point.[95] Although Syme was a noted scholar at Oxford and prolific author, the particular work cited by Meyers is obscure. I could not locate a copy for sale or elsewhere on the web. Thus, I can't substantiate the proof given by Syme for a Roman troop reduction, much less quantify it. The Roman Empire was a vast enterprise. How big was the supposed troop reduction? One, two, three legions? Where did the reductions occur? Spain, Gaul, Germania, Galacia, Greece, Africa, Syria? The claim lacks the proper detail allowing us to weigh it with the other known facts surrounding the death of Herod. Thus, there is no evidence that the number of Roman legions in the Syrian province shrank during this period. If Caesar disbanded a legion in Africa or Spain would that necessarily be evidence there was no local revolt elsewhere in the empire? Local revolts of varying magnitudes perpetually occurred somewhere in the vast Roman Empire. I find this point in the category of a red herring.

---

[93] Antiquities XVII 6:4.
[94] *Chronological, Nativity, and Religious Studies* by David W. Beyer published in Chronos, Kairos, Christos II (Mercer University Press (1998) at page 88.
[95] The Crisis of 2 BC by R. Syme (Munich: Beck 1974) at page 3.

This brings us to the final point—the Jewish revolt ended in 1 BCE.[96] Josephus records this particular Jewish revolt starting during a Passover.[97] The revolt supposedly corresponds with the 1 BCE eclipse in March of that year. So, for proponents of the 1 BCE date, the revolt started in April of 1 BCE, conflagrated into a war involving three Rome legions, many thousands of allied troops covering the separate lands of Judea, Samaria, and Galilee, then ended all before the close of that year (i.e., it lasted a mere 8-9 months). Any fair assessment of Josephus leads one to the conclusion that this Jewish revolt lasted several years. For instance, Varus (Roman governor of Syria) went to Jerusalem from Antioch on three separate occasions to put down this revolt having thought on each of the prior two visits that the situation was under control allowing him to return to his provincial capital. I put the length of the conflict described by Josephus at two to three years from start to finish. There was no way the revolt described by Josephus wrapped up in eight months. See *Supplement 1* to this book (outline of passages from Antiquities on this topic).[98]

The final nail in the coffin to the theory dating Herod's death to 1 BCE is archeological evidence of coins and monuments showing Herod Archelaus, Herod Antipas, and Herod Philip[99] all dated the beginning of their reigns to 4 BCE.[100] Herod's sons did not receive kingdoms until after their father's death; therefore, this is strong evidence that Herod died on or before 4 BCE. I've read the argument that Archelaus predated his reign to 4 BCE because

---

[96] See The Birth of Christ Recalculated by Ernest Martin (Foundation for Biblical Research 1980).

[97] Antiquities, XVII 9:3.

[98] To put the engagement in historical perspective, the revolt against Rome led by King Antigonus the Hasmonean started in 40 BC and was not finally suppressed until 37 BC. The most famous Jewish revolt against Rome started in 66 CE and led to the destruction of the Temple in 70 CE. Further, Jews in the countryside during the great revolt were not finally suppressed until Masada fell to the Romans in 73 CE.

[99] I use the name "Herod Philip" to denote Philip the Tetrarch and "Herod Boethus" for his half-brother Herod, who was the grandson of High Priest Boethus.

[100] See Christianity and the Roman Empire by Ralph Martin Novak (Continuum International 2001) at page 285.

that was the year he became coregent. That argument does not hold water for two reasons. It fails to explain why Herod's other sons who received kingdoms but were never coregent (i.e., Herod Antipas and Herod Philip) also dated the beginning of their reigns to 4 BCE. Further, the coins and monuments contain the specific title awarded to each by Caesar Augustus[101] after the death of Herod. For instance, Archelaus expected to be named king but received the title "ethnarch" from Caesar. This is very persuasive evidence that Herod died during 4 BCE.

Conclusion: The proof presented in support of the position that Herod died in 1 BCE is extremely weak. Stronger proof exists for dating the death of Herod to 4 or 5 BCE.

Dating Herod's Death to the Winter of 4 BCE

After trashing the 1 BCE proposed date for Herod's death, the evidence (listed below) points to either 4 or 5 BCE. I accept the aforementioned coin and monument evidence establishes 4 BCE as the latest possible date on which Herod could have died. Here are the pieces of the chronology puzzle that must be shoehorned into the solution to the date of Herod's death. Next to each piece of evidence, I note whether it tends to favor either 4 or 5 BCE.

Evidence	Date favoring
Coins and monuments	4 BCE
Lunar eclipse in Palestine	4 or 5 BCE
Year deprived Matthias ben Theophilus of high priesthood	4 or 5 BCE
Reigned 34 years from death of Antigonus	3 or 4 BCE
Reigned 37 years since declare king by Roman senate	3 or 4 BCE

A review of the above chart shows 4 BCE as the most likely date for the death of Herod. The coin evidence narrows our search down to a small window of dates. The one piece of

---

[101] "Ethnarch" in the case of Archelaus and "Tetrarch" for Antipas and Philip.

evidence scholars most often point to when advocating for a 5 BCE date is the lunar eclipse of Josephus. There were two lunar eclipses in 5 BCE and another two in 4 BCE. See tables from NASA's Goddard Space Flight Center on the next page. Putting all the evidence together, these four lunar eclipses are the only viable candidates to be the one mention by Josephus.

Reproduced below are tables from NASA's Goddard Space Flight Center showing calculations for the dates of lunar eclipses occurring during 5 and 4 BCE.[102] Please note that astronomers count years before the Common Era differently than the Gregorian method by inserting a year zero that the Gregorian calendar lacks. The below tables follow this convention; therefore, year "-4" is 5 BCE in the Gregorian numbering system and "-3" equates to 4 BCE. Also, lunar eclipses only occur when there is a full moon so focus on the third column from the left. The letter "t" denotes total eclipse and "p" partial.

Year	New Moon			First Quarter			Full Moon			Last Quarter		
-4										Jan	2	15:42
	Jan	9	06:55	Jan	16	08:21	Jan	24	13:06	Feb	1	02:03
	Feb	7	17:32	Feb	15	03:27	Feb	23	05:09	Mar	1	09:23
	Mar	8	04:44 P	Mar	15	22:45	Mar	23	18:16 t	Mar	30	14:54
	Apr	6	16:51 P	Apr	14	16:57	Apr	22	04:31	Apr	28	20:07
	May	6	05:57	May	14	09:16	May	21	12:29	May	28	02:29
	Jun	4	20:00	Jun	12	23:11	Jun	19	19:13	Jun	26	11:13
	Jul	4	10:55	Jul	12	10:34	Jul	19	01:58	Jul	25	23:05
	Aug	3	02:28	Aug	10	19:40	Aug	17	09:56	Aug	24	14:26
	Sep	1	18:09 P	Sep	9	03:12	Sep	15	20:05 t	Sep	23	09:02
	Oct	1	09:15 P	Oct	8	10:10	Oct	15	08:54	Oct	23	05:58
	Oct	30	23:08	Nov	6	17:49	Nov	14	00:21	Nov	22	03:28
	Nov	29	11:32	Dec	6	03:09	Dec	13	17:59	Dec	21	23:19
	Dec	28	22:39									

---

[102] Tables from the Goddard Space Flight Center website. "Algorithms used in predicting the phases of the Moon and eclipses are based on Jean Meeus' Astronomical Algorithms (Willmann-Bell, Inc., 1998). All calculations are by Fred Espenak, and he assumes full responsibility for their accuracy."

Year	New Moon	First Quarter	Full Moon	Last Quarter
-3		Jan 4 14:44	Jan 12 12:53	Jan 20 15:36
	Jan 27 08:52	Feb 3 04:33	Feb 11 07:40	Feb 19 03:38
	Feb 25 18:32 T	Mar 4 20:15	Mar 13 00:45 p	Mar 20 11:55
	Mar 27 03:58	Apr 3 13:16	Apr 11 15:00	Apr 18 17:40
	Apr 25 13:37	May 3 06:56	May 11 02:15	May 17 22:19
	May 25 00:11	Jun 2 00:20	Jun 9 11:11	Jun 16 03:17
	Jun 23 12:25	Jul 1 16:31	Jul 8 18:55	Jul 15 09:51
	Jul 23 02:51	Jul 31 06:49	Aug 7 02:37	Aug 13 19:13
	Aug 21 19:21 A	Aug 29 19:03	Sep 5 11:08 p	Sep 12 08:18
	Sep 20 12:57	Sep 28 05:30	Oct 4 21:01	Oct 12 01:33
	Oct 20 06:16	Oct 27 14:38	Nov 3 08:37	Nov 10 22:19
	Nov 18 22:12	Nov 25 23:03	Dec 2 22:13	Dec 10 20:40
	Dec 18 12:17	Dec 25 07:25		

Lunar Eclipse And Herod's Death

The March eclipses of 5 and 4 BCE are problematic because Josephus lists a series of events occurring after Herod died but before the next Passover in April. See *Supplement 2* for list of 17 separate recorded events. In 4 BCE, Passover occurred on April 10 leaving a maximum of 28 days for all the events described by Josephus to occur after the eclipse but prior to Passover. The time gap in 5 BCE between the March eclipse and Passover was even shorter. I find it extremely unlikely all of the events described by Josephus happened within 28 days. Josephus records in his histories just an overview of the highlights meaning more events occurred in thus period than the 28 items recorded. To my eyes, the list of events is more suited to months in duration, not days. For this reason, I remove the two March eclipses from the list of possible choices. This narrows the field down to the eclipses of September 15, 5 BCE and September 5, 4 BCE.

One can see from the tables that the September eclipse of 5 BCE was total (i.e., a more significant event to the naked eye) while the 4 BCE eclipse was partial. Does this fact lead us to favor the 5 BCE eclipse over the one in 4 BCE? It's well documented in histories of the Roman world from this time period that priests looked into the sky for omens at the time of important events. The range of events recorded as important omens were vast--an eagle taking flight, a shooting star, an eclipse, a conjunction of stars. These omens were reported back to the people by the priests as proof that the gods were for or against something. I submit these reports of astrological events in the sky were an early form of propaganda. As propaganda, the magnitude of the event observed in the sky did not necessarily correlate with the importance of the supposed corresponding human event. Josephus records that Herod removed the high priest Matthias ben Theophilus from office at the time of a lunar eclipse. As explained in Chapter 10 of this book, I believe the father of Josephus was also a high priest named Matthias ben Theophilus who served at the outbreak of the great Jewish Revolt in 66 CE (or roughly 70 years later). The Matthias who was removed from office as high priest by Herod in 4 BCE may very well have been an ancestor of Josephus, which helps explain the historian's special interest in the events of his short tenure as high priest. This fact also helps explain why Josephus could have latched upon a minor lunar eclipse to show that God was displeased with the removal of Matthias ben Theophilus from the office of high priest.

The language found in <u>Antiquities</u> on this issue infers Herod died close in time to a lunar eclipse visible in Judea and that this celestial event was also tied to the execution of two rabbis. As with much of Josephus, what he actually said is murkier than the popular perception. The pertinent passage from Josephus appears in Book XVII, Chapter 6 of <u>Antiquities</u>. Section 2 of Chapter 6 relates how two pious rabbis (Judas and Matthias) led a crowd in tearing down a golden eagle erected by Herod upon the Temple gate in Jerusalem, as it violated Jewish religious law against graven images. The two rabbis and 40 of their followers were arrested for this act. Section 3 of Chapter 6 tells us the two rabbis were transported from Jerusalem to Jericho and burned alive in front of the leading men of Judea upon Herod's orders. Section 4 of Chapter 6 deals with the punishment Herod handed out to the high priest at the time the rabbis pulled down the golden eagle at the Temple (i.e., Matthias ben Theophilus).

> But Herod deprived this Matthias of the high
> priesthood, and burn the other Matthias, who
> had raised the sedition, with his companions,

alive. <u>And that very night there was an eclipse and the moon.</u>[103] [Emphasis added.]

Did the eclipse occur when the high priest was sacked by Herod, when the rabbis were burned alive in Jericho, or simultaneously with both events? It's difficult to say for sure but section 4 of Chapter 6 deals almost exclusively with Herod changing high priests while cryptically mentioning one of the two rabbis who was burned to death, perhaps only to distinguish this individual from the high priest of the same name. Coupling that point with the probable family relationship between Josephus and Matthias ben Theophilus leads me to conclude that Josephus meant the eclipse of the moon occurred on the day Herod removed Matthias ben Theophilus from the high priesthood. Even though Josephus relates the removal of the high priest after he recounts the rabbis being burnt alive, this does not mean the events occurred in that order. In Chapter 6 of this book, I give an example of Josephus listing a series of related events out of historical order (relating to the end Pontius Pilate's term in Judea). It is not an uncommon occurrence in the works of Josephus.

An important point is made by establishing that the lunar eclipse occurred when the high priest Matthias ben Theophilus was removed from office as opposed to when the rabbis were burned at the stake in Jericho. The high priest ruled in Jerusalem and the crowd destroyed the golden eagle in Jerusalem. The most volatile periods for rebellious activity at the Temple were during religious festivals. Rosh Hashanah (Yom Teruah) occurs in September followed closely by the Day of Atonement (Yom Kippur). I believe the rabbis incited the crowd to tear down the golden eagle from the Temple gate in early September of 4 BCE. Herod would have still been in Jerusalem at this time (not yet having departed for his winter palace) and took swift action against the high priest removing him from office. With two important religious festivals close at hand and Jerusalem soon to swell with visiting Jews making crowd control problematic for the authorities, Herod

---

[103] <u>Antiquities</u> XVII 6:4 (167).

wisely refrained from immediately executing the rabbis in Jerusalem and, instead, removed them to Jericho to avoid inciting the crowd. As winter came on, Herod executed the rabbis at his winter palace in Jericho.[104] Thus, there was a time gap of a few months between the eclipse and the execution of the rabbis in Jericho.

Under my theory Herod died in his winter palace late in 4 BCE, most likely in late November. Support for this month comes from the Hebrew scholion interpreting the Megillat Ta'anit. The Megillat Ta'anit is a list of Jewish holidays and other special days of commemoration written in Aramaic around the time of the destruction of the Temple in 70 CE.[105] According to the scholion, the ancient Jews celebrated the anniversary of Herod's death on 7 Kislev (Hebrew month falling in November-December).[106] The Hebrew date 7 Kislev converts to November 24th for the calendar year of 4 BCE.[107] This proposed timeline requires a dying Herod to linger near death for several months (from September to November) after the rabbis incited the crowd to pull down the golden eagle from the Temple gate, a problematic but not fatal flaw. All of us know of individuals sent to hospice to die but who live on for many months past when the doctors predicted they would die. My own grandmother defied death in this fashion while succumbing to cancer. In the case of Herod, I can easily believe he stubbornly clung to life for the express purposes of seeing his son Antipater put to death.

---

[104] Josephus very specifically states that the rabbis first sent to Jericho before being executed in front of all the leading men of the country. Antiquities XVII 6:3 (160).

[105] The Bible As It Was by James L. Kugel (Belknap Press of Harvard University Press 1999) at page 590.

[106] The History of the Jewish People in the Age of Jesus Christ, Volume 1 by Emil Schürer, Géza Vermès, and Fergus Millar (T&T Clark Ltd. 1973) at page 328, footnote 165; Studies in the Jewish Background of Christianity by Daniel R. Schwartz (Mohr Siebeck 1992) at page 160, footnote 10.

[107] This calculation was made using an online tool found at http://www.olenberg.org to convert the Hebrew calendar date of Kislev 7 in the year 3758 to the Gregorian date of November 24, 4 BCE.

60

After relating the events leading up to the death of Herod, Josephus states the following.

> When he had done those things, [Herod] died, the fifth day after he had caused Antipater to be slain; **having reigned, since he procured Antigonus to be slain, thirty-four years; but since he had been declared king by the Romans, thirty-seven.**[108] [Emphasis added.]

This presents another problem. We know from other sources that the Roman senate declared Herod king in 40 BCE and Antigonus died in 37 BCE. Counting 37 and 34 years, respectively, from those historical dates brings us to 3 BCE; however, there was no lunar eclipse in 3 BCE.[109] Is there a way to harmonize the above-quoted passage from <u>Antiquities</u> with a 4 BCE death for Herod?

The answer to the conundrum lies in the method by which Josephus counted regnal years (i.e., the years of reign of a king). An example of the method employed by Josephus comes from his discussion of the Battle at Actium. "At this time it was that the fight happened at Actium, between Octavius Caesar and Antony, in the <u>seventh year</u> of the reign of Herod."[110] However, we know from Roman historians that the Battle at Actium occurred in 31 BCE or six years after Herod took the throne in Jerusalem in 37 BCE. How does Josephus deduce this to be Herod's seventh regnal year? Under the nonaccession-year system, the first partial calendar year of a king's reign was counted as his first regnal year.[111] For instance, Herod captured Jerusalem in June of 37 BCE and, under the nonaccession-year system, his first regnal year ran from June through December of 37 BCE. The calendar year of 36

---

[108] <u>Antiquities</u> XVII 8:1 (191).

[109] According to the aforementioned NASA tables, there were no partial or total lunar eclipses in 3 BCE, only penumbral eclipses which cannot be detected with the naked eye.

[110] <u>Antiquities</u> XV 5:2.

[111] <u>The Mysterious Numbers of the Hebrew Kings</u> by Edwin Richard Thiele (Kregel Academic & Professional 1994) at pages 43-44.

BCE would be year 2 of Herod's reign under this system. This explains how Josephus calculated 31 BCE as the seventh year of Herod's reign and indicates Josephus used the nonaccession-year system. If 31 BCE was the seventh year of Herod's reign, then 4 BCE was the 34th year of his reign.

After Herod's death at Jericho and burial at Herodium, one logically assumes Archelaus was in a big hurry to get to Rome and have his appointment as king in Herod's last testament confirmed by Caesar.[112] Yet Archelaus did not leave for Rome until after the following Passover, which occurred on March 15 in 3 BCE. Why wasn't Archelaus off for Rome to secure the Jewish throne from Caesar the moment Herod died? First, the Aegean Sea was too rough for passage to Rome in the winter months. Second, Archelaus conducted an elaborate funeral for his father followed by an official state mourning period. I find three months a reasonable period for the funeral, mourning period, feasts, consolidating power with the military, making nice with leading men of Jerusalem, taking possession of Jewish lands outside of Judea (i.e., Galilee, Samaria and Idumea) and, finally, preparing for the trip to Rome. Assuming Herod died in late November of 4 BCE, this three month period takes us to late February of 3 BCE. With an important religious festival close at hand in mid-March, it makes sense that Archelaus stayed in Jerusalem a few extra weeks desiring to get past the threat of a revolt during Passover before sailing for Rome. Further, with the Aegean Sea unnavigable in winter, it is unlikely Archelaus could have sailed for Rome before March even if he desired to do so.

Conclusion: The lunar eclipse referred to by Josephus occurred on September 5, 4 BCE. Herod died in late winter of 4 BCE (most likely November) at his winter palace in Jericho. The Jewish revolt against Archelaus broke out during the following Passover in March of 3 BCE. The revolt gradually increased in intensity over two years starting out as a local matter with only one Roman legion engaged but conflagrated into a vast war covering three separate territories (Judea, Galilee and Samaria) with three

---

[112] Josephus even refers to this in Jewish Wars II 1:1.

Roman legions engaged in battle. Varus stamped out the last remnants of this revolt in 1 BCE.[113]

Dating the Birth of Jesus

Having concluded Herod died in November of 4 BCE, it should be a piece of cake to fit the birth of Jesus into our timeline, right? To borrow a phrase from Hertz Rent-A-Car commercials, not exactly. Most scholars date the birth of Jesus to a matter of days or months <u>before</u> the death of Herod because the *Gospel of Matthew* has the magi showing up at Jerusalem after the birth of Jesus inquiring of "Herod the king" the birth location for the new king of the Jews. There are two problems presented by a 4 BCE date for the birth of Jesus—(a) no celestial event occurred during 4 BCE that one may ascribe to the Star of Bethlehem and (b) no Roman census as mentioned in *Luke* occurred in 4 BCE. Another issue to consider is the virgin birth, which I reject as myth. If Jesus had a biologic father, then his mother Mary must have been married to said father otherwise Jesus was a bastard. I can't fathom a bastard convincing any segment of the Jewish population he was the messiah, much less Pontius Pilate accepting the bastard as a legitimate Jewish king. Further, no self-respecting Jew would marry a woman whose husband still lived. That was the religious crime John the Baptist railed against Herod Antipas for. I've made the case earlier herein that the father of Jesus was Antipater ben Herod; however, he died five days before Herod. The point being that Joseph the carpenter could not have married or even betrothed Mary the mother of Jesus until after Antipater had been executed. If Herod died in November of 4 BCE (and Antipater five days before him) then Jesus was born no more than nine months after that date. To work within our theory, Mary bat Antigonus became pregnant by Antipater ben Herod while he was imprisoned by Herod just prior to his execution in late 4 BCE. The execution of Antipater left Mary a pregnant widow who was

---

[113] <u>See</u> Supplement 3 for a discussion of the issue of coin evidence Varus' governorship of Syria.

then betrothed to Joseph the carpenter. Jesus was thereafter born in the summer of 3 BCE in Judea.

Early Church Fathers Placed the Birth of Jesus in 3 BCE

Ancient Christian writers almost unanimously date the birth of Jesus to 3 or 2 BCE, which is after Herod's death in 4 BCE. The dates given were not an exact calendar year as we use today but, rather, the number of years from the start of the reign of Caesar Augustus or an important event (such as the death of Marc Antony).[114]

Author	Stated Birth of Jesus	Time Period Author Wrote
Irenaeus	3 BCE	180 CE
Tertullian	3/2 BCE	198 CE
Clement of Alexandria	3 BCE	200 CE
Julius Africanus	3/2 BCE	Early 3rd century
Origen	3 BCE	Early 3rd century
Eusebius	3/2 BCE	Early 4th century
Epiphanius	2 BCE	Late 4th century

Census of Quirinius

According to *Luke*, Jesus' birth occurred in the time of the "first census taken while Quirinius was governor of Syria."[115]

---

[114] <u>Christianity and the Roman Empire</u> by Ralph Martin Novak (Trinity Press International, 2001) at page 299. All dates given in the table come from Novak with the exception of Irenaeus. Novak ascribes to Irenaeus a date of 3 or 4 BCE depending on whether one counts using nonaccession-year or accession-year systems. But a check of the actual Irenaeus quote yields a date of 3/2 BCE. "Our Lord was born about the 41st year of the reign of Augustus." Irenaeus, <u>Against Heresies</u>, Bk. III, XXI 3. Although Julius Caesar was assassinated on March 15, 44 BCE, Marc Antony controlled Rome immediately after Caesar's death leaving the teenage Octavian (later Augustus) with no official role in government. It was not until November 26 of 43 BCE that Octavian became triumvir jointly ruling with Antony and Lepidus. Counting from November of 43 BCE, the 41st year of his reign ran from November of 3 BCE to November of 2 BCE.

[115] *Luke* 2:1-2.

64

Problem: Publius Sulpicius Quirinius served as the Roman governor of Syria from 6-12 CE (i.e., at least nine years after the accepted date for the birth of Jesus). Quirinius did in fact perform a Judean census after Herod Archelaus was removed from the throne in 6 CE. However, I don't know of a single serious scholar who dates the birth of Jesus to 6 CE nor does this statement from *Luke* mesh with Josephus. In researching this issue, one finds strenuous arguments that Quirinius twice served as governor of Syria, both at Jesus' birth in 3 BCE and later in 6 CE. There is ZERO evidence for this argument either in the form of archeological proof or in the recorded histories.[116]

The Roman governor of Syria in the years immediately before and after the death of Herod was Quintilius Varus. The most obvious and logical solution to the problem is that *Luke* confused "Quirinius" (Publius Sulpicius Quirinius) with "Quintilius" (Publius Quintilius Varus). Despite all protests to the contrary, the evidence weighs heavily in favor of Varus being governor of Syria in the 4-3 BCE timeframe. See *Supplement 3* below. And, further, we have historical evidence for an empire-wide Roman registration and loyalty oath in 3 BCE prior to the senate proclamation awarding Augustus Caesar the title, "Father of My Country".[117] No historical evidence exists for a Roman census conducted in 4 BCE.

For these reasons, the Roman census mentioned in chapter 2 of *Luke*'s gospel refers to the one conducted by Publius Quintilius Varus in 3 BCE.

---

[116] Some argue a stone inscription referred to as the Lapis Tiburtinus found near the Tiber River references an individual who twice served as governor of Syria and, inexplicably, this unnamed person must be Quirinius. Not only is the person who is the subject of the inscription never identified but, also, the inscription never says this unnamed Roman official served twice as governor of Syria. You can read the translation yourself here: http://www.infidels.org/library/modern/richard_carrier/quirinius.html#Tiburtinus

[117] *The Nativity and Herod's Death* by Ernest L. Martin published in Chronos, Kairos, Christos edited by Jack Finegan, Jerry Vardaman, and Edwin M. Yamauchi (EISENBRAUNS 1989) at page 89.

The Star of Bethlehem

The stories of the Magi and the Star of Bethlehem are recorded in but one gospel—*Matthew*. As such, I find them less reliable as an historical event. Nevertheless, scholars have expended considerable detective work searching for the star said to herald the birth of Jesus. But was it a star or some other astrological phenomenon that spawned *Matthew*'s account? The following quote gives us a clue: "They (the Magi) went their way; and lo, the star, which they had seen in the east went on before them, **until it came and stood over where the child was.**"[118] Emphasis added. *Matthew* describes a celestial body processing across the sky then stopping at a fixed point. This description fits the movement of planetary bodies within our own solar system, which progress across the sky until they stop for a short period before regressing[119] in the opposite direction. Ancient astrologers studied and documented the phenomena of planets appearing to stand still before switching from progression to regression. For this reason, I find the argument that the Star of Bethlehem refers to an unusual conjunction of planetary bodies within our solar system superior to theories of a comet or other celestial events.

But what planet(s) should our inquiry focus upon? "Jupiter often was associated with the birth of kings and therefore called the king planet."[120] For a 12-month period spanning August of 3 BCE to August of 2 BCE, a series of close conjunctions occurred involving the planet Jupiter. Of particular interest were conjunctions of Jupiter and Venus occurring on **August 12, 3 BCE** (4.3' of separation) and on June 17, 2 BCE (0.5' of separation). In ancient mythology, Venus represented the mother goddess. The close conjunction of these planets would have held

---

[118] Matthew 2:9.

[119] "Retrogression is the period of time during which a planet in our solar system appears to be moving backward as we see it against the fixed backdrop of the stars. The phenomenon is entirely due to our Earth-based perspective and was well known to ancient astronomers." Retrograde Planets: Traversing the Inner Landscape By Erin Sullivan (Red Wheel 2006) at page 3.

[120] *The Real Star of Bethlehem*, Chapter 4 by Associates For Spiritual Knowledge. http://www.askelm.com/star/star004.htm, quoting Gospel of Matthew by William Hendricksen (Baker Academic 1981) at page 153.

special significance to ancient astrologers. The August 12, 3 BCE conjunction fits my timeline for the birth of Jesus while the conjunction the following year (2 BCE) does not.

How much does the conjunction of Jupiter and Venus in 3 BCE help us date the birth of Jesus? About as far as I'm willing to go on this point is conclude a celestial phenomenon consistent with *Mathew*'s description of the Star of Bethlehem occurred in late summer, 3 BCE. This matches up with the empire-wide Roman census conducted in 3 BCE.

Magi meet with "Herod the king"& Herod Slaughters the Innocents

If Jesus was born in 3 BCE and Herod the Great died in 4 BCE, how does the theory account for *Matthew* recording that "Herod the king" met with the Magi and slaughtered the innocents in Bethlehem <u>after</u> the birth of Jesus? It's a definite conundrum; however, one potential solution exists. Just as Julius Caesar's name became a Roman title for the office of emperor used by his successors, so too did descendants of Herod the Great who ruled Jewish territories use the name "Herod" as a title of quasi-kingship. In the generation after Herod the Great, Rome awarded the title "Herod" to his sons Archelaus, Antipas, and Philip. That brings us to the question of whether *Matthew* referred to Herod the Great or one of his sons when he wrote "Herod the king"? Antipas and Philip, rulers of smaller territories, never claimed to be kings. Archelaus, on the other hand, was named king in Herod's last will and proclaimed king by the Jewish military immediately after the death of his father. Caesar Augustus later downgraded the title of Archelaus to "Ethnarch" (i.e., ethnic ruler). However, when referencing "Herod the king" at verses 1 and 3 of Chapter 2, we know *Matthew* was <u>not</u> referring to Herod Archelaus because 21 verses later *Matthew* spoke of "Archelaus" reigning over Judea.[121] The *Gospel of Mark* mistakenly referred to Antipas as "King Herod"[122] but *Matthew* never made this mistake. *Matthew* correctly called Antipas "Herod the Tetrarch".[123]

---

[121] *Matthew* 2:22.
[122] *Mark* 6:14.
[123] *Matthew* 14:1.

We know from Josephus that Archelaus and Antipas sailed for Rome after the first Passover subsequent to the death of Herod the Great leaving their brother Philip in charge of the kingdom.[124] According to my theory, Jesus was born in the summer of 3 BCE at a time when Archelaus and Antipas were in Rome. Thus, Herod Philip was in charge of the Jewish kingdom when Jesus was born. The only possible reconciliation with the *Gospel of Matthew* is if Matthew meant Herod Philip when he wrote the words "Herod the king". Matthew referred to Herod Philip one time in his gospel, incorrectly naming him as the first husband of Herodias.[125] We know from Josephus that Philip's half-brother Herod Boethus was the correct first husband of Herodias.[126] I take this as evidence that Matthew was confused as to the identity of Herod Philip. While not the strongest of proofs, it is plausible that the evangelist incorrectly referred to Herod Philip as "Herod the king". While his brothers Archelaus and Antipas were in Rome arguing their case to Caesar during the probate of Herod's will, Philip was acting king of the entire Jewish kingdom. We know from Josephus that Caesar did not render a swift verdict in the case of Herod's will as Malthace, one of Herod's wives and the mother of both Archelaus and Antipas, died in Rome after Caesar had heard arguments from the parties but before rendering a verdict.[127] Also, news of the Jewish revolt reached Rome at this time further delaying Caesar's disposition of Herod's will thereby keeping both Archelaus and Antipas in Rome for many months. Both assuredly were still in Rome through the summer of 3 BCE (assuming Herod died the previous winter).

Herod Philip was acting ruler of the Jewish kingdom in August-September of 3 BCE and it is plausible that Matthew meant Herod Philip when using the phrase "Herod the king",

---

[124] Antiquities, XVII 9:3 (219).

[125] *Matthew* 14:3.

[126] Antiquities, XVII 1:2 (14) and Jewish Wars, I 28:2 (557). Josephus clearly named Herod the grandson of High Priest Boethus as the first husband of Herodias. Herod the Great later disinherited Herod Boethus after he divorced this son's mother (Mariamne bint Boethus). Herod Boethus and Herod Philip the Tetrarch were half-brothers (sons of Herod the Great by different mothers).

[127] Antiquities XVII 10:1 (250).

while describing the meeting with the Magi and Slaughter of the Innocents.

Antigonus ben Antipater

If Jesus indeed was the son of Antipater ben Herod, then the name Jesus was an alias. Antipater had at least one son older than Jesus that Josephus informs us was married to a daughter of Pheroras (Herod's brother). The standard Herodian practice was to name the eldest son for his paternal grandfather and the second son for the maternal grandfather. Jesus was the eldest son of his mother Mary. Antipater presumably already had a son named Herod. Therefore, it follows that Jesus' birth name (and the one on file with the Temple authorities) was **Antigonus ben Antipater.**

Pantera

The Talmud describes a character some suggest to be Jesus the Nazarene. Yeshua is the Aramaic form of Jesus. The Rabbinic literature states that Yeshua (Jesus) was the product of adultery between his mother Miriam and a Roman soldier whose name is alternatively given as Pantera, Panthera, Pandera, or Pantiri.[128] This evidence garnered increased attention in modern times when a grave stone of a Roman legionnaire was unearthed in Bingerbrück, Germany in 1859 with the inscription, "Tiberius Julius Abdes Panthera, an archer, native of Sidon, Phoenicia, who in 9 AD was transferred to service in Rhineland."[129] Some proclaimed this to be the grave stone of the father of Jesus.

I suggest "Pantera" is an adulteration of "Antipater". Jesus' father Antipater was raised in Rome having been banished there by Herod in 41 BCE at the age of 5, remaining in Rome until 29 BCE (age 17). Further, Josephus records Antipater making two extended trips back to Rome after rejoining the Jewish royal family. Antipater spent more time in Rome than any of Herod's other

---

[128] Jesus in the Talmud by Peter Schäfer (Princeton University Press 2007) at pages 96-98.

[129] See The Jesus Dynasty: The Hidden History of Jesus, His Royal Family by Prof. James Tabor (Simon & Schuster 2007) at Chapter 3.

sons. Children of subject kings living in Rome were raised in close contact with the Roman royal family. All aristocratic children of Rome received military training. Antipater undoubtedly was trained to lead Roman soldiers. Further, he was close with Caesar Augustus, the royal family, and members of Caesar's court. One can surmise Antipater was fluent in Latin and Greek. The point being that, from the viewpoint of the Pharisee priesthood, Antipater was Herod's Roman son. Upon his return to Palestine, Antipater likely served in the Roman military before later taking up residence in his father's court.

What of the Talmud's claim that Jesus was an illegitimate child even though Josephus recorded Antipater married to the daughter of Antigonus? Remember that Pharisees were known as doctors of Jewish law. As all of the male members of Mary's family had been executed by Herod, it's easy to imagine the Pharisees taking technical issue with the legality of the marriage contract between Antipater and Mary. What male possessed authority under Jewish law to give her away in marriage? Did this person sign the marriage contract? The unusual situation under which Mary's marriage to Antipater occurred lends itself to legal attack under the Jewish law of the day. Essentially, the Pharisees smeared Jesus with the Pantera rumor found in the Talmud; however, to be fair, one reads Jesus throwing some heavy punches back at the Pharisees (i.e., "you brood of vipers"[130]).

Finally, assuming for sake of argument that Jesus was the illegitimate son of a Roman solider, he could not have obtained Roman citizenship in this fashion. Roman citizenship was only passed down from birth if the child's parents were married under Roman law _and_ both parents were legal Roman citizens.[131]

---

[130] *Matthew* 12:34.

[131] There are several reasons why Jesus could not have attained Roman citizenship as the illegitimate son of a Roman soldier named Pantera. First, common legionnaires who were not citizens from birth did not obtain Roman citizenship until after having served 20 years and receiving military discharge. Second, Mary would have to be a Roman citizen in addition to Pantera and, also, they must be married under Roman law in order to pass citizenship to their child. The wives of retired legionnaires were not given Roman citizenship through their husbands.

Further, Roman soldiers who were not Roman citizens at birth did not obtain Roman citizenship until their discharge from the military and were not allowed to marry while still active members of the legion. Thus, a child fathered by a Roman soldier serving in Judea by a Jewish woman would not be born a Roman citizen. Without Roman citizenship, no explanation exists for why Jesus was taken to Pontius Pilate for trial. In order for this to be the case, it follows that Antipater both legally married Mary bat Antigonus and obtained Roman citizen for her.

Timeline—Conception and Birth of Jesus In Historical Context
The table below summaries the historical dating argued for in this chapter relative to the death of Herod and birth of Jesus.

Date	Event
Nov. 4 BCE	Mary bat Antigonus conceived Jesus by Antipater ben Herod while imprisoned by his father Herod in Jericho.
Nov. 4 BCE	Herod executed Antipater. Herod died of natural causes at his winter palace in Jericho. Herod buried at Herodium.
March 3 BCE	Jews revolt starts during Passover after Archelaus turned the soldiers loose on the crowd and they killed thousands of Jews. Archelaus and Antipas sailed for Rome to participate in adjudication of Herod's will by Caesar Augustus leaving the Jewish kingdom in control of their brother Herod Philip.
Spring 3 BCE	Varus, governor of Roman province of Syria, put down the Jewish revolt and returned to Antioch leaving an extra Roman legion in Judea.

May 3 BCE	Procurator Sabinus[132] took over as top Roman administrator in Jerusalem and reignited the Jewish revolt against Rome during Pentecost. Revolt initially confined to Jerusalem but later spread to the entire Jewish kingdom including Samaria, Galilee and Perea.
Aug. 3 BCE	Jesus born in Bethlehem, a town between Herod's summer palace of Herodium and Jerusalem.
Sept. 3 BCE	Mary presented her first-born son to Anna and the priests at the Temple.

What happened to Mary bat Antigonus after the execution of her husband Antipater? I guaranty one thing, she wasn't released by the Herodians. Her royal Hasmonean lineage stood as a threat to the legitimacy of the Herodian dynasty. She certainly was imprisoned. Why didn't the Herodians just execute her out of hand? Caesar Augustus didn't allow subject persons of high royal birth to be executed without his authorization. Such executions led to civil wars, which reduced Roman tax revenues and drained assets. Caesar Augustus reserved to himself the authority to adjudicate disputes between rulers and royal persons of his subject kingdoms. Further, Caesar Augustus was close with Antipater (her dead husband). The Romans became aware of Mary when she appeared at her husband's trial before Governor Varus (as recorded in Josephus). Archelaus, the new king, had a bigger problem on his hands than worrying about Mary. He was named the new king in Herod's will but Caesar Augustus still had to confirm the appointment. Only Augustus held authority to name rulers in subject kingdoms. Certainly Archelaus did not wish to

---

[132] Josephus uses the name "procurator" in reference to Sabinus. Jewish Wars II 2:1. But a check of the list of Roman consuls shows a Sabinus having served as consul in 4 BCE. It makes sense that this is the same Sabinus now in the important Roman province of Syria after his term as consul ended. Perhaps he was scheduled to take over the Syrian governorship but Varus but that was delayed when the Jewish revolt broke out.

make any move that would antagonize Caesar. I reason Archelaus left the country for Rome putting the Mary issue on hold. He likely knew upon departing Judea that Mary was with child. I further speculate he issued orders to his brother Herod Philip to execute Mary's child when it was born. The Herodians stood a better chance of getting away with killing the royal child because its existence was unknown to the Romans (and the Herodians intended to keep it this way).

Speculation on the Fate of Mary bat Antigonus

In March of 3 BCE, the first Jewish revolt started in Jerusalem but was quickly put down by Governor Varus with two Roman legions. I theorize the pregnant Mary bat Antigonus was still imprisoned at this juncture. How do we know this? Mary would have left the country if given the opportunity, which means Jesus would have been born abroad. Further, the Herodians intended to keep Mary and her royal blood under lock and key. The reasoned inference from the birth of Jesus at Bethlehem is that Mary moved to Herod's nearby summer palace during the summer of 3 BCE, which was the normal practice for Herodian royals of the day. Also, I am sure the Herodians worried about trouble in Jerusalem during the revolt so moving Mary to a more secure location such as Herodium made sense on that front as well. Herodium was more of a fortress than a palace. The Jewish revolt renewed in Jerusalem during Pentecost of 3 BCE and spread. It's a fair assumption that Herodian troops stationed at Herodium were moved to Jerusalem, then under siege by insurrectionists. Someone sprang Mary out of captivity in Herodium as the revolt intensified over the summer. I surmise it to have been Hasmonean priests (her relatives) aided by Parthian operatives during the general turmoil of the Jewish revolt. Why Parthians? The magi were priests of the Parthian state religion and appear at the birth of Jesus. They came bearing gifts for the grandson of their former client king Antigonus. Upon rescue from Herodium, Mary was very pregnant and went into labor on the road after her escape. They pulled into the closest town outside of Herodium, which was

Bethlehem. Mary gave birth and her party later moved on to another hiding location in Judea.

The Herodians discovered Mary's escape from Herodium and tracked her movements to Bethlehem. There they heard from locals that she gave birth to a son. Remember that Mary survived Herod's purge of Hasmoneans in 37 BCE through deception (i.e., the royal baby was hidden with another family). Antigonus separated the child Mary from the immediate royal family leaving her with a local couple in Jerusalem. It's reasonable to assume the Herodians feared the same trick occurring again with the birth of Jesus. Herod Philip (or perhaps even Archelaus via letter from Rome) ordered all young male children in Bethlehem executed to ensure that history did not repeat itself. Bethlehem was a small village. Considering the depth of political killings that occurred during the reign of Herod and his descendants, this would not rate as a major event. Our modern day opinion of Herod is of a great builder who was a pathologic killer. I don't share the view that Herod was pathologic, while accepting as fact the vast scores of persons killed by Herod including members of his own family. Within the framework of my theory, I see a rational political reason for the Herodians ordering the execution of the children of Bethlehem (if it occurred at all). The bloodline of Antigonus posed a serious threat to their rule. The possibility existed that the infant Jesus was stashed among the children of Bethlehem.

A strange thing occurred after Bethlehem. Mary, Joseph the carpenter, and the baby Jesus were clearly on the run from the Herodians. The Bible tells us that, after their narrow escape at Bethlehem, Mary took the baby to Jerusalem instead of immediately fleeing the country. An entire cohort (600 to 700 Roman soldiers) was housed at Fortress Antonia overlooking the Temple. The Temple was the most heavily policed location in the Jewish kingdom. If one were running from the authorities, it was the last place to go. Of course, Jewish law dictated that the child be presented at the Temple after Mary completed a 40 day purification period. But under normal circumstances the risk of death would have been too high to even contemplate such action. How can we account for Mary taking her newborn son to the

Temple? Josephus records the Jewish revolt to have been restarted by Procurator Sabinus at Pentecost and growing with time. The Jewish nationalists eventually gained control of the entire district surrounding Jerusalem. This must have occurred at precisely the time when Mary was running from the authorities with her child. The soldiers hunting for Jesus were recalled to fight the insurgents. As the revolt gained strength, Jerusalem and the roads leading there became free of Herodian and Roman soldiers allowing Mary to travel to the Temple and present the baby in accordance with Jewish law.

Perpetual Virgin

The canon of the Catholic Church venerates Mary as a perpetual virgin, i.e., she conceived Jesus without human intercourse and throughout her life never engaged in human intercourse. The official Catholic Catechism from the Vatican website puts it thusly.

> The deepening of faith in the virginal motherhood led the Church to confess Mary's real and perpetual virginity even in the act of giving birth to the Son of God made man. In fact, Christ's birth "did not diminish his mother's virginal integrity but sanctified it." And so the liturgy of the Church celebrates Mary as Aeiparthenos, the "Ever-virgin".

If the Catholic Church admitted that Jesus had brothers or sisters through Mary, it destroys their contrived perpetual virginity doctrine. Why is perpetual virginity important? Because in the view of orthodox Christianity Jesus was a god and not a man, therefore, his mother needs to be superhuman. The Catholic Church and Protestant denominations cling to the fantasy that Jesus lacked siblings in the face of gospel passages such as the following: "Then [Jesus'] mother and his brothers arrived, and standing outside they sent word to Him and called him."[133]

---

[133] *Mark* 3:31.

Further, Paul's *Epistle to the Galatians* specifically refers to James as "the Lord's brother."[134] Also, several ancient historians specifically identified James as the brother of Jesus—i.e., Josephus, Hegesippus, and Eusebius.

Why does the Roman Catholic Church steadfastly cling to the patently weak argument that James the Just was a mere cousin of Jesus? Because the status of James as the brother and true successor of Jesus Christ as leader of the incipient Christian church after the crucifixion undermines the authority of the Pope, who traces his authority to Peter. The story goes that Peter appointed the first bishop of Rome who became leader of the entire Christian faith upon the death of Peter with authority over, and to appoint, all other Christian bishops in the world. If Peter was not the successor of Jesus, the alleged chain of authority leading from Jesus to the Roman Catholic Pope is broken.

More On Mary's Other Son, James The Just

James the Just stands as a substantial historical figure attested to outside of the New Testament in numerous texts from the first few centuries after the crucifixion of Jesus. Hegesippus wrote the follow about James in the second century of Common Era.

> After the apostles, James the brother of the
> Lord surnamed the Just was made head of
> the Church at Jerusalem. Many indeed are
> called James. This one was holy from his
> mother's womb. He drank neither wine nor
> strong drink, ate no flesh, never shaved or
> anointed himself with ointment or bathed.
> He alone had the privilege of entering the
> Holy of Holies, since indeed he did not use
> woolen vestments but linen and went alone
> into the temple and prayed in behalf of the
> people, insomuch that his knees were reputed
> to have acquired the hardness of camels'

---

[134] *Galatians* 1:19.

> knees by reason of his constantly bending the
> knee in adoration to God, and begging
> forgiveness for the people. Therefore, in
> consequence of his pre-eminent justice, he
> was called the Just.[135]

The striking point from this passage is the strict religious piety attributed to James the Just. He appears to have been under a Nazarite oath from a young age.[136] This description fits that of a priest, not a craftsman's son from Galilee.

There are two references to Jesus Christ found in existing copies of the histories of Josephus. The first--gushing over Jesus with "if it be lawful to call him a man, for he was a doer of wonderful works"[137]—is generally regarded by scholars to be a fraud surreptitiously inserted into the text at a later date. Josephus was not a Christian. He proclaimed himself to be a devout Jew who would never blaspheme by inferring that a man was God. A second passage in Josephus mentioning Jesus is generally regarded by scholars to be authentic.

> Ananus ... assembled the Sanhedrin of
> judges, and brought before them the brother
> of Jesus, and some others; and when he had
> formed an accusation against them as
> breakers of the law, he delivered them to be
> stoned.[138]

Notice that the focal point of the passage is James while Jesus is only mentioned in passing as the brother of James. Further, Josephus says that, upon the recommendation of the Roman prefect Albinus, Jewish King Agrippa removed Ananus from the high priesthood for having brought James before the Sanhedrin and executed him. Why was the Roman prefect of Judea in such an uproar over the conviction and execution of James? The Sanhedrin held jurisdiction for enforcement of Jewish law

---

[135] Hegesippus, Fragment from Book V quoted in De Viris Illustribus by St. Jerome.
[136] More discussion of the Nazarite oath in Chapter 10.
[137] Antiquities XVII 3:3 (63).
[138] Antiquities XX 20:1 (200).

regarding Jews. Not only was Albinus upset but he demanded the high priest be removed, a very serious change in local government. One can only conclude than James was such an important figure in Jerusalem that the Romans feared the turmoil his execution would touch off.[139] This only makes sense from a Roman perspective if James was a Hasmonean prince of royal blood. Thus, in my view, James must have also been a grandson of King Antigonus to draw such high level attention from the Roman authorities.

Consider the words of Jesus recorded in the *Gospel of Thomas* found within the collection of texts known as the Nag Hammadi Library.

> The disciples said to Jesus, "We know that you are going to leave us. Who will be our leader?" Jesus said to them, "No matter where you are you are to go to James the Just, <u>for whose sake heaven and earth came into being</u>."[140] [Emphasis added.]

A curious statement indeed. "For whose sake heaven and earth came into being", this can only mean that James the Just was of very high royal birth. It indicates that James was also the son of Mariamne bat Antigonus and, further, that Jesus intended James as his successor. The position of James as successor of Jesus is also supported by the *Epistle of Clement to James*, part of the <u>Clementine Homilies</u>. It's introduction reads as follows.

> Clement to James, the lord, and the <u>bishop of bishops, who rules Jerusalem, the holy church of the Hebrews, and the churches everywhere</u> excellently rounded by the providence of God, with the elders and deacons, and the rest of the brethren, peace be always. [Emphasis added.]

---

[139] James was executed in 63 CE and the great Jewish revolt commenced in 66 CE. Although then turbulent times in Judea, it difficult to directly connect the two events.

[140] *Gospel According to Thomas*, Logion 12, The Gnostic Society Library translated by Stephen Patterson and Marvin Meyer.

There can be no doubt the author of this letter viewed James as the undisputed leader of the world-wide Christian church (also known as the Nazarenes). The Roman Catholic Church denies Clement authored this epistle although it accepts the *Epistle of Clement to the Corinthians* (a/k/a *First Clement*) as authentic even though his name appears nowhere on that document and, further, the epistle contains several citations to the Old Testament, something odd for an individual such as Clement who was born and raised in Rome (and was presumably a gentile). However, another Clementine text, the *Epistle of Clement to the Corinthians*, espouses a doctrine important to the Roman Catholic Church, the concept that bishops are not elected by the people but, rather, appointed by Church leaders. And who appoints the Church leaders? The theory goes that the apostles appointed their successors who further inherited the right to appoint their own successors. So it has gone through the centuries from antiquity to the present day. In practice the Roman Catholic Church is a classic oligarchy answerable to no one. As stated earlier, its entire legitimacy rests on the tenuous notion that Jesus appointed Peter as his successor. So you can see why the RCC must denounce the *Epistle of Clement to James* and further the *Gospel of Thomas*. The RCC maintains Peter converted the young Clement of Rome to Christianity. He became a disciple of Peter, was perhaps a member of the Roman royal family, and is also said to have served as the fourth bishop of Rome (i.e., the fourth Pope).

The RCC's position that Jesus appointed Peter to succeed him as head of the Nazarene movement with James the Just merely serving as the first bishop of Jerusalem rests solely upon one short passage from the *Gospel of Matthew*, "And I tell you that you are Peter [meaning rock], and on this rock I will build my church."[141] Nowhere else in the New Testament is Peter named the successor of Jesus. In fact, *Acts of the Apostles* and Paul's epistles paint quite a different picture noting that both Peter and Paul reported as subordinates to James the Just, who was clearly head of the entire incipient Christian Church.

---

[141] *Matthew* 16:18.

My view is that James the Just was both a descendant of King Antigonus and a Kohen priest. Jesus, with his Herodian father, was <u>not</u> Kohanim. From the Roman perspective, Jesus was of higher birth but, in Jewish eyes, the ancestry of James exceeded that of Jesus. James did not bear the stain of Herod as did his brother Jesus. I believe James was slated to serve as high priest in the hoped for reign of Jesus as king of the Jews.

Joseph The Carpenter

I struggled attempting to peer through the fog of time and Christian myth to glimpse the historic Joseph, adoptive father of Jesus. We're told the genealogy found in the *Gospel of Matthew* is that of Joseph the carpenter. Unfortunately, *Matthew's* genealogy contains the name of the accursed Jeconiah in addition to David and Solomon. For this reason, the *Matthew* genealogy is illegitimate for a Jewish king. I conclude it is a complete fabrication. Why? Joseph the carpenter was the father of James the Just and James was a Kohen priest. Therefore, by definition, Joseph had to be a Kohen priest. Kohanim were of the tribe of Levi but David was of the tribe of Judah. The genealogy from *Matthew* is not that of a Kohen priest nor acceptable for a Jewish king.

Who was Joseph then and how did he come to be Mary's husband? Earlier in this chapter, I argued that Mary was adopted by a Kohen priest after the death of her father the king. Building off of that premise, the logical party to collect Mary after the execution of her first husband would have been her adoptive Hasmonean family. Only they could legally marry her to a second husband. Jewish marriage contracts of the Second Temple period worked somewhat like Muslim marriage contracts in Islamic countries today. A senior male member of the bride's family was the only one authorized to give her away in marriage. In fact, the bride's signature on the contract was not necessary. A man and woman could be betrothed without ever having met one another. The Bible discusses Joseph wishing to "quietly divorce" Mary after learning she was pregnant.

> His mother Mary was pledged to be married
> to Joseph, but before they came together, she

> was found to be with child through the Holy
> Spirit. Because Joseph her husband was a
> righteous man and did not want to expose
> her to public disgrace, he had in mind to
> divorce her quietly.[142]

How did Joseph miss her pregnancy when he married her? One possibility is that Mary was not yet showing. However, it is equally likely that Mary and Joseph were married without even having seen each other (or least not met in a number of years). Working from the theory's premise, Mary was in a Herodian prison when betrothed to Joseph. The ranking male member of her adoptive family signed the marriage contract on her behalf. She was freed from the prison by her family, perhaps with the assistance of Parthian agents (which explains why the magi knew where to find her). It is only then that Joseph discovered she was pregnant. Obviously, Joseph was a reluctant groom, probably forced into the marriage by his powerful father who was also a Kohen priest.

The description of Joseph as a carpenter conflicts with my characterization of him as being from a family of Temple priests. A potential solution to this conflict lies in the practices of the Essenes. Joseph, Mary and the infant Jesus fled Judea to live in exile in Egypt. After a number of years, they returned not to Judea but to Galilee because they deemed it a safer location for the family. In Galilee, Joseph would have been cut off from his religious profession at the Temple, including the fat stipends awarded to elite Temple priests. Jesus, James, and John the Baptist all showed signs of Essene influence. We know very little of Joseph the carpenter; however, we do know that Essenes practiced trades. The following description of the habits of Essene monks comes to us from Philo of Alexandria.

> They are above all men devoted to the
> service of God, not sacrificing living animals,
> but studying rather to preserve their own
> minds in a state of holiness and purity. No
> one, in short, attends to any employment

---

[142] *Matthew* 1:18-19.

whatever connected with war, or even to any of those occupations even in peace which are easily perverted to wicked purposes.[143]

The different members of this body have different employments in which they occupy themselves. Some of them ... are devoted to the practice of agriculture, others again are shepherds, or cowherds, and experienced in the management of every kind of animal, some are cunning in what relates to swarms of bees, and <u>others again are artisans and handicraftsmen</u>.[144] [Emphasis added.]

Note that Essene monks, as recorded by Philo, not only engaged themselves in prayer and religious study but also engaged in an earthly craft of some kind. Philo's description of "artisans and handicraftsmen" reasonably includes carpenters. My view is that Joseph the Kohen priest became Joseph the Essene monk at some point after the birth of Jesus. The tradition of monastic life with a rural, Spartan life that includes manual labor in a basic trade lives on to this day in the Christian faith. A recent magazine article describes a sect of the Monks of the Most Blessed Virgin Mary of Mt. Carmel as follows:

They belong to an order rooted in the 16th century that requires they sustain themselves through mostly manual labor. They dress in handmade full length robes, sleep in small individual housing units called hermitages with no radio, no TV, no Internet. They raise and grow most of their own food, funding their operation by making and producing their own brand of coffee ... .[145]

---

[143] Philo, *Every Good Man Is Free* XII (75) and (78).

[144] Philo, *Hypothetica* (11.8-11.9).

[145] Bob Moen, "Catholic Monks In Wyoming Face Opposition Over Monastery Plans", Huffinton Post, 09/25/10 edition.

As stated above, I think strong circumstantial evidence exists for the argument that Joseph was a Kohen priest. Further, the occupation of carpenter is completely compatible with an individual who was also a Jewish Essene monk of the first century of Common Era; however, labeling such an individual as merely a carpenter misdirects by omission.

This leads us to the next question of why was Joseph's identity masked? His father must have been an important individual in Jerusalem in my opinion, probably a former high priest. The writers or editors of the New Testament engaged in a pattern of suppressing the full identity of Jesus over the centuries. Portraying Joseph as a mere Galilean carpenter instead of a Kohen priest is just more of the same.

Chapter 5
Mary Magdalene
(Mariamne bat Aristobulus)

This book contains numerous controversial theories but the most contentious and speculative likely concerns Mary Magdalene. An important Herodian-Hasmonean princess inexplicably disappears from the histories of Josephus at a young age. She was Mariamne bat Aristobulus, the sister of King Herod Agrippa I, King Herod of Chalcis, and Princess Herodias (wife of Herod Antipas). As a child, she was married to Antipater ben Herod (her uncle) and, after his execution, then to Herod Archelaus (another uncle). She divorced Herod Archelaus in her early 20s and disappeared from the historical record. Antipater was coregent when married to Mariamne and Archelaus ethnarch (i.e., ethnic ruler of the Jews). Mariamne married higher ranking Herodian husbands in her two marriages than did her sister Herodias, which indicates she was the older sister. I propose she later converted to the Nazarene movement and married Jesus. We know her today as Mary Magdalene. She was the first cousin of Jesus and the former wife of his deceased father.

Jewish Kings Must Marry And They Preferred Hasmonean Wives
As a claimant to the Jewish throne, Mosaic Law required Jesus to be married—"Be fruitful and multiple".[146] If one accepts that Jesus aspired to the Jewish throne, the suggestion he was not

---

[146] Genesis 1:28.

married is ludicrous in my opinion. No Jewish king prior to Jesus was recorded as being unmarried.[147] Once accepting that Jesus the Herodian-Hasmonean prince had a wife, the question turns to qualifiers that can aid us in our search for his princess. We know Herod married a Hasmonean princess (Mariamne bat Alexander) and made her his queen. Recall that Josephus referred to Herod as a man of common ancestry but said the Hasmoneans were of "royal blood". One can deduce the value Herodian princes placed on Hasmonean wives simply by reviewing the list of Herodian rulers and identifying their known wives. The Hasmonean princesses on the list are highlighted.

Herodian Ruler	First Wife	Second Wife
Herod the Great (King)	Doris (Idumean princess)	Mariamne bat Alexander
Antipater (Coregent)	Mariamne bat Aristobulus	Mariamne bat Antigonus
Archelaus (Ethnarch)	Mariamne bat Aristobulus[148]	Glaphyra, daughter of King Archelaus of Cappadocia
Antipas (Tetrarch)	Phasaelis, daughter of King Aretas of Nabatea	Herodias bat Aristobulus
Herod Philip (Tetrarch)	Salome bat Herod (daughter of	

---

[147] After Jesus, Herod Agrippa II ruled fringe areas of the Jewish kingdom. He never married allowing his sister Berenice (a Hasmonean princess) to act as his defacto queen. Some historians speculate Agrippa II was either gay or carried on an incestuous affair with his sister.

[148] Josephus names the first wife of Herod Archelaus merely as Mariamne, neglecting to identify her father or mother despite this being a common family name. See Jewish Wars II 7:4. The logical Mariamne of this generation to have been the first wife of Archelaus, principal heir of Herod the Great, was Mariamne bat Aristobulus. Archelaus as prime heir surely had a Hasmonean wife and Mariamne bat Aristobulus was the only Hasmonean Mariamne unaccounted for in this generation. Josephus regularly gave the father's name when introducing Hasmonean women so this omission was unusual for him. I believe Josephus intentionally failed to identify Mariamne's father in an attempt to obscure her identity.

	Herodias)	
Herod of Chalcis (King)	Mariamne bat Joseph	Berenice bat Agrippa
Agrippa I (King)	Cypros bat Phasaelus	

Notice that every Herodian ruler on this list had at least one Hasmonean wife. In two cases, the Herodian ruler divorced women married prior to ascending to power in order to acquire a Hasmonean wife while on the throne (Herod the Great divorced Doris and Herod Antipas divorced Phasaelis).[149] The one odd case was Herod Archelaus, the main heir named in Herod's last will, who divorced his Hasmonean wife. Shortly after Archelaus divorced Mariamne bat Aristobulus, the Romans removed him from office sending him into exile in France. The above represents solid evidence that Herodians required Hasmonean wives to serve as legitimate Jewish rulers.

Please also note that only one name appears on this list twice, **Mariamne bat Aristobulus**. She married Antipater when he was the prime heir in Herod's will. After Antipater's execution, she became the wife of the new crown prince and prime heir of Herod (Archelaus). She was Herod's oldest granddaughter by his Hasmonean sons. Her younger sister Herodias, by comparison, married the #2 heir in Herod's successive wills.[150] The first husband of Herodias was Herod Boethus, grandson of the high priest Boethus. Herod Boethus was the #2 heir under Antipater in Herod's will that existed prior to the arrest of Antipater. Thereafter, Herod the Great replaced both Antipater and Herod Boethus in his will with sons Archelaus and Antipas, prime and second heir respectively. Herodias famously divorced Herod

---

[149] Mariamne bat Joseph died while married to Herod of Chalcis.

[150] Her first husband had been Herod Boethus, grandson of the high priest Boethus. Herod Boethus was the #2 heir under Antipater in Herod's will that existed prior to the arrest of Antipater. Thereafter, Herod the Great replaced Antipater and Herod Boethus in his will with sons Archelaus and Antipas, prime and second heir respectively. Herodias famously divorced Herod Boethus to marry Antipas.

Boethus to marry Antipas. Under both of Herod's wills Mariamne bat Aristobulus married the prime heir (Antipater and Archelaus, successively) while her younger sister married the secondary heir (Herod Boethus and Antipas). This demonstrates the high royal status of Mariamne bat Aristobulus. She was only in her twenties when she divorced Herod Archelaus yet Josephus fails to mention her again in his histories, quite strange.

"Magdalene"

The accepted interpretation of the term "Magdalene" as applied to Mary Magdalene is that it referred to her city of birth, i.e., the city of Magdala on the northwest shore of the Sea of Galilee. I don't agree with that theory. Natives of Galilee in this period were known as Galileans, natives of Samaria as Samaritans, natives of Nabatea as Natabateans, and natives of Israel as Israelites. I cannot locate a single example from the Jewish kingdom of a descriptive suffix of "ene" added to a place name to indicate that an individual was a native of that locale.[151] To highlight the oddness of this interpretation, it equates to calling a person from Galilee a "Galilene". Further, Magdala was no more than a small town during the time of Jesus. Identifying Mary as a resident of a small little-known town in Galilee would not aid the general public in identifying this Mary. It would be like referring to President Bill Clinton as a Hopean (i.e., native of the small rural town of Hope, Arkansas). It adds no context to the description of the person. Not so when large cities are involved such as Philo of Alexandria or Clement of Rome or Cleopatra of Jerusalem. These cities were touchstones that the wider world of that day was familiar with. Remember that Galilee in the time of Jesus was a Jewish backwater. It had been a Greek territory forcibly converted to Judaism by the Hasmoneans roughly 100 years prior to the birth of Jesus. Magdala was an insignificant location in the context of

---

[151] Some may argue that natives of Nazareth were referred to as Nazarenes, thus, the precedent for Magdalene. As explained in chapter 8, I see this as a misinterpretation of the term "Nazarene". I believe it refers to a religious movement and not a city. Nazareth was no more than a small hamlet in the time of Jesus.

the wider Jewish world. If a resident of Magdala, she would have been known as Mary the Galilean (if given a name through reference to her place of birth). We have many examples in Josephus of figures identified as Galileans but none from small towns in Galilee.

The word Magdala means tower in Aramaic (Migdal being the Hebrew equivalent). Thus, I view the term "Magdalene" as a title. It means Mary the towering one or, put another way, Mary the great. She must have been of high royal blood to have been granted such a title. Mariamne bat Aristobulus was the wife of two kings and the princess of the highest royal blood of her generation. Jesus was the only man alive in his day who was the grandson of two Jewish kings. Not even James the Just could claim that. If Jesus required a high-status Hasmonean wife for his attempt to capture the Jewish throne, Mariamne bat Aristobulus fits this description perfectly. Further, she disappeared from the histories of Josephus in 6 CE making her the best candidate for the Hasmonean wife of Jesus, claimant to the Jewish throne. However, I reason this marriage as strictly political. As discussed in chapter 8, I have concluded that the marriage of Mary and Jesus did not compromise the Nazarene requirement of celibacy. Anything other than a chaste marriage renders Jesus a hypocrite to the brand of Jewish faith he preached. In 30 CE, Mary Magdalene would have been around 43 years of age (see age computation in next section). I theorize Jesus and Mary had a celibate yet loving marriage that allowed Jesus to both pursue the Jewish throne yet maintain his Nazarene ideals.

Mary Magdalene's Ancestry

Per Josephus, the historical figure I identify as Mary Magdalene was the granddaughter of Mariamne bat Alexander and Herod the Great.[152] Her father was Aristobulus ben Herod who Herod executed in 7 BCE. She was the great, great granddaughter of two Hasmonean high priest / kings (Hyrcanus II and

---

[152] Herod had another wife named Mariamne who is generally referred to as Mariamne II when discussing the family of Herod. This Mariamne was the daughter of a high priest but not of Hasmonean descent.

Aristobulus II). Further, she was also the grandniece of a Hasmonean high priest (Aristobulus III). Two of her brothers became kings—Herod Agrippa I and Herod of Chalcis. The below chart contains her wing of the Herodian family.

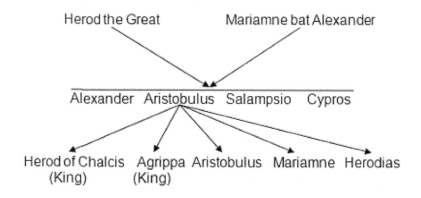

Although a child, she was betrothed to Antipater, the eldest son of Herod (i.e., her uncle) who was also coregent. The match was strange for any family except Herod's in that Antipater goaded Herod to murder this girl's father. After Antipater's execution, she married Herod Archelaus who was then Herod's primary heir. That's quite a resume for a woman still of childbearing years upon divorce from Archelaus in 6 CE.

The birth date of Mariamne bat Aristobulus is not known; however, we shall operate under the reasoned assumption that she was older than her sister Herodias given her priority in husbands. Further, Mariamne was the name of the maternal grandmother of this child. Per Herodian naming patterns, the eldest daughter was named after the maternal grandmother. Her father, Aristobulus ben Herod, was executed in 7 BCE at the age of 24 leaving five children (3 boys, 2 girls). The only son of Aristobulus with a known date of birth was Herod Agrippa, born in 10 BCE. Obviously, he was not the oldest child of Aristobulus.[153] Let's assume Mariamne was the oldest child of Aristobulus and use age

---

[153] Born in 10 BCE, three years before his father's death. There were five children all from the same mother. Therefore, Agrippa had older siblings.

17 as the earliest date Aristobulus started having children. That would put Mariamne's birth date in 14 BCE[154] making her seven years of age upon her father's death in 7 BCE. This, of course, is a rough approximation as history does not record the precise date of the birth of Mariamne bat Aristobulus.

Mariamne bat Alexander
Born	57 BCE
Married Herod	37 BCE
Died	29 BCE

Aristobulus ben Herod
Born	31 BCE
Died	7 BCE

Mariamne bat Aristobulus
Born	14 BCE
Married Antipater	7 BCE
Married Archelaus	4 BCE
Divorce Archelaus	6 CE

Although it may seem impossible that Mariamne bat Aristobulus married Antipater ben Herod when she was seven years of age, this squares with Josephus' description of the young orphaned children of Aristobulus. Particularly instructive is this line from Josephus quoting Herod, "I also betroth to thy son, Antipater, the daughter of Aristobulus [Mariamne], be thou therefore a father to that orphan."[155] Obviously, Herod was speaking of a pre-pubescent child in this passage.

Although three generations stood between Mariamne bat Aristobulus and a Hasmonean high priest-king, she was, nonetheless, a high-ranking princess sure to be prized as a wife by the Herodian princes. After the execution of her first husband Antipater, she married Herod Archelaus, another uncle, who was then Herod's principal heir. It was a measure of her high status that she was chosen as wife twice by the highest-ranking Herodian

---

[154] Born in 31 BCE, Aristobulus was 17 years of age in 14 BCE.
[155] Jewish Wars, I 28:2.

royal in the generation immediately after Herod the Great. For me, it's a near certainty the young Princess Mariamne bat Aristobulus eventually married a third Herodian prince after Archelaus yet Josephus is silent. She was only around 20 years of age when she divorced Archelaus in 6 CE. In my view, this silence regarding a person of such high royal standing is indicative of deception as opposed to a lapse in attention to detail.

Mary Magdalene and the Tribe of Benjamin.

In his best seller The Da Vinci Code, Dan Brown asserts Mary Magdalene was of the tribe of Benjamin.[156] If true, this fact would appear to contradict my theory of Mary Magdalene as a Herodian-Hasmonean princess in that the Hasmoneans were of the tribe of Levi, not Benjamin. My research succeeded in turning up scant evidence to support the Mary Magdalene as Benjamite princess contention. The only thing I could find was reference to a 14th century manuscript said to be a copy of a 9th century biography of Mary Magdalene written by a Roman Catholic archbishop stating she came from the tribe of Benjamin and was related to the Hasmonean royal house.[157] As previously stated, these are contradictory claims because the Hasmoneans were of the tribe of Levi. Unless more evidence exists for the Mary Magdalene as Benjamite theory of which I am unaware, it doesn't appear to carry much weight.

The one reason I refrain from totally dismissing the theory out of hand is the fact that Paul of Tarsus claimed to be of the tribe of Benjamin.[158] I discuss Paul further below and express the view that Paul was a Herodian-Hasmonean prince like Jesus. Herod's father came from the kingdom of Idumea (Edom). The Idumeans were known to have intermarried with Jews of Judea

---

[156] See Chapter 58, p. 248; See also The Woman with the Alabaster Jar by Margaret Starbird (Bear & Company 1993)

[157] Life of Mary Magdalene by Rabanus Maurus (AD 766-856), Archbishop of Mayence. This is a fourteenth-century manuscript held by the University of Oxford said to be a copy of a ninth century work.
http://witcombe.sbc.edu/davincicode/magdalen-legend-cult.html

[158] Romans 11:1.

(where the Benjamite homeland was located). Perhaps Herod claimed to be of the tribe of Benjamin leading to Paul's assertion that he was a member of this tribe? I'll leave that possibility out there for later investigation.[159]

"From whom seven demons had gone out"

Both *Luke* and *Mark* record seven demons having been cast out of Mary Magdalene.[160] *Luke* also relates an incident where an unnamed woman washed the feet of Jesus with her tears and dried them with her hair a few versus before *Luke* introduces Mary Magdalene along with two other women. The Pharisees who witnessed this act of a woman washing the feet of Jesus inferred she was a prostitute.[161] Pope Gregory (speaking in the sixth century CE) stated that Mary Magdalene and the prostitute wiping the feat of Jesus in *Luke* were one in the same person. I can see how the Pope made that conclusion but it's a stretch in my opinion. Here are the counterarguments. Why fail to give the woman a name in *Luke*, Chapter 7 but then use her name a dozen or so versus later if they are the same person? Three women are named as having been "healed of evil spirits" in *Luke*, Chapter 8. How can one conclude that the prostitute of *Luke*, Chapter 7 referred to Mary Magdalene and not one of the other women named in *Luke*, Chapter 8? The Vatican quietly reversed the position of Pope Gregory in 1969 agreeing that the prostitute crying upon the feet of Jesus was not Mary Magdalene. Hollywood apparently did not get the memo on this point. *The Greatest Story Ever Told* (1965) with Max von Sydow as Jesus and *The Last Temptation of Christ* (1988) with Willem Dafoe as Jesus both portray Mary Magdalene as a prostitute prior to conversion by Jesus. Although disagreeing with its biblical interpretation, I'm a big fan of *The Greatest Story Ever Told*.

---

[159] Note: In Chapter 9, I discuss the intermarriage of the Idumean royal house with King Solomon. Herod was NOT a descendant of the Idumean royal house.

[160] *Luke* 8:2 and *Mark* 16:9.

[161] *Luke* 7:36-50.

Largely based on the statement from Pope Gregory, Dan Brown called out the Catholic Church in the <u>Da Vinci Code</u> for perpetrating a "smear campaign" against Mary Magdalene.[162] I have many disagreements with the Catholic Church but this is not a fight I see any merit in. The Catholic Church has consistently been a biblical strict constructionist. In two places the Gospels state that seven demons were cast out of Mary Magdalene. For a strict constructionist, this means Mary Magdalene was an evil person before her association with Jesus. I disagree with the interpretation placed on these passages by the Catholic Church but understand a logical basis for their position. One can only come to another understanding of Mary Magdalene and her background by accepting that the phrase casting out seven demons is allegorical, not literal. In my view, the reference to the casting out of seven demons from Mary identifies her as a high initiate.

<u>Mary As Inner Initiate Of Jesus</u>

Philo of Alexandria read the Torah as wrapped with allegory.[163] Philo and Jesus were contemporaries although we have no evidence the two ever met. Nonetheless, Jesus extensively used allegory and symbolism in his many parables. In light of the use of symbolism in the Gospels, one must accept the possibility that references to "seven demons" cast of out of Mary Magdalene were symbolic.

I see a connection between the phrase "seven demons" in the New Testament Gospels and the discussion of the "seven powers of wrath" found in the *Gospel According to Mary Magdalene*. We learned of this work from the Papyrus Berolinensis 8502 text acquired by German scholar Carl Reinhardt in 1896. It is generally considered to be a Gnostic gospel. In the gospel text, the disciples come to Mary Magdalene after the departure of Jesus and ask her to tell them about special instruction Jesus gave her. Much of the surviving text is fragmentary but it describes Mary first receiving instruction from Jesus then having a discussion directly with "the

---

[162] <u>Da Vinci Code</u> by Dan Brown (Anchor 2009) at pages 243-44.
[163] <u>The Bible: A Biography</u> by Karen Armstrong (Atlantic Monthly Press 2007) at page 49.

soul". The soul relates to Mary a journey passing through various "powers". The third power is called ignorance and the fourth wrath, although wrath came in seven forms.

> The first form is darkness, the second desire, the third ignorance, the fourth is the excitement of death, the fifth is the kingdom of the flesh, the sixth is the foolish wisdom of flesh, the seventh is the wrathful wisdom. These are the seven powers of wrath.[164]

As one can see from the above passage, each of the seven powers of wrath consists of a negative element of the material world. As the soul passes through each of these forms of the powers, it gets closer to what the text calls the "root" or, said another way, closer to the source of all existence. The description of the soul passing through these "powers" on its way back to the Godhead is reminiscent of the seven seals found in *Book of Revelation*.[165]

The concept of passing through layers or rooms during one's journey from the material world to the realm of God is conveyed by the popular term "Seventh Heaven", which comes to us from Jewish mysticism.

> This concept we find only in rabbinic literature, where it plays an important role, especially in the early form of Jewish mystical thought known as "Hechalot" or "Palace" mysticism. In the Hechalot tradition, it is the task of the mystical initiate to ascend by meditative techniques through the seven heavens one after another, overcoming angelic challenges in each, and then to pass safely through the seven "palaces" of the seventh heaven in order to reach the base of God's throne.[166]

---

[164] *Gospel According to Mary Magdalene* 8:19.
[165] *Revelation* 5.
[166] *In Seventh Heaven* by Philologos, The Jewish Daily Forward (July 10, 2007) found by the author at forward.com.

Paul of Tarsus speaks of varying levels of heaven in a cryptic reference to a man "caught up to the third heaven" where he "heard inexpressible words, which a man is not permitted to speak."[167]

Philo of Alexandria has a long discussion of the number seven in his text, *On The Creation*.

> And such great sanctity is there in the number seven, that it has a pre-eminent rank beyond all the other numbers of the first decade. ... But seven alone, as I said before, neither produces nor is produced, on which account other philosophers liken this number to Victory. ... But Hippocratres the physician says that there are seven ages of man, infancy, childhood, boyhood, youth, manhood, middle age, old age.[168]

Philo also calls the number seven "the perfecter of things".

One allegorical interpretation of the reference in the New Testament to expelling "seven demons" from Mary Magdalene is that she attained perfection by overcoming the seven demons that block one's path from this world to the seat of God. These demons are the human imperfections we all possess at birth and must purge to reach higher levels of existence. We are all born in ignorance possessed of these demons and must move from death to life as Jesus put it. These are the stages one travels through on the road to enlightenment. Thus, far from being a mark of shame, casting out seven demons signifies completion of the human journey to perfection. Of course, only another initiate in the inner teachings of Jesus would understand this allegorical meaning. In the *Gospel according to Mary Magdalene*, the surviving eleven apostles of Jesus were ignorant of his inner teachings.

---

[167] 2 *Corinthians* 12:2-4.
[168] *On the Creation* XXXIII (99) and (100), XXXVI (105).

Chapter 6
Crucifixion of Jesus

In constructing the thesis of this book I read the New Testament in conjunction with the histories of Josephus placing related events from the two sources side by side. Most Christian scholars date the crucifixion of Jesus to between 30 and 33 CE. By correlating clues from the New Testament with historical dates found in Josephus, I propose a less popular date for the crucifixion of Jesus—36 CE. This chapter analyzes the chronology of the last days of Jesus including the mechanics of his arrest with a fresh look at the role of Judas in the crucifixion based upon the *Gospel of Judas*, a recently uncovered ancient manuscript.

Dating the Start of the Ministry of John the Baptist

One thing the Gospels are explicit upon is that Jesus was crucified after John the Baptist began his ministry. The opening verse of Chapter 3 of *Luke*'s gospel gives us a historical description of when the ministry of John the Baptist began, it reads:

> Now in the fifteenth year of the reign of Tiberius Caesar, when Pontius Pilate was governor of Judea, and Herod was tetrarch of Galilee, and his brother Philip was tetrarch of the region of Ituraea and Trachonitis, and Lysanias was tetrarch of Albilene, in the high priesthood of Annas and Caiaphas, the word

of God came to John, the son of Zacharias,
in the wilderness.[169] [Emphasis added.]

Here are the known historical dates corresponding to the events referenced in *Luke*.

Fifteen year of the reign of Tiberius Caesar	29 CE[170]
Pontius Pilate governor of Judea	26 – 37 CE[171]
Herod Antipas tetrarch of Galilee	4 BCE – 39 CE
Herod Philip tetrarch of Ituaea and Trachonitis	4 BCE – 34 CE
Lysanias tetrarch of Albilene	???
High priesthood of Annas and Caiaphas	36 CE

The last event on the list does not match with the others as I interpret that phrase (see discussion immediately below). Throw it out from the list and we have *Luke* telling us John the Baptist started his ministry in 29 CE. Thus, the public career of Jesus Christ began on or after 29 CE. This point is generally accepted by scholars.

In The High Priesthood of Annas[172] and Caiaphas

The last item on *Luke*'s list is a conundrum. The high priest holding office in 29 BCE when John the Baptist started his ministry was Joseph Caiaphas (18-36 CE). When *Luke* used the term "Caiaphas the high priest", he likely referred to Joseph Caiaphas as he was the only individual generally known to have served as high priest with the name Caiaphas. This was his family name, not his first name. Also, just one priest served as high priest at any given time, no joint office holders. However, when the

---

[169] New American Standard Version (1976).

[170] Tiberius succeeded Augustus Caesar upon his death in 14 CE.

[171] Archeological evidence indicates Pilate's rank was prefect, not governor. I extend his time as prefect to early 37 BCE because Caesar Tiberius died in March of 37 CE as Pilate was on route home to Rome after removal from office.

[172] *Luke* spells the name Annas whereas Josephus has it as Ananus. They both refer to the same famous family of Jewish high priests.

changeover from one high priest to another occurred during a year, then two high priests would each serve for parts of that year (but not together concurrently). I believe *Luke* refers to a year where there was a change in high priests resulting in two having served in the same year when the gospel uses the phrase "in the high priesthood of Annas and Caiaphas".

Scholars generally contend *Luke's* use of "Annas" refers to Annas ben Seth, high priest from 6-15 CE. I don't agree with the scholars. There were three other high priests with terms between Annas ben Seth and Joseph Caiaphas.[173] The point being that the terms of Annas ben Seth and Joseph Caiaphas in no way overlapped or intersected. Further, why would *Luke* refer to Caiaphas by his family name yet call Annas ben Seth by his first name in the same sentence? A modern day equivalent would be use of the phrase "in the presidency of Bush and Barack" to refer to the year both George W. Bush and Barack Obama were president of the United States (i.e., 2009). This is inconsistent usage.

The most logical reading of the phrase "in the high priesthood of Annas and Caiaphas" (when one forgets about timeline issues) is that *Luke* refers to the single year where these two high priests both served for parts of said year. This occurred in the 36 CE. Joseph ben Caiaphas served for part of the year and Jonathan ben Annas for the remainder. If we substitute Jonathan ben Annas for his father ben Seth and inject it into the quote from *Luke* using my interpretation, we get "in the year Jonathan ben Annas and Joseph ben Caiaphas were high priest" (i.e., 36 CE). That makes abundant sense until one stops and looks at the dates of the other events given in the passage from *Luke*. There is no way to fit 36 CE in with the other dates. Herod Philip the Tetrarch died in 34 CE and the date corresponding to the 15th year of the reign of Tiberius is 29 CE.

Although the date 36 CE does not fit with the beginning of the ministry of John the Baptist, I find it to be a very significant date nonetheless. Under my theory, it is the date the Romans

---

[173] Ishmael ben Fabus, Eleazar ben Ananus, and Simon ben Camithus.

crucified Jesus the Nazarene.[174]   Luke apparently slipped this important historical marker into the wrong section of his Gospel.

On the issue of Luke using the last or family name when referring to a high priest, we can see this pattern in *Acts*. The consensus opinion is that Luke authored *Acts* as well as his own gospel. *Acts* refers to Annas and Caiaphas together in a passage describing the arrest of Peter and John after the crucifixion of Jesus.

> The next day the rulers, elders and teachers of the law met in Jerusalem. Annas the high priest was there, and so were Caiaphas, John, Alexander and the other men of the high priest's family. They had Peter and John brought before them and began to question them: "By what power or what name did you do this?"[175]

Notice *Acts* only identifies Annas as "the high priest". It lists Caiaphas with other distinguished attendees, probably past high priests. "John" most likely refers to Jonathan ben Annas, who was high priest from 36-37 CE. If Jonathan was a former high priest at the time, then "Annas the high priest" means his brother Theophilus ben Annas who served from 37-41 CE. Comparing this passage from *Acts* to the above-quoted passage from *Luke* buttresses the conclusion that *Luke* does NOT refer to Annas ben Seth but, rather, one of his sons who also served as high priest. Under the generally accepted timeline, Caiaphas would have still been high priest when Peter and John were arrested yet *Acts* names him as a past high priest. Clearly, "Annas the high priest" referred to in *Acts* was a son of Annas ben Seth. It logically follows that the same construction applies to the *Gospel of Luke*.

---

[174] See also N. Kokkinos, Crucifixion in A.D. 36: The Keystone for Dating the Birth of Jesus, published in Chronos, Kairos, Christos, edited by J. Finegan, J. Vardaman and E.M. Yamauchi (Eisenbrauns 1989) pages 133-63.
[175] *Acts* 4:5-7.

TABLE OF JEWISH HIGH PRIESTS

High Priest	Term In Office
Simon ben Boethus	24 BCE – 5 BCE
Matthias ben Theophilus	5 BCE – 4 BCE
Joazar ben Boethus	4 BCE
Eleazar ben Boethus	4 BCE – 3 BCE
Josua ben Sie	3 BCE – 6 CE
Annas ben Seth	6 – 15 CE
Ishmael ben Fabus	15 – 16 CE
Eleazar ben Annas	16 – 17 CE
Simon ben Camithus	17 – 18 CE
Joseph ben Caiaphas[176]	18 – 36 CE
Jonathan ben Annas	36 – 37 CE
Theophilus ben Annas	37 - 41 CE
Simon Cantatheras ben Boethus	41 – 43 CE
Matthias ben Annas	43 CE
Aljoneus[177]	43 – 44 CE
Jonathan ben Annas	44 CE
Josephus ben Camydus	44 – 46 CE
Annas ben Nebedeus	46 – 52 CE
Jonathan	52 – 56 CE
Ishmael ben Fabus	56 – 62 CE
Joseph ben Simon	62 – 63 CE
Annas ben Annas	63 CE
Joshua ben Damneus	63 CE
Joshua ben Gamaliel	63 – 64 CE
Matthias ben Theophilius	65 – 66 CE

---

[176] Son-in-law of Annas ben Seth.

[177] Aljoneus may have been from the Caiaphas family. See "To Bury Caiaphas, Not to Praise Him" by Prof. David Flusser of Hebrew University of Jerusalem posthumously published in *Jerusalem Perspective Online* (01 Jan. 2004): "Thus, two high priests are known who belonged to the Caiaphas family, the earlier one being Joseph (18-36 C.E.). It is even probable that the high priest Elionaeus was the son of Joseph Caiaphas."

Dating the Crucifixion of Jesus

Dating the crucifixion is even murkier territory than the birth of Jesus. My analysis on this point rests heavily upon Josephus for dating events referred to in the New Testament. Let's start with a relevant historical date that we do know. *Luke* tells us exactly when John the Baptist started his public ministry— 29 CE.[178] If Jesus had a short one-year public ministry, the bare minimum accepted by scholars, then the earliest possible date for the crucifixion would be 30 CE. Further, the Romans removed Pontius Pilate as prefect of Judea in 37 CE. These facts render a potential timeframe within which to work of 30 to 37 CE.

Most assume Jesus began his ministry the same year as John the Baptist but I think not. John clearly possessed a large following when Jesus began his own ministry with a small core of followers. Further, the synoptic Gospels say Jesus came to John to undergo his baptism ritual. Why? What sins did Jesus commit for which this purification was necessary? The *Gospel of John* records no baptism of Jesus by John. [179] Instead, in John's gospel Jesus came to the Jordan where John baptized and John hailed Jesus as the Christ. Then Jesus walked off with two disciples of John the Baptist but no baptism. My take is that Jesus sought approval from John the Baptist for political reasons, as a means of tapping into John's vast popular support. In Second Temple Judea, religious parties were defacto political parties. Jesus naturally sought support from the leading populist rabbi of the day in his campaign for the Jewish throne. It's analogous to Barack Obama currying support from American Evangelical Christian leaders of the present day while running for president of the United States.

---

[178] "Now in the fifteenth year of the reign of Caesar Tiberius, when Pontius Pilate was governor of Judea," the word came to John. Luke 3:1. The reign of Tiberius began in 14 CE making the start of John's public ministry 29 CE. Pontius Pilate was governor of Judea 26-37 CE.

[179] In the gospel of John, Jesus is never actually baptized by John. Check the interplay between John the Baptist and Jesus recorded in *John* 1:19-34 and again in 3:22-36.

The War Between Antipas and Aretas

The two most popular dates proposed by scholars for the crucifixion are 30 and 33 CE. My principal piece of evidence in opposition is the war between Antipas and Aretas. Herod Antipas divorced the daughter of King Aretas IV of Nabatea to marry Herodias (his Hasmonean niece), which prompted Aretas to declare war on Antipas. How does this war relate to the New Testament? Herod Antipas beheaded John the Baptist for condemning his marriage to Herodias.[180] The marriage of Antipas to Herodias triggered the war with Aretas as well as the beheading of John the Baptist. Josephus gives us two datable events around the time of the war between Antipas and Aretas--the death of Philip the Tetrarch in 34 CE and the appointment of Lucius Vitellius as president of Syria in 35 CE.[181] It's clear from Josephus that the war between Aretas and Antipas occurred after Vitellius was appointed president of Syria by the emporer.[182]

I date the war to 35 CE and surmise the war closely followed the beheading of John the Baptist. By dating the war, we date the execution of John which greatly aids us in dating the crucifixion. Josephus describes the situation as follows.

> So Aretas made this the first occasion of his enmity between him and Herod, who had also some quarrel with him about their limits at the country of Gamalitis. So they raised armies on both sides, and prepared for war, and sent their generals to fight instead of themselves; and when they had joined battle, all Herod's army was destroyed * * *.
> Now some of the Jews thought that the destruction of Herod's army came from God,

---

[180] Herodian men regularly married their nieces. That wasn't the particular transgression of Antipas attacked by John the Baptist. The problem was that Herodias' first husband, Herod Boethus (1/2 brother of Antipas) was still alive when she married Antipas. This violated Jewish law.

[181] See <u>Antiquities</u> XVIII, Ch. 5.

[182] After Antipas was defeated by Aretas, he wrote to Emperor Tiberius complaining about it. The emperor, in turn, wrote to Vitellius telling him to make war on Aretas. <u>Antiquities</u> XVIII 5:1 (115).

and that very justly, as a punishment of what he did against John, that was called the Baptist: for Herod slew him, who was a good man.[183]

To my eyes, Josephus describes a short war. Antipas ruled both Galilee and Perea[184] while Aretas ruled Nabatea. Perea and Nabatea bordered each other. Once the armies were raised; battle would have been joined during the next campaigning season. Thus, I reason the entire sequence of events described by Josephus and listed below occurred during a one-year cycle.

– One Year –

- Antipas divorces daughter of King Aretas to marry Herodias
- John the Baptist criticizes marriage on Jewish legal grounds
- Aretas declares war on Antipas
- Aretas and Antipas raise armies
- Antipas arrests John the Baptist and executes him
- Aretas defeats Antipas on the field of battle
- The Jewish people conclude God punished Antipas by this defeat for his wrongful execution of John the Baptist

Working from this chain of events given by Josephus, John the Baptist was executed not long <u>before</u> Aretas defeated Antipas in 35 CE, most likely in 34 CE.

Dirty Dancing

Another fact tending to support dating the execution of John the Baptist to 34 CE is the curious gospel story of Herodias' daughter dancing in a manner "pleasing" to Herod Antipas at his

---

[183] <u>Antiquities</u>, XVIII 5:1.
[184] Josephus informs us that John the Baptist was executed by Herod Antipas at his castle Macherus in Perea. <u>Antiquities</u> XVIII 5:2.

birthday party then requesting John the Baptist's head as a gift.[185] The only daughter of Herodias known to history is Salome who married her uncle Philip the tetrarch.[186] Reasoned assumption has the adult Salome living as a widow in the palace of her stepfather Herod Antipas <u>after</u> the death of her husband in 34 CE. Salome remarried another Herodian prince after Philip so my reasoned assumption is that she was not in residence with Herod Antipas as an unmarried woman for long. These facts fit with the thesis that Antipas executed John the Baptist in the closing months of 34 CE or early 35 CE.

Public Ministry of Jesus

Securing a date for the beheading of John the Baptist aids us in framing the timeline of Jesus. The NT Gospels state the public ministry of Jesus began when John was still alive then continued on after John's execution. Scholars offer differing opinions on the length of the public ministry of Jesus, anywhere from one to three years. I find it difficult to confine the movements of Jesus described in the *Gospel of John* to one year. *John* has Jesus going to Jerusalem for two separate Passovers[187]; therefore, *John* indicates at least a two year ministry (or one year plus several months). Unfortunately, *John* omits the execution of the Baptist from his narrative. *Mark* places the story of the execution of the Baptist early in his narrative, Chapter 6 of 16. The last time *John* mentions the Baptist alive is in Chapter 3 of 21. I conclude John the Baptist was executed early in the public ministry of Jesus. If Jesus had a two year ministry and John the Baptist was executed in 34 CE, these facts point to 36 CE as the date of the crucifixion of Jesus. Also, this date coincides with the "high priesthood of Annas and Caiaphas" from *Luke*.

I draw further support for this conclusion from Josephus. Inherent in the self-proclamation of Jesus as Jewish king was insurrection against Rome. As explained below, the weakest point of the Roman administration in Palestine for many years on either

---

[185] *Matthew* 14:6-11.
[186] <u>Antiquities</u>, XVIII 5:4.
[187] John 2:13 and 5:1.

side was 35-36 CE during which period several legions from the Syrian province marched over five hundred miles into Parthia (discussed in next paragraph). With Roman military strength temporarily depleted in the province, this period stood as a particularly advantageous date for a Jewish revolution. Thus, a public ministry for Jesus of two years from 34 to 36 CE fits the historical information from Josephus.

Rome attacks Parthia (Persia) With Legions From the Syrian Province

The Emperor Tiberius ordered Lucius Vitellius, Roman proconsul of the province of Syria, to march several Roman legions from Syria deep into Parthia for the purpose of placing the Roman puppet Tiridates III on the Parthian throne. Josephus records these legions moving east of the Euphrates River into present day Iraq. Vitellius put down a tax revolt in the subject kingdom of Cilicia located well north of Palestine on his return from the long campaign east to Babylon. Our historical sources date these campaigns against Parthia and Cilicia to 35 CE. Thereafter in early 37 CE, Vitellius marched into Palestine at the head of two Roman legions[188] with orders from Rome to kick some Nabatean butt in retaliation for the war on its client, Herod Antipas. Luckily for the Nabateans, before Vitellius and his two legions made it to the Nabatean capital of Petra, the emperor Tiberius died. Vitellius ordered both legions back to their barracks in Syria upon hearing the news to await instructions from the new emperor.

I believe this to be an important historical fact in dating Jesus' attempt to seize the Jewish throne. The perfect time from a military standpoint was 36 CE. It was the low-point for Roman power in the region. At least two legions, 50% of the entire Roman troop strength for the Syrian province, were engaged in a campaign over 500 miles to the east. Further, a large Jewish army

---

[188] See Antiquities XVIII 5:3. The date 37 CE is derived from Josephus telling us in Antiquities XVIII that, while in Jerusalem at this time, Vitellius fired Jonathan as high priest and installed his brother Theophilus in that post. We know from other sources that Jonathan ben Ananus was replaced as high priest by Theophilus ben Ananus in 37 CE.

allied with the Romans under Antipas had just been defeated by Aretas, king of Nabatea, thus reducing the number of local auxiliary troops available to the Romans in Judea. During this period the Roman emperor Tiberius didn't even live in Rome thereby weakening his administration of the empire. Further, Tiberius previously executed his long-term and trusted minister (Sejanus) adding to the administrative turmoil in the provinces as officials loyal to Sejanus were purged. The year 36 CE represented a small window of opportunity for Jewish insurrectionists.[189] Jesus and his followers took their shot at restoring the Hasmonean dynasty, while Roman military strength in the province was temporarily reduced. It's difficult to sustain a 30 or even 33 CE date for the crucifixion if one cross-checks the New Testament against Josephus and other Roman historian.

Josephus Muddies the Waters

Josephus confuses the matter by reporting events in chapters 4 and 5 of Book XVIII of Antiquities out of chronologic order. Below are the historical events in the order listed by Josephus in chapters 4 and 5 next to the known dates of each.

- Removal of Pontius Pilate (Winter or Spring of 37 CE)
- Vitellius in Jerusalem just prior to Passover (March 37 CE)[190]
- Vitellius ordered to march on Parthia by Tiberius (Spring 36 CE)
- Vitellius and Antipas meet with Parthians at Euphrates (Summer 36 CE)
- Death of Herod Philip the tetrarch (34 CE)

---

[189] Our date of 36 CE also fits in with the potential dates for the crucifixion based on the Jewish festival calendar: "Based on inferences from gospel accounts, Jesus was executed by crucifixion on Friday, 14th day of the Jewish month of Nisan under the administration of Pontius Pilate. Pontius Pilate held his position from 26-36 and the only years in which Nisan 14 fell on a Friday are 27, 33, and 36 and possibly in 30 depending on when the new moon would have been visible in Jerusalem. Scholars have defended all of the dates." http://www.wikinfo.org/index.php/Jesus_Christ.

[190] Josephus states that Vitellius came to Jerusalem "at the time of the festival which is called Passover." Antiquities XVIII 4:3 (90).

- War between King Aretas of Nabatea and Antipas (35 CE)
- Vitellius in Jerusalem with legions preparing to attack Aretas when emperor Tiberius dies (March 37 CE)

Let's reorder these events to get a clearer picture of what happened during this crucial period in Jewish history.

- Lucius Vitellius serves as Roman consul (34 CE)
- Death of Herod Philip (34 CE)
- Antipas divorces daughter of Aretas and marries Herodias (34 CE)
- Antipas beheads John the Baptist (34 CE)
- Vitellius becomes proconsul / president of Syrian province (35 CE)
- War between Antipas and Aretas, Aretas wins (35 CE)
- Vitellius, backed by two Roman legions, places Tiridates III on Parthian throne (35 CE)[191]; Vitellius forced to move legions from Parthia to Cilicia to quash local revolt leaving Tiridates to his own devices (35 CE)
- Artabanus gathers army and pushes Tiridates out of Parthia (35 CE)
- Vitellius returns to Babylon reaching peace agreement with Artabanus, the Parthian king previously deposed by the Romans (36 BCE)
- Jesus crucified at Passover (36 CE)
- Vitellius replaces Caiaphas as high priest (36 CE)
- Pilate conducts punative raid against Samaritans (36 CE)
- Vitellius returns to Palestine with two legions for punitive war on Aretas of Nabatea, removes Pilate from office (37 CE)
- Tiberius dies (37 CE)

I shall leave the topic of Vitellius and the movement of his legions for now moving forward to the immediate events of the arrest and crucifixion of Jesus in Jerusalem. However, we shall

---

[191] Encyclopaedia Britannica: a Dictionary of Arts, Sciences, and General Literature, Volume 18 by Thomas Spencer Baynes (1888) at page 601.

return to Vitellius later in this chapter when discussing the possible reasons why the quest of Jesus and his followers for the Jewish throne failed.

Daily Chronology of Crucifixion

An inherent controversy exists in attempting to square the four NT gospel accounts of the crucifixion and, further, determine the day of the week upon which the crucifixion occurred. All appear in agreement that Jesus arose from the dead on the Jewish "first day", which is Sunday.[192] The Gospels also tell us that Jesus was brought down from the cross and buried just before sundown and the start of a Sabbath.[193] The standard Jewish Sabbath is on Saturday (commencing at sundown on Friday), thus, under normal circumstances, this would mean Jesus was crucified on a Friday; however, *Matthew* 12:38-40 throws a wrench into that timeline. *Matthew* states Jesus was in the tomb three days and three nights just as Jonas lay in the belly of the whale. If buried Friday evening and resurrected Sunday morning, then Jesus was only in the tomb for two nights, not the required three.

A possible solution to the paradox lies in the special high Sabbath occurring on the first and last day of the Passover Feast— the 15th and 21st of Nisan, respectively. If 15 Nisan fell on a day other than Saturday, then this day was also treated as a Sabbath by Jewish custom.[194] *John* 19:31 specifically refers to the Sabbath in question being a "high day", i.e., not just a normal Saturday Sabbath. If the Passover fell on a Friday in the year Jesus was crucified thereby making it a special high Sabbath, then the *Gospel of Matthew* can be made to confirm with the other three NT Gospels through the following sequence.

---

[192] *John* 20:19 and *Luke* 24:12.
[193] *Mark* 15:42 and *Luke* 23:54.
[194] See The Betrothed Bride of Messiah by Rick Deadmond (Xulon Press 2007) at page 78 for discussion of 15 Nisan as high Sabbath.

Wednesday 13 Nisan	Last supper; Jesus and his party move to the Mount of Olives; Jesus arrested late in evening.
Thursday 14 Nisan	Jesus tried before Pilate, crucified, and taken down from cross before sundown; Passover feast eaten this evening.
Friday 15 Nisan	First day of Passover, special high holy Sabbath
Saturday 16 Nisan	Normal Sabbath
Sunday 17 Nisan	"First day" upon which Jesus rises from his tomb.

This chronology allows Jesus to be crucified on the eve of the High Sabbath, spend three nights in the tomb, and then arise on the "first day" (Sunday).

In the first edition of this book, I stopped the analysis on this issue here. However, it later occurred to me that an online tool that converts Hebrew calendar dates to Gregorian[195] could be used to determine what day of the week 15 Nisan fell on from 29 to 36 CE. The below table contains the results.

Year	Hebrew Calendar	Gregorian Calendar
29 CE	Nisan 15, 3789	Sun 4/15/29
30 CE	Nisan 15, 3790	Thu 4/4/30
31 CE	Nisan 15, 3791	Tue 3/25/31
32 CE	Nisan 15, 3792	Tue 4/13/32
33 CE	Nisan 15, 3793	Sat 4/2/33
34 CE	Nisan 15, 3794	Tue 3/21/34
35 CE	Nisan 15, 3795	Tue 4/10/35
36 CE	Nisan 15, 3796	Sat 3/29/36

As one can see from the table, Passover did not fall on a Friday in any year during the potential window (i.e., from the start of John the Baptist's ministry to the removal of Pilate as prefect of Judea).

---

[195] http://www.olenberg.org/forms/calendar_candles.html.

Thus, we are left with no other conclusion than that *Matthew* incorrectly states Jesus was in the tomb for three nights and three days. The other Gospels indicate he was crucified on a Friday and emerged from his tomb on a Sunday (two nights and three days). In only two years out of those possible did 15 Nisan fall on a Saturday, with Passover beginning the previous evening (on Friday)—33 and 36 CE. I conclude Jesus was crucified in one of these two years and support 36 CE as the best candidate due to the overlay of Josephus upon the information given to us in the Bible.

<u>Did Jesus Know He Was To Be Arrested That Evening?</u>

Jesus famously predicted at the last supper that one of his disciples would betray him.

> Now when evening had come, he was reclining at the table with the twelve disciples. And as they were eating, he said, "Truly I say to you that one of you will betray me." And being deeply grieved, they each one began to say to him, "Surely not I, Lord?"[196]

"Betrayal" is a broad concept and can mean many things. I imagine if Peter had gone out and slept with a prostitute during Passover or Andrew fell down drunk in the town square, Jesus would have viewed it as a betrayal. But the Gospels give us other clues that Jesus expected to be arrested the evening of the last supper including the threat of violence. Seven verses after the above quote from *Matthew* predicting betrayal, Jesus states that he will not drink fruit of the vine again until "I drink it new with you in my father's kingdom."[197] Either Jesus was giving up wine for life after the last supper or he expected to die soon. We can infer the later when this comment is placed in the context of *Luke's* description of the last supper.

---

[196] *Matthew* 26:20-22.
[197] *Matthew* 26:29.

> And [Simon Peter] said to [Jesus], Lord, with you I am ready to go <u>both to prison and to death</u>. ...
>
> And he said to them, "When I sent you out without purse and bag and sandals, you did not lack anything, did you?" And they said, "No nothing." And he said to them, "But now, let him who has a purse take it along, likewise also a bag and let <u>him who has no sword sell his robe and buy one</u>.
> ...
> And they said, "Lord, look, here are two swords." And he said to them, "It is enough."[198] [Emphasis added.]

I interpret the above exchange as follows. Both Jesus and Peter understand that Jesus was likely to be arrested that night. Peter attempted to put on a brave face telling Jesus, "I am ready to go both to prison and death" with you. Jesus previously instructed his disciples to travel without bag or purse and, instead, rely on the kindness of fellow brothers in the towns they visited. [199] However on this evening, Jesus told the disciples to bring all their possessions. Why? Solution: they may have to go into hiding in the wilderness where they could not rely upon assistance of fellow brothers. Further, Jesus ordered everybody to bring a sword as they ventured out for the evening. In fact having a sword was so important that those without swords should sell their robes to obtain swords. When told the disciples could only come up with two swords, Jesus curiously responded "It is enough". If a confrontation was expected with the authorities, how could two swords be enough? A potential explanation comes from the *Gospel of Judas* discussed below.

---

[198] *Luke* 22:33-38.
[199] See *Luke* 9:3.

<u>Spending the Night On the Mount of Olives</u>

Jews coming to Jerusalem for high religious festivals were so numerous that the city lacked sleeping accommodations for all. Josephus describes a tent city at Jerusalem presumably outside the city walls comprised of many thousands of festival goers.[200] During Passover in the year of Jesus' birth, Herod Archelaus sent the Jewish Herodian cavalry against the tent city killing 3,000 ordinary Jewish citizens. Josephus does not tell us where the tent city was located but surely it was not the Mount of Olives. The rocky terrain of the Mount of Olives and adjoining Kidron Valley were completely unsuited for the movement of mounted soldiers. Did Jesus choose the Mount of Olives to afford greater safety to his group against attack by Roman and / or Jewish cavalry? This appears to be a logical conclusion based on the facts.

A more fundamental question is why Jesus and his inner circle of followers spent the night outside on and near the Mount of Olives? The apostles rented a room for the evening where the last supper was held. Why not just spread out on the couches there? Why not return to the nearby town of Bethany to the home of Lazarus? Two potential solutions to the question come to mind. First, fearing arrest, setting up on the Mount of Olives afforded more protection. Secondly, I infer from the size of the contingent that came to arrest Jesus in the dead of night that Jesus was camped on the Mount of Olives with a very large group of followers, perhaps 1000 or more persons. The Gospels present Jesus as a man who served others, who shared the pains and toils of his followers. Would such a man rest comfortably for the evening in a private home in Jerusalem leaving the remainder of his followers to fend for themselves for the night on the Mount of

---

[200] During the first Passover after Archelaus succeeded his father Herod, Archelaus turning Herod's royal troops loose on the crowd at the Temple. Josephus tells us that a continent of cavalry, in addition to the foot soldiers attacking at the Temple, were sent against Jews in their tents outside the Temple. The cavalry killed 3,000. One can safely assume the tent city was many times larger than the number killed. I assume those killed in the tent city when attack occurred were ordinary citizens (perhaps women and children) because the true radicals were inside the Temple protesting against Archelaus at the time. <u>Antiquities</u> XVII 9:3 (217).

Olives? I think not. The Jesus we know from the Gospels would rough it outdoors with his followers.

Party That Arrested Jesus

Turning to the mechanics of the arrest, each of the four Gospels describe the arrest of Jesus yet *John* is markedly different than the others. Below are the pertinent quotes from each gospel.

- *Matthew* 26:47--"a great multitude with swords and clubs, from the chief priests and elders of the people"
- *Mark* 14:43--"a multitude with swords and clubs, from the chief priests and the scribes and the elders"
- *Luke* 22:52--"chief priests and officers of the temple and elders who had come against him"
- *John* 18:3--"Roman cohort, and officers from the chief priests and the Pharisees, came there with lanterns and torches and weapons" (emphasis added).

Matthew, *Mark*, and *Luke* omit any reference to the Romans describing only local officials--chief priests, elders and officers of the temple. *John*, on the other hand, adds an important additional element to the scene--a "Roman cohort" plus the Pharisees. A Roman cohort numbered six to seven hundred heavily armored soldiers. It was an imposing and professionally trained force. The determination by the authorities that a Roman cohort was needed to arrest Jesus indicates that a very large group of followers surrounded him at the time of his capture. I surmise no less than one thousand followers of Jesus were camped on the Mount of Olives on this fateful night as heavily armored Roman legionnaires could easily subdue a lightly armed mob many times their own number.

Location of the Arrest

There is an unusual element to the arrest of Jesus that, to my knowledge, has gone unnoticed in the voluminous commentary on the life of Jesus. Below are the four gospel accounts of the movements of Jesus immediately prior to his arrest at the Garden of Gethsemane.

- *Matthew:* "And after singing a hymn, they went out to the Mount of Olives. [Conversation occurs on the Mount of Olives between Jesus and the disciples.] Then Jesus came with them to a place called Gethsemane and said to his disciples, "Sit here while I go over there and pray." And then he took with him Peter and the two sons of Zebedee, and began to be grieved and distressed."[201]

- *Mark:* "And after singing a hymn, they went out to the Mount of Olives. [Conversation occurs on the Mount of Olives between Jesus and the disciples.] And they came to a place named Gethsemane and he [Jesus] said, "Sit here until I have prayed." And he took with him Peter and James and John, and began to be very distressed and troubled."[202]

- *Luke:* "And he came out and proceeded as was his custom to the Mount of Olives; and the disciples also followed him. ... And he withdrew from them about a stone's throw, and he knelt down and began to pray."[203]

- *John:* "When Jesus had spoken these words [at the last supper], he went forth with his disciples over the ravine of Kidron, where there was a garden, and he and his disciples went into it."[204]

Matthew and *Mark* are very similar, Jesus traveled from the last supper out of the city to the Mount of Olives and, then, down to the Garden at Gethsemane. *Luke* never mentions the Garden at Gethsemane. *John* leaves out the stop at the Mount of Olives. I reason the omissions of detail in *Luke* and *John* were errors and that *Matthew* and *Mark* record the full sequence of events. The Gospels of *Matthew*, *Mark* and *John* place Jesus in the Garden at Gethsemane located at the foot of the Mount of Olives when he was arrested.

---

[201] *Matthew* 26:30, 36.
[202] *Mark* 14:26, 32-33.
[203] *Luke* 22:39-41.
[204] *John* 18:1.

In years past I assumed the Garden at Gethsemane was located somewhere on the top of the Mount of Olives as that is the impression one gets from the Gospels. Only after recently studying topographical maps and reading eyewitness accounts of the terrain did I discover my error. The Garden at Gethsemane lies near the foot of the western slope of the Mount of Olives. The Mount of Olives rises over 2,700 feet above sea level. I haven't been able to find a reading on height above sea level for the Garden at Gethsemane; however, the topography of Jerusalem shows a significant drop-off in the area of the Kidron Valley adjacent to the garden. I estimate the drop from the summit of the Mount of Olives to the garden as measuring more than 1000 feet in elevation. For comparison's sake, 1000 feet is in excess of a 70 story building. The point being that the Mount of Olives possessed serious elevation making any military assault on its summit by heavy infantry at night an extremely difficult proposition. Further, as the name implies, the Mount of Olives was said to be heavily forested with olive trees in antiquity. Chances are the approaches to the summit of the mount were restricted to a few paths through the trees making them highly defensible from the summit.

The below-figure displays the Garden at Gethsemane with other known locations on the eastern edge of Jerusalem.

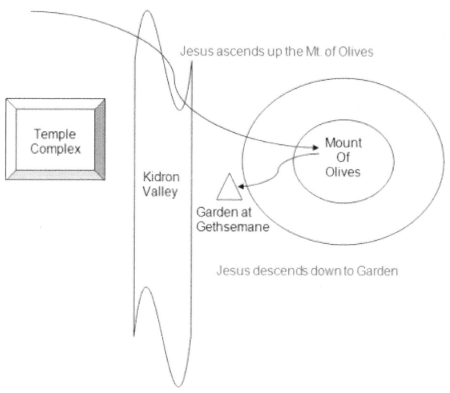

Jesus ascends up the Mt. of Olives

Temple Complex

Kidron Valley

Mount Of Olives

Garden at Gethsemane

Jesus descends down to Garden

The followers of Jesus were camped out on top of the Mount of Olives for safety as they feared attack that night by the authorities. Jesus, in fact, told his companions to bring their swords with them. Yet, later that night Jesus abandoned the sanctuary of the hilltop descending at least 1,000 feet to the west (i.e., toward the city) down to the foot of the mount presumably with a small group of followers. *Matthew*, *Mark*, and *Luke* have Jesus further separating himself from the main body of disciples once they reached the Garden at Gethsemane. When arrested, Jesus was guarded by only three disciples. Why in God's name would Jesus do that when he knew the authorities were coming for him that evening? This is the only time the Garden at Gethsemane is mentioned in the NT. Careful study of the movements of Jesus immediately prior to his arrest leave the reader with one logical explanation for his actions, Jesus intentionally put himself into a position to allow for his easy capture. How did the Temple authorities and Romans know they would find Jesus down in the Garden at Gethsemane during the early morning hours of 14 Nisan? Reason dictates Jesus and Judas prearranged his arrest at that location at that time. It's implausible that an entire Roman cohort marching in the night just happened upon Jesus and a few disciples tucked among the trees in the Garden at Gethsemane. The solution of a prior understanding between Jesus and Judas is also suggested in the recently rediscovered *Gospel of Judas*.

Gospel of Judas

This work was rediscovered in the 1980s but a translation has only recently been published. The document comes with a shadowy provenance although thought to have been found in the Egyptian desert not far from Nag Hammadi. The text is in Coptic on papyrus and radiocarbon dated to between 220 and 340 CE. The academic community, to my knowledge, accepts this manuscript as an authentic ancient gospel of an early Christian sect, the Gnostics. The canonical gospels of the NT present Judas as the betrayer of Jesus, an evil person who betrayed Jesus. The *Gospel of Judas* (as the title suggests) portrays a different Judas, a trusted and high ranking disciple of Jesus. Below is a quote from this work consisting of Jesus addressing his disciples.

> "Truly I say to you, no generation of people that are among you will know me." [The disciples became angry upon hearing this. Jesus responded,] "Why has this agitation led you to anger? Your god who is within you has provoked you to anger with your souls. Let any one of you who is strong enough among human beings bring out the perfect human and stand before my face."[205] [Emphasis added.]

Only Judas was able to "bring out the perfect human" and stand before Jesus. Then Jesus told Judas to "Step away from the others

---

[205] The Gospel of Judas edited by Kasser, Meyer and Wurst (National Geographic Society 2006) at pages 21-22.

and I shall tell you the mysteries of the kingdom." This passage marks Judas as an inner initiate of the Jesus movement, one who received secret wisdom from the master. In Scene 3, Judas tells Jesus he saw a vision of the other disciples stoning him. After a long discussion between Jesus and Judas of Gnostic cosmology, Jesus states: "But you will exceed all of them. For you will sacrifice the man that clothes me."[206] The final paragraph of the gospel has Judas going to the high priest and receiving money for turning over Jesus.

For Gnostics, the human body of flesh and bone is merely a vehicle or suits of clothes in which the true person resides. This true inner self is sometimes referred to as the garment of light.[207] The words of Jesus at the end of the *Gospel of Judas* (i.e., "For you will sacrifice the man that clothes me"), from the Gnostic viewpoint, mean Judas shall do a service for Jesus by sacrificing the earthly body of Jesus thereby freeing the inner self. The unavoidable import of the *Gospel of Judas* is that Judas acted according to the instructions of Jesus when turning him over to the chief priests. I further infer from the vision Judas had of the other disciples killing him that the author of the *Gospel of Judas* believed Judas was murdered by the other disciples after the arrest of Jesus and did not commit suicide.

Where did it all go wrong?

Why would Jesus turn himself in to the authorities knowing the act would likely lead to his death by a violent and painful end? I see it as a heroic act on the part of Jesus designed to save the

---

[206] Ibid at page 43.

[207] "You cover yourself with light as though it were a robe." *Psalms* 104:2. "Now after six days Jesus took Peter, James, and John his brother, led them up on a high mountain by themselves; and He was transfigured before them. His face shone like the sun, and his garments became as white as the light." *Matthew* 17:1-2. "In no other manner will one be able to be begotten of Him in this grace, unless he is clothed in the Perfect Light and Perfect Light is upon him. [Thus clad], he shall go [forth from the world]." *Gospel of Philip*. See also 2 Enoch 22:8--"And the Lord said to Michael, 'Go, and extract Enoch from his earthly clothing and anoint him with my delightful oil, and put him into the clothes of my glory."

lives of his family and followers. By sacrificing himself to the Sanhedrin / Romans Jesus averted a larger retaliation against his followers. Perhaps Judas arranged this with the chief priests before turning Jesus over. His surrender also meant Jesus lost hope in the probability of his mission succeeding. One can only assume that Jesus and his followers carefully studied the political landscape before marching into Jerusalem and Jesus proclaimed himself the messiah. I doubt it was a suicide mission given that he prepared his whole life for his destiny in Jerusalem and the women of his family accompanied him during his critical last days. Something happened during those final days in Jerusalem that altered the probabilities against Jesus. I speculate that the forces opposing Jesus on the Sanhedrin disclosed to the public that Jesus was the grandson of Herod. That disclosure bled away the rabble leaving Jesus with only his hard core supporters, not enough to overcome the combined Roman – Herodian forces in Jerusalem during Passover in 36 CE.

Another theory is that the unexpected return of Roman legions under Proconsul Vitellius from Parthia turned the tables against Jesus. In 35 CE, the Romans placed a puppet on the Parthian throne (Tiridates III); however, the previous Parthian king (Artabanus III) was not captured. Artabanus fled east and grew stronger when Vitellius withdrew the Roman legions from Parthia in order to put down a revolt in Cilicia (southern Turkey). Artabanus quickly pushed Tiridates out of Parthia without the backing of his Roman masters. By the time Vitellius returned to Parthia in 36 CE after taking care of matters in Cilicia, the Romans unexpectedly made peace with Artabanus throwing their client Tiridates under the bus. It appears Vitellius thereafter made a beeline from Babylon (where the peace treaty with Artabanus was concluded) for Jerusalem, where the Romans removed Joseph Caiaphas as high priest. Further, Josephus discusses Passover in conjunction with this visit of Vitellius to Jerusalem. What if the Passover festival-goers in 36 CE learned that Vitellius along with two Roman legions were nearing the city just as Jesus proclaimed himself king? This grim news would have bled away the rabble and casual followers of Jesus. It also would explain why Jesus turned himself over for capture by the Romans only a few days after declaring himself king. This chain of events appears plausible in my view.

<u>Role of Herod Antipas In Crucifixion</u>

After his arrest, the gospels contain divergent facts leading to the nailing of Jesus to the cross. Below are the chain of events found in each NT Gospel moving Jesus from arrest to crucifixion.

Gospel	Jesus, Chain of Custody After Arrest
Matthew	• Brought before Caiaphas at undisclosed location • Trial in Sanhedrin • Trial by Pontius Pilate
Mark	• Before high priest, chief priests, and elders in undisclosed location • Trial by Pontius Pilate
Luke	• Brought to home of high priest • Trial in the Sanhedrin • Questioned by Pontius Pilate • Interview by Herod Antipas[208] • Trial by Pontius Pilate
John	• Brought before former high priest Annas • Brought before high priest Caiaphas • Trial by Pontius Pilate

As you can see, *Luke* contains the most complete list of events, including a curious interview between Jesus and Herod Antipas prior to the trial of Jesus by Pilate.

Luke tells us that when Pilate learned that Jesus was a citizen of Galilee, he sent Jesus to Herod Antipas as that was his jurisdiction. First question, why didn't Herod Antipas just go ahead and execute Jesus under his own authority as he had John the Baptist? Antipas executed John the Baptist merely for

---

[208] *Luke* 23:5-12.

criticizing his marriage to Herodias (his divorced niece). Clearly Antipas held the authority to execute citizens of his territory yet failed to act in the case of Jesus. This is additional evidence that Jesus was a Roman citizen thereby depriving both the Sanhedrin and Antipas of the authority to execute him.

But the peculiar nature of the interview as told by *Luke* does not stop there. Antipas interviewed Jesus but the prisoner said nothing in response. Interview concluded Antipas sent the Jesus back to Pilate who executed him. The passage concludes with this observation.

> Now Herod and Pilate became friends with one another that very day; for before they had been at enmity with each other.[209]
> [Emphasis added.]

A Jew became friends with a Roman prefect like Pontius Pilate in only one fashion, by paying a bribe. It is no different in the modern world of organized crime. How does a New Jersey businessman become friends with Tony Soprano? The only reasonable inference to be drawn from the above-quoted language from *Luke* is that Pilate first balked at executing Jesus and instead sent the prisoner to Antipas. Then Antipas bribed Pilate to perform the deed. This incident points out the degree to which Herod Antipas felt threatened by Jesus. Again, what was the source of the political threat posed by Jesus? I submit the facts fit the hypothesis that Jesus was of royal Herodian-Hasmonean blood. Antipas was Samaritan on his mother's side, a bloodline far inferior to that of Jesus for one claiming the Jewish throne.

Crucifying a King

I thank my friend Jan Van Puffelen in the preface to this book for conducting early debates with me on the theory. In response to my inference of Jesus' Roman citizenship, he raised the point that Roman magistrates could not crucify Roman citizens. It was a punishment reserved for non-citizens under Roman law. If Jesus was a Roman citizen, how was he legally crucified by Pilate?

---

[209] *Luke* 23:12.

I chewed on this issue for several days before reaching a comfort level with it. If Jesus was the grandson of Herod, it would have been an even greater violation of Roman law for Pilate to execute Jesus without approval from the emperor. Final authority for the execution of members of the royal family of any subject kingdom was reserved to Caesar. We see this principal at work with the trial and execution of three of Herod's sons (Antipater, Alexander, and Aristobulus). Using an outlandish analogy, the situation is like a drug dealer who sells both heroin and marijuana. We have no need to dwell on the lesser crime (marijuana) when a far larger one (heroin) presents itself with the same perpetrator. So the more crucial issue stands as how Pilate rationalized executing Jesus knowing he was of Herodian royal blood?

My hypothesis is that Pontius Pilate played along with the supposition that Jesus was the son of Joseph the carpenter in exchange for a sizable bribe from Herod Antipas. If Jesus was supposed to be the son of Mary and Joseph the carpenter, he was a Hasmonean royal descendant of King Antigonus but not of Herod. Examining the situation from the perspective of Roman records, I highly doubt Jesus was ever recorded on the Roman provincial tax or census records as a son of Antipater ben Herod. Mary and Joseph fled Judea to Egypt at the birth of Jesus to protect him from the authorities (although they presented the baby at the Temple before fleeing the country). The family returned to the more distant Galilee, not Judea, presumably for the protection of Jesus. Logic dictates they did not identify Jesus as the grandson of Herod to the Romans and Herodians. However, the fact that the chief priests adamantly pressed Pilate with the point that they lacked authority to execute Jesus indicates the chief priests knew the identity of the father of Jesus. One can infer from this that Jesus was in fact registered in the Temple archives as a son of Antipater ben Herod.

How does Pilate ignore the birth registry information contained in the Temple archives? The answer most likely turns on evidentiary procedure in that it was never entered into the trial record at the Praetorium. The chief priests from the Sanhedrin refused to enter the Praetorium where Jesus was tried because the building contained graven images. They merely stood outside the building and petitioned Pilate to execute Jesus. Whatever they said to Pilate wasn't part of the trial record. Let's assume the NT Gospel accounts of the trial of Jesus before Pilate are correct. Pilate is said to have asked Jesus, "Are you the king of the Jews?" Jesus replied, "It is as you say."[210] Pilate accepts this testimony without follow-up questions to Jesus regarding the basis for his royalty. Why did Pilate not ask Jesus the identity of his father? Perhaps he already knew but did not wish the information entered into the trial record. Even if Pontius Pilate secretly learned the true identity of Jesus as a grandson of Herod, Pilate possessed plausible denial of this information as Jesus publicly connected himself only with King Antigonus (as the messiah of Levi), not Herod. Without evidence in the record connecting Jesus to the family of Herod, Pilate was free to execute Jesus on the charge of insurrection. If Jesus had publicly acknowledged before Pilate that he was the grandson of Herod then his case would have gone to Rome for adjudication (as occurred in the case of Paul of Tarsus). Yet Jesus remained silent regarding his ancestry.

How could a grandson of Antigonus be legally executed under Roman law but not a grandson of Herod when both were Jewish kings? Antigonus was declared an enemy of Rome when he formed an alliance with the Parthians. This allowed Marc Antony, then proconsul of the Eastern provinces, to execute Antigonus in 37 BCE under his own authority without sending Antigonus to the Roman senate for trial. Declaring a foreign ruler an "enemy of Rome" deprived that person of the protection of Roman law (including Roman citizenship). Therefore, a descendant of Antigonus who was not also a member of Herod's family fell outside the protected class of Jewish royals even though he was of royal blood. Further, Roman citizenship was only conferred at the birth of the child if both parents were Roman citizens. Mary surely became a Roman citizen when she married Antipater ben Herod. However, nothing in the background of Joseph the carpenter indicates he was a Roman citizen. A son of Mary and Joseph

---

[210] Mark 15:2 (New American Standard Version).

would not have possessed Roman citizenship from birth; however, a son of Antipater ben Herod and Mary would have. I theorize that the Roman records recorded Jesus as a son of Joseph the carpenter and a citizen of Galilee. On that basis, Pilate determined he possessed jurisdiction to execute Jesus. Further, I reason Pilate ignored the rumors floating around Jerusalem that Jesus was the grandson of Herod in return for a massive bribe from Antipas. Pilate was near the end of his term in Judea, which only heightened his amenability to bribery. This was his last big score before heading back to private life in Rome.

The Fate of Pontius Pilate

The generally accepted date for the termination of Pontius Pilate's tenure as prefect of Judea is 36 CE. After carefully reading Josephus and matching it with the known time of death of Caesar Tiberius, I place the removal of Pilate by proconsul Vitellius in 37 CE.

> So Vitellius sent Marcellus, a friend of his, to take care of the affairs of Judea, and ordered Pilate to go to Rome, to answer before the emperor to the accusation of the Jews. So Pilate, when he had tarried ten years in Judea, made haste to Rome ... but before he could get to Rome Tiberius was dead.[211] [Emphasis added.]

We know exactly when Tiberius died, i.e., March 16, 37 CE. Consider further that it would have taken at least 20 days for that information to reach Jerusalem from Rome. It's rather clear that Pilate was removed from office close in time to the death of Tiberius, such that Pilate was en route to Rome from Judea when the event occurred (or departed Caesarea before news of the emperor's death reached Judea from Rome).

The first action of Vitellius upon arriving in Judea was to remove Pilate. He also replaced Jonathan Annas as high priest with his brother Theophilus Annas. Josephus says this occurred at

---

[211] Antiquities XVIII 4:2 (89).

the time of an "ancient [Jewish] festival"[212] but fails to name which one. Passover occurred on March 19 in 37 CE, or three days before Tiberius died on March 16. The logical ordering of events has the Roman army marching for Petra a matter of days before the news of Tiberius' death reached him. The distance was relatively short between Jerusalem and Petra; therefore, his army could not have been on the march long for it to have been in transit at the time the news arrived. At this time, Pontius Pilate was already traveling back to Rome but did not arrive there prior to the death of Tiberius. Given that the removal of Pilate is connected with both a Jewish festival and the death of Tiberius, it's unlikely he was removed in 36 CE yet failed to reach Rome before the death of Tiberius on March 16, 37 CE. It's clear to me that Pilate was removed in February or March of 37 CE.

Lucius Vitellius became proconsul of Syria in 35 CE. Pontius Pilate must have known proconsul Vitellius intended to place his own man in charge of the wealthy prefecture of Judea. With his long tenure in Judea nearing an end, the desire to collect as many gifts (bribes) from the Jews as possible before departing office in Judea certainly would have weighed on the mind of Pilate during Passover in 36 CE when Jesus came to trial. In my view, this fact fits nicely with the inference in *Luke* that Antipas paid a bribe to Pilate for the execution of Jesus.

Both Josephus and Philo wrote that Pontius Pilate was a cruel administrator who abused his power. Thus, Pilate's reluctance to crucify Jesus as recorded in the Gospels is at odds with the reports we have from other historians upon his character. And what became of Pilate upon his return to Rome? Not much is known. The Christian historian Eusebius, writing in the early third century, states that Pilate was "involved in such calamities that he was forced to become his own executioner" during the reign of Emperor Claudius.[213] One reaps what he sows.

---

[212] Antiquities XVIII 5:3 (122).
[213] *History of the Church*, II.7.

Chapter 7
Paul of Tarsus
(Phasaelus ben Timius)

I debated not discussing Paul in this work for fear of being labeled one who finds a Hasmonean under every Judean stone; however, Paul of Tarsus stands as a colossus in Christianity. Any discussion of early Christianity demands inclusion of Paul of Tarsus. The case for Paul as a Herodian-Hasmonean carries the same weight as that for Jesus in my opinion. The first to identify Paul of Tarsus as a member of Herod's family was, I believe, Professor Robert Eisenman of California State University at Long Beach.[214] Paul (originally known as Saul) is an interesting historical character who switched sides in the middle of a religious war. Initially he persecuted the Jesus movement in some official capacity for the Sanhedrin. Later, he allegedly saw the light on the road to Damascus transforming himself into a major leader of the Nazarene movement. In addition to laying out the evidence for Paul as a Herodian, this chapter summarizes the conflict between Paul and James the Just that developed after the crucifixion of Jesus.

---

[214] *Paul as Herodian* by Prof. Robert Eisenman, Institute for Jewish-Christian Origins (1996).

Paul of Tarsus, Great-grandson of Herod

I place Paul of Tarsus within a specific branch of Herod's family—i.e., Herod's nephew Phasael[215], husband to his oldest Hasmonean daughter Salampsio. Before delving further into Phasael and Salampsio, I submit the following evidence in support of the case that Saul / Paul was a Herodian prince:

1. In his epistle to the Romans, Paul gives salutations to "my kinsman Herodian."[216] Similarly, he writes, "Greet those who are in the household of Aristobulus."[217] Aristobulus was the name of a Jewish Hasmonean king and several descendants of Herod were named Aristobulus. See Herod's family tree (Figure 1 to this book). Each Aristobulus within the Herodian clan was also of Hasmonean blood.

2. The identity of Paul's companion in Antioch: "Manean who was a foster-brother of Herod the Tetrarch."[218]

3. Paul was a Roman citizen. Few Jews outside of the house of Herod were Roman citizens. Roman citizenship was gained by a Jew in three ways: (a) being a member of Herod's family, (b) service in the Roman military, (c) purchase Roman citizenship from a government official. However, Paul says he was a Roman citizen "by birth".[219] Roman citizenship by birth was not purchased or gained through military service. Descendants of Herod were citizens by birth.

4. Paul's acquaintance and friend Epaphroditas might well be the person of the same name who was a secretary to Nero (and who helped Nero commit suicide). He was greeted in one of Paul's letters[220] along with "Caesar's household".

---

[215] A derivative of Phasael is Phasaelus. It may mean son of Phasael. I use Phasael for the nephew of Herod and Phasaelus for Phasael's grandson.
[216] Romans 16:11.
[217] Romans 16:10.
[218] *Acts* 13.1.
[219] *Acts* 22.27-8.
[220] *Phil.* 2:25-30; 4:10-18.

5. Josephus refers to "Saulus, a kinsman of Agrippa" said to be of the royal family.[221] Professor Eisenman opines that "Saulus" of Josephus is in fact Paul of Tarsus.

6. Paul tells us he was born in the Diaspora as the son of a middle-class craftsman of the tribe of Benjamin, meaning Paul was not an hereditary member of the Levitical priesthood. Despite this, Paul gained official position with the Sanhedrin (perhaps as a voting member) at an age much younger than normally expected of Pharisaic legal scholars who rose up through the ranks of rabbis via merit. *Acts* says Paul was a young man at the stoning of Stephen. I reason he was no more than 27 at the occurrence of this event yet members of the Sanhedrin were required to be community elders, usually at least 40 years of age.

No one element of this proof hits a home run. It's the totality of the evidence when taken together that forms the strength of the case. What is particularly clear after reading the six points above is that Paul of Tarsus was not the person portrayed in the Bible—i.e., a lowly tradesman[222] from the provincial town of Tarsus. It is inconceivable to me that a Jew of low birth from Asia Minor was a Roman citizen by birth and, later, found his way onto to the Sanhedrin as a voting member at such an astonishingly young age. The Herodians and Romans named the members of the Sanhedrin. That body was dominated by senior rabbis and Levitical priests.

Paul as Member of Sanhedrin

The Sanhedrin was something of a Jewish religious uber high court. Below are facts inferring that Paul was a member of the Sanhedrin or at least an official of the Sanhedrin authorized to make arrests.

---

[221] <u>Antiquities</u>, XX 9:4.
[222] In *Acts* 18:3, Paul is said to be a tentmaker.

1. Paul (Saul) was one of the officials who witnessed the stoning of Stephen (Acts 7:59), an action ordered by the Sanhedrin.
2. Paul "cast his vote" against the Nazarenes (early name for Christians) who were condemned to death. The only Jewish counsel with authority to condemn a Jew to death was the Sanhedrin. Ergo, Paul voted as a member of the Sanhedrin to condemn the Nazarenes to death.[223]
3. Paul went before the high priest requesting and receiving letters authorizing "official" prosecution of Nazarenes in Damascus.[224]
4. Paul was a disciple of Nasi Gamaliel, the president of the Sanhedrin.[225]

At a minimum, one can say with confidence that Paul was an official within the Sanhedrin power structure who was commissioned to take official acts on behalf of the chief priests. I lean toward the conclusion that Paul was a voting member of the Sanhedrin. However, confusion exists over the term "Sanhedrin" requiring further clarification. There were two types of Sanhedrin. We mostly associate the phrase with the Great Sanhedrin located in Jerusalem; however, there were lesser Sanhedrin located outside of the capital.

> By whom members of the Sanhedrin were appointed is not clear from the Talmud. Naturally they were chosen primarily on account of their learning, but it seems that priests had a prior claim, other things being equal. In the period of the Hasmoneans, Sadducean or Pharisaic elements seem to have predominated in the Great Sanhedrin

---

[223] "Indeed, I myself thought I must do many things contrary to the name of Jesus of Nazareth. This I also did in Jerusalem, and many of the saints I shut up in prison, having received authority from the chief priests; and when they were put to death, I cast my vote against them. And I punished them often in every synagogue and compelled them to blaspheme; and being exceedingly enraged against them, I persecuted them even to foreign cities." *Acts*, 26:9-11.
[224] *Acts* 9:1–2.
[225] *Acts* 22:3.

> according to the disposition of the ruling
> prince.[226] [Emphasis added.]

At the very least, members of the Sanhedrin were required to be outstanding scholars of the Torah. Notice also the highlighted phrase at the end of the above quote, "according to the disposition of the ruling prince." In the days of Herod and his successors, the Herodians appointed the members of the Sanhedrin. So to be a member of the Sanhedrin you were learned in the Torah, most likely of priestly ancestry, and had connections with the ruling Herodians. Those qualifications don't square with Paul's self-described background as a tentmaker from the provinces. If, on the other hand, Paul was a descendant of Herod and also of Hasmonean (priestly) blood then his appointment to the Sanhedrin appears more plausible.

Paul states in his *Letter to the Philippians*, I was "circumcised the eighth day, of the nation of Israel, of the tribe of Benjamin, a Hebrew of Hebrews; as to the Law, a Pharisee."[227] Emphasis added. Benjamin was the tribe of the first Jewish king, also named Saul, and smallest of all the Jewish tribes. The Hasmoneans were of the tribe of Levi. Thus, Paul's statement in *Philippians* seems on its face to disqualify him from being of Hasmonean descent. Let us dig deeper. The most curious portion of the quote from *Philippians* is the phrase, "Hebrew of Hebrews". I interpret this phrase as akin to the way an attorney may be referred to as a "lawyer's lawyer". The latter phrase means a lawyer of exceptional ability who commands respect from his fellow lawyers. Thus, I interpret Paul as telling us he was a Jew from an outstanding and respected family, a "Jew's Jew" so to speak. To me, this is a coded reference to Paul's Hasmonean heritage. The Hasmoneans were the preeminent Jewish family of the period. How could he be both a member of the tribe of Benjamin and also of Hasmonean blood? Tribe identity was determined by one's father. Paul's statement in *Philippians* could be consistent with Hasmonean heritage if his

---

[226] Rabbi J. Shachter, Introduction to translation of Sanhedrin, Babylonian Talmud Tract published by Come and Hear™.

[227] *Philippians* 3:5.

130

father was from the tribe of Benjamin while his mother was Hasmonean. Very few Hasmonean princesses married outside the Herodian family. Paul's self-identification with the tribe of Benjamin indicates to me that his father was not a Herodian (or at least not mixed Herodian-Hasmonean).

Inference of Wealth

Two cryptic references in the New Testament hint that Paul of Tarsus possessed wealth. On Paul's second trip to Jerusalem, he met with the leaders of the Church and they "only asked us [Paul and Barnabas] to remember the poor."[228] It seems like a strange request of Nazarene missionaries given the injunction of Jesus to his disciples to travel with the bare minimum of possessions.

> And He said to them, "Take nothing for your journey, neither a staff, nor a bag, nor bread, nor money; and do not even have two tunics apiece."[229]

What money would Paul possess to give to the poor? To my knowledge, the New Testament records only two incidents of a specific individual being told to give to the poor—(a) the above-mentioned incident with Paul and (b) Jesus' instruction to a rich man who wanted to know the path to God.[230] Further, we have the incident from *Acts* where the Roman prefect Felix solicited a bribe from Paul while under arrest in Caesarea.[231] Felix kept Paul under arrest in Judea for two years waiting for the payment of a bribe. Why would a Roman prefect expect to receive a bribe from an itinerant Nazarene missionary? Paul should have lived a life of poverty. The incident makes much more sense if Paul were indeed a Herodian prince whose father was a wealthy merchant. Even if Paul lacked the means of paying a large bribe to Felix, the expectation would have been that his family would ransom him from prison. Finally, we have Paul's own admission that he was a

---

[228] *Galatians* 2:10.
[229] *Luke* 9:3.

Roman citizen from birth identifying his Jewish family as one of material means.

The Family Tree of Paul of Tarsus

The search for Paul's mother within the Herodian family tree starts with the Hasmonean women. Why Hasmonean? I can't fathom a descendant of Herod being appointed to the Sanhedrin (a body of priests and rabbis) unless he possessed Jewish royal blood. Further, Herod had dozens of grandchildren and even more great-grandchildren. Paul's bloodline must have been extraordinary to distinguish him from the vast multitude of Herodians thereby marking him for special promotion onto the Sanhedrin.

Herod had one Hasmonean wife, Mariamne bat Alexander. Thus, our search narrows in on the descendants of Herod through his wife Mariamne the Hasmonean. Next we filter this branch for Hasmonean women who married outside of the Herodian family. If Paul's father lived in Tarsus and was of the tribe of Benjamin, he was unlikely to have been a Herodian. *Acts of the Apostles* gives an additional clue in our search for Paul's ancestry--"Saul, who was also known as Paul."[232] After conversion to the Nazarene movement, Saul was exclusively thereafter known as Paul. The Herodian name most reasonably connected to both the names Saul and Paul was Phasael or Phasaelus, oldest brother of Herod. Narrowing the search further, we find Herod's nephew Phasael ben Phasael married to Herod's oldest Hasmonean daughter Salampsio. Oddly, according to Josephus, Phasael ben Phasael did not name one of his sons Phasael. Herodians stuck to established naming patterns, so it was unusual for Herod's nephew to deviate. Taking Josephus at face value regarding the names of the children of Phasael and Salampsio, I theorize Paul of Tarsus was a grandson of this couple (and a great grandson of Herod) putting Paul one generation behind Jesus in the Herodian extended family tree. Using these parameters, I identify Paul's mother as Alexandra, the oldest daughter of Salampsio because she married outside of the

---

[230] *Luke* 18:22.
[231] *Acts* 24:26.
[232] *Acts* 13:9.

Herodian clan. Her husband (and the person I identify as Paul's father) was Timius of Cyprus. Below is the branch of Herod's family tree I associate with Paul.

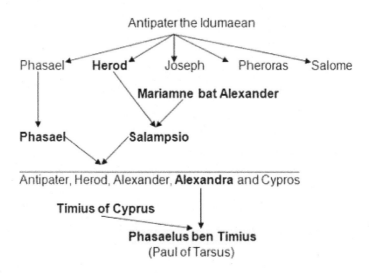

Cyprus sounds much like Tarsus. Both were in the Mediterranean outside of the Jewish kingdom. Tarsus was located in modern day Turkey and, in Roman times, was the capital of Cilicia. One can almost conflate the words Timius and Cyprus into Tarsus, but not quite. Further, Cyprus was the first location Paul the Nazarene apostle visited on his recorded missionary journeys. Was Cyprus in fact the homeland of Paul? An ancient tradition from the Ebionites also helps us tie Paul of Tarsus to Timius of Cyprus. I have assumed to this point that Paul's father was Jewish as he proclaims to be of the tribe of Benjamin. The name Timius is Greek. Hellenized Jews took Greek names so the name Timius alone is not determinative but does raise an eyebrow.

The Ebionites, or poor ones, were successors of the Jerusalem church headed by James the Just after the crucifixion of Jesus. They venerated Jesus as the Messiah (but not as a divine being) and followed Jewish law as interpreted by Jesus. They viewed Paul as a wicked teacher who deviated from the teachings of Jesus. The Roman Church declared the Ebionites heretics in the fourth century CE. Doesn't that strike you as the tail wagging the dog, the Roman church declaring its authority over the Jerusalem church? The scriptures of the Ebionites were burned by the Roman Catholic Church; however, scraps of their writings were preserved by Roman apologists who published attacks against the Ebionites. One such work is that of Bishop Epiphanius. In his *Panarion*, he quotes the Ebionites as saying that Paul was "Greek and of gentile parentage but that he later became a proselyte."[233] If the Ebionites learned the name of Paul's father to be Timius of Cyprus, one easily sees their conclusion that Paul was Greek. His father had a Greek name and hailed from a Greek island.

Josephus makes one brief mention of Timius of Cyprus, "Alexandra's [husband] was Timius of Cyprus, a man of some importance, in union with whom she died childless."[234] I reason Timius was a wealthy Greek-Jewish merchant who bought himself a Hasmonean bride. Josephus specifically states that Timius and Alexandra had no children. Thus, my hypothesis identifying Paul's parents only works if Josephus or later editors purposefully altered Antiquities to hide Paul's ancestry. I operate under the assumption that Antiquities was altered to shield the identity of Saul / Paul.

Working from these facts, we can understand Paul's choice of career. The first son of Timius and Alexandra should have been named after the father of Timius with the second son after the father of Alexandra. Thus, the name Phasaelus belongs to the second son of Timius and Alexandra. Jewish tradition contains the law of primogeniture by which the eldest son receives the lion's share of the inheritance. Paul, as the second son, would have been cut out of Timius' wealthy family business that passed to his older brother. For an upwardly mobile Jew of royal blood cut out of the family business, becoming a rabbi was the logical alternative career course. Paul was not eligible for the priesthood despite his Hasmonean blood as his father was not born of priestly lineage. That steered Paul to the Sanhedrin where his Herodian

---

[233] Reprinted in The Panarion of Epiphanius of Salamis, Volume 1 by Frank Williams (Brill Academic Publishers 1987) at page 140.
[234] Antiquities 18.130-41.

134

connections were a boost and one was not strictly required to be Kohanim as a prerequisite for high position.

Just to back up and explain the difference between a Temple priest and a rabbi. The Jewish priesthood at this time was strictly hereditary. One must come from the tribe of Levi to be eligible for the priesthood and, further, be a patrilineal descendant of Aaron (i.e., Kohanim) to be eligible for all positions of importance within the Temple priesthood. Rabbis, on the other hand, were scholars of the Torah. To my knowledge, there were no hereditary requirements that stood as prerequisites for a rabbinical student in the Second Temple period. The New Testament identifies Jesus as a rabbi. As his father was Herodian, he lacked the proper ancestry to become a Temple priest just as was the case with Paul.

Birth of Paul of Tarsus (11 CE)

If I have correctly identified the historical Paul of Tarsus, we can use the above family tree to set some parameters on the date of his birth. Mariamne bat Alexander married Herod in 37 BCE at the age of 20 and was executed by him in 29 BCE. Salampsio was Mariamne's oldest daughter so, reasoned guess, she was born around 33 BCE. Let's further assume that Salampsio began having children by Phasael at or near the age of 20. We know Alexandra was Salampsio's oldest daughter but not where she fell in relation to her brothers. If we assume Salampsio gave birth to her first child at age 20, then her first child was born in 13 BCE. To be conservative, I added two years to this date accounting for the fact that Alexandra may have been a middle child (with older brothers). This method renders an estimated birth date for Alexandra bat Phasael of 11 BCE. If Alexandra married at age 18 with her second son born (Phasaelus) at age 21, then Paul was born around 11 CE. This date falls within the generally accepted range.

Mariamne bat Alexander
Born	57 BCE
Married Herod	37 BCE

Died	29 BCE
Salampsio bat Herod	
Born	33 BCE
Married Phasael	15 BCE
Alexandra bat Phasael	
Born	11 BCE
Married Timius	7 CE
Phasaelus ben Timius	
Born	11 CE

Stoning of Stephen / a "young man named Saul"

The date of Paul's conversion from Sanhedrin thug to noble leader of the Nazarene faith has always been murky. We know from *Acts* that Saul / Paul remained on the side of the Herodian forces when the Sanhedrin stoned Stephen, a Nazarene follower of Jesus.[235] Based on where the story of Stephen falls in *Acts*, it is generally assumed his execution occurred one to two years after the crucifixion of Jesus. By dating the crucifixion to 36 CE, this places the death of Stephen in 37-38 CE during the reign of Caligula. *Acts* mentions Paul (Saul) within the passages on the stoning of Stephen as follows, "the witnesses laid aside their robes at the feet of a young man named Saul."[236] Emphasis added. In 38 CE, I reason Paul to have been 27 years of age. Although 27 years old might not have been considered young among the general Jewish population of the day, it was indeed young for a rabbi. They functioned as elder theologians specializing in the minutiae of Jewish law. Those who sat on the Sanhedrin were senior rabbis and Jewish elders. Thus, preferential treatment by the ruling prince (who was then Herod Agrippa) was required to elevate a young man such as Paul to the position of voting member of the Sanhedrin.

---

[235] "And Saul was in hearty agreement with putting [Stephen] to death." *Acts* 8:1.

[236] *Acts* 7:58.

<u>Aunt Cypros and Agrippa</u>

An interesting consequence of pushing the date for the crucifixion of Jesus back to 36 CE is that it also places Paul's early Nazarene career under a new Roman emperor, Caligula (37 – 41 CE). Assuming I have correctly placed him within the family tree of Herod the Great, Paul's relationship to Agrippa holds interesting implications. One of the first moves made by Caligula upon taking the throne was to name his childhood friend Herod Agrippa the new king of Batanaea and Trachonitis, territories previously ruled by his uncle Herod Philip. Later, Herod Agrippa gained dominion over Lysanaias, Galilee, Perea, Samaria and Judea. Thus, he became nearly as powerful as Herod the Great. Herod Agrippa's wife was Cypros bat Phasael, the younger sister of Paul's mother Alexandra. During part of his reign, Herod Agrippa appointed the members of the Sanhedrin. You don't suppose Aunt Cypros put in a good word with Agrippa for her nephew Paul? This premise solves the mystery of how a lowly tentmaker's son of the tribe of Benjamin from the Jewish Diaspora who was much too young for the position ended up a voting member on the Sanhedrin.

Herod Agrippa (the elder) appears as a major villain in *Acts*. The passage reproduced below relates his execution of James ben Zebedee.

> Now about that time Herod the king [Herod Agrippa I] laid hands on some who belonged to the church in order to mistreat them. And he had James the brother of John put to death with a sword. When he saw that it pleased the Jews, he proceeded to arrest Peter also. Now it was during the days of Unleavened Bread. When he had seized [Peter], he put him in prison.[237]

As a nephew of Herod Agrippa, it is an easy connection between Paul and the persecution of the nascent Nazarene movement by Agrippa. This squares with Paul's own description of his activities

---

[237] *Acts* 12:1-4.

prior to "seeing the light" on the road to Damascus. *Acts* describes Saul / Paul laying waste to the Nazarene church after the execution of Stephen, "Saul began ravaging the church, entering house after house, and dragging off men and women, he would put them in prison."[238] According to the generally accepted timeline of Paul's life, shortly after Stephen's execution by the Sanhedrin Paul converted to the Nazarene faith. The main justification for placing Paul's conversion close in time to the last recorded event in *Acts* of Paul still aligned with the Sanhedrin is attempted conformity with Paul's self-described timeline given in *Galatians*.

Paul's Timeline Problem, "an interval of fourteen years"

Many a scholar of early Christian history has wrestled mightily with the timeline of Paul's post-conversion life as found in *Acts* and his epistles, especially a particular statement found in *Galatians*--"after an interval of fourteen years I went up again to Jerusalem with Barnabas."[239] The first question relative to the 14 year interval is the starting point for counting. In *Galatians*, Paul discusses his two trips to Jerusalem in close proximity within the text of the epistle. Paul made one trip three years after his conversion but introduced a second trip to Jerusalem by saying it occurred after "an interval" of fourteen years. The plain language of *Galatians* leads one to conclude the 14 years length was the time between trips to Jerusalem. Accounting for the three years transpiring before the first trip to Jerusalem leaves us with 17 total years to work into Paul's timeline.

Acts also discusses Paul's second Jerusalem trip. It tells us "Barnabas and Saul" came to the elders in Jerusalem. Notice that Paul takes second billing to Barnabas in this early stage of his Christian career. Additionally, *Acts* states this trip to Jerusalem was occasioned by a prophesy of famine.

> [A seer named Abagus] stood up and began to indicate by the spirit that there would certainly be a great famine all over the world.

---

[238] *Acts* 8:3.
[239] *Galatians* 2:1. These are just a few of many I randomly selected.

> And this took place in the reign of Claudius.[240]

The church in Antioch took up a collection for their brethren giving it to Paul and Barnabas for delivery to Jerusalem. Herod Agrippa dies in the next chapter of *Acts* (Ch. 12) while Paul and Barnabas are still on their trip to Jerusalem.[241] We know Herod Agrippa died mysteriously in 44 CE. Further, Josephus records a famine beginning in Palestine in 46 CE.[242] I believe this to be the famine prophesized by Abagus in *Acts*. Although one encounters difficulty dating the events in the life of Paul, in this instance the facts line up placing Paul's second Jerusalem trip in 44 CE. The text of *Acts* places the death of Agrippa during Paul's second trip to Jerusalem post-conversion. I find no compelling evidence tending to indicate an alternate date (except the impossible desire to stretch out events so they fit the 14-year interval). Therein lays the problem. If *Galatians* is believed and we work backward from 44 CE, then Paul's first visit to Jerusalem post-conversion occurred in 30 CE and he converted to the Nazarene movement three years earlier in 27 CE. **Absolutely impossible!** *Luke* identifies 29 CE as the start of the ministry of John the Baptist.

Even collapsing the ministries of both John and Jesus down into one single compact year, maintenance of any sense of reason makes it impossible to date the crucifixion prior to 30 CE. My approach is to throw out the 14-year interval given in *Galatians* as an error of a copyist or perhaps Paul himself. Once the 14-year interval is stricken, Paul's timeline becomes a more sensible endeavor.

---

[240] *Acts* 11:28.

[241] *Acts* 11:30 records Paul and Barnabas leaving for Jerusalem. *Acts* 12:21 records the death of Agrippa and, a few verses later, *Acts* 12:24 records the return of these two men to Asia Minor from their mission to Jerusalem.

[242] Antiquities XX:2 (51-52). Josephus does not give a precise date of the famine; however, based upon the terms of Roman officials discussed in the same chapter as the famine, most scholars this Judean famine to 46 CE. See Rabbi Paul: An Intellectual Biography by Bruce Chilton (Doubleday Religion 2004) at page 144.

Expulsion of the Jews From Rome by Claudius

When Paul arrived in Corinth during his second missionary journey, he found Aquila and Priscilla who had been deported from Rome by Claudius.[243] This matches up with a statement from the Roman historian Suetonius: "Since the Jews constantly made disturbances at the instigation of Chrestus, he [Claudius] expelled them from Rome."[244] Scholars have studied this issue ad nauseum generating heavy disagreement upon the date of the Jewish expulsion, whether only Christians were expelled, or whether the expulsion took place at all. "Suetonius [does not supply] us with enough information to date the expulsion; the later writer Orosius would date it to A.D. 49. Orosius is not famous for his impeccable accuracy, but such a date receives some confirmation from *Acts*."[245] Adding fuel to the flame Cassius Dio, another Roman historian writing in the third century CE, described a lesser punishment upon the Jews (i.e., banning assembly and closing of synagogues) exacted by Claudius near the start of his reign in 41 CE. Dio never mentioned an expulsion of Jews. It appears the events described by Dio are different than the expulsion mentioned by Suetonius.[246]

Suetonius and *Acts* both describe an expulsion of Jews from Rome. Orosius puts this event in 49 CE which fits with what we can piece together of Paul's timeline from *Acts* and his letters; however, Christian scholars scoff at that date. Dio wrote more than 100 years after the composition of *Acts* and, also, after Suetonius. Further, Suetonius mentions the existence of Christians in Rome as the underlying cause for the uproar in the Jewish community. Keeping in mind my dating of the crucifixion of Jesus to 36 CE, it's very difficult to imagine a sizable Christian community already established in Rome by 41 CE (a mere five

---

[243] *Acts* 18:2.

[244] Christianity and the Roman Empire: Background Texts by Ralph Martin Novak (Trinity Press International 2001) at page 20; See The Church In Rome In The First Century by George Edmundson (Bibliolife 1913) at page 9 supporting the equation of "Chrestus" with christus.

[245] Antioch and Rome: New Testament Cradles of Catholic Christianity by Raymond Edward Brown, John P. Meier (Paulist Press 1983) at page 102.

[246] Beginning from Jerusalem, Christianity in the Making by James D. G. Dunn (Wm. B. Eerdmans Publishing Company 2008) at pages 506-07.

years after the crucifixion). Paul was the main evangelist to the Gentiles and no one believes he began his missionary work west of Judea prior to 41 CE. In my view, we lack a compelling reason for rejecting the date of 49 CE for the Jewish expulsion from Rome given by Orosius. Further, this date meshes with another event from *Acts* for which we have independent dating evidence—Paul's appearance before proconsul Lucius Gallio.

Dating Paul's Appearance Before Proconsul Gallio

Paul went to Greece during his second missionary journey staying in Corinth for 18 months according to *Acts*.[247] I date his arrival in Corinth to early 50 CE because Aquila and Priscilla (the two deportees from Rome) were already in Corinth when Paul arrived.[248] This dating for Paul's arrival in Rome also aligns with an acceptable dating for his appearance before Lucius Gallio. While in Corinth, the local Jewish population brought Paul before the Roman proconsul Lucius Gallio accusing him of a crime. A surviving inscription written by Claudius to the people of Delphi mentions proconsul Gallio and provides us with independent evidence for the date of Gallio's term in office. The Delphi Inscription states that Claudius received a report from Lucius Gallio, his friend and proconsul of Achaea (Roman province of Greece). The text of the inscription dates it's authorship by Claudius to the 12th year of his reign and the 26th time he was acclaimed emperor. These two events fall between January 25 and August 1, 52 CE.[249]

Roman proconsuls of this period generally served for one year (occasionally two years) with their terms starting and ending at the onset of summer (May or June). The question remains whether Gallio reported to Augustus on the matter of Delphi at the beginning or end of his term? On this point, Seneca (younger brother of Gallio) wrote that Gallio developed a fever in Achaia and '"took to ship immediately', insisting the disease was 'not of

---

[247] *Acts* 18:11.
[248] *Acts* 18:2.
[249] Christianity and the Roman Empire: Background Texts by Ralph Martin Novak (Trinity Press International 2001) at page 21.

the body, but of the place.'"[250] Did Gallio take to ship from Greece before his term ended never to return as proconsul? That's the implication Seneca's letter. If so, Gallio served no more than a few months in his post as proconsul before leaving Greece. As proconsul terms began in May or June that means Gallio left Greece mid to late summer of the same year. Putting together the evidence of the Delphi inscription and the Seneca letter, the best date for Gallio's short term as proconsul of Greece was the summer of 51 CE. That fits with the tail end of Paul's time in Greece. The pieces of puzzle fit if Gallio left Greece in late fall of 51 CE sailing around the Mediterranean for his health for several months taking him into the winter (during which time long-distance travel by ship ceased in the Eastern Mediterranean). Gallio then returned to Rome in the early spring of 52 CE reporting to Nero upon his arrival.

The following summarizes my sequencing of the events surrounding Paul's 18-month period in Corinth.

- **Winter 50 CE**--Paul arrives in Greece.
- **Summer 51 CE**--Paul appears before proconsul Gallio.
- **Winter 51-52 CE**--Gallio reports to Claudius; Claudius shortly thereafter writes to the people of Delphi.

Dating the Council of Jerusalem

Besides Herodian persecution, one of the greatest challenges faced by the incipient Nazarene church was deciding whether gentile converts were required to fully comply with Jewish law, including circumcision. At one time, Romans outlawed circumcision assessing the same criminal penalty for circumcision as for castration.[251] Asking prospective converts of the Roman

---

[250] First Corinthians: A New Translation by Joseph A. Fitzmyer (Yale University Press 2008) at page 42.

[251] Emperor Hadrian outlawed castration but did not specifically address whether circumcision fell under this ban. See Ulpianus, *On the Duties of Proconsul*, Book VII. His adoptive son Antoninus Pius who went on to become emperor (138-161 CE) specifically exempted Jews allowing them to circumcise "their own children" but "anyone who performs this operation upon persons of a different religion will incur the penalty for castration." Modestinus, *Rules*, Book VI. This would seem to outlaw the circumcision of converts as only children of Jews

world to get their penis sheared surely put a damper on recruitment. Paul, as head of gentile recruitment, vehemently opposed mandating Jewish dietary laws and circumcision upon gentile converts. On the other side of the issue stood staunch Jewish traditionalist who viewed the Nazarenes as a Jewish religion whose members must comply with the laws of Moses as interpreted by Jesus. They were referred to as the Circumcision Party (or Judaizers). The church leaders called a major conference in Jerusalem to resolve the dispute. Dating the conference has been a hotly debated question for academics.

The timeline of Paul's missionary journeys help us pinpoint the date of the Jerusalem Council. Paul demonstrated a pattern of checking back in with his superiors in Jerusalem at the conclusion of each missionary journey. He met with James and Peter in Jerusalem prior to his first missionary journey to Galatia. That trip ended with a second stop in Jerusalem in 44 CE. We know the date because *Acts* ties it to the death of Herod Agrippa I. From *Galatians*, we see that the circumcision issue was still not a settled during Paul's second stop in Jerusalem because he made a point of writing how the church leaders in Jerusalem did not require his traveling companion Titus (a Greek) to be circumcised. Paul then departed Judea on his second missionary journey going through Galatia on his way to Greece.

Paul left Greece after the trial before Gallio in the summer of 51 CE and returned to Judea. *Acts* places the Council of Jerusalem directly after Paul's return from Judea from Greece. Thus, the facts point to 52 CE as the date of the Council of Jerusalem. As Paul harps on the circumcision issue in *Galatians*, an issue settled by James at the Council of Jerusalem, I believe it was written before the Council. Taking all factors into account, I find 52 CE to be the most likely date for the Council of Jerusalem and date Paul's *Epistle to the Galatians* to 50 CE.

---

allowed the practice. Further, Pius would not have had to legislate a special exemption for Jewish circumcision unless it was outlawed under Hadrian.

<u>Dating Paul's Arrest in Jerusalem</u>

Acts relates Paul held prisoner by the Romans in Caesarea for two years before Porcius Festus succeeded Felix as prefect.[252] Thus, by dating the changeover in the Roman administration in Judea from Felix to Festus, we date Paul's arrest. Josephus mentions the changeover from Felix to Festus in <u>Antiquities</u>. Although no date is directly attached to this event by Josephus, in the immediately preceding paragraph he states, "About this time king Agrippa gave the high priesthood to Ishmael, who was the son of Fabi."[253] Ishmael became high priest in 56 CE. As Josephus occasionally departs from reporting events in completely linear fashion, this reference from <u>Antiquities</u> is suggestive but not determinative that the changeover from Felix to Festus occurred near 56 CE. Eusebius, another ancient author, also dates the changeover from Felix to Festus to 56 CE (i.e., the second year of Nero's reign).[254] No Roman historian gives a date other than 56 CE for the changeover from Felix to Festus.

One finds many published citations to 60 CE as the date Paul sailed for Rome from Judea with zero evidence given for this date.[255] I am perplexed how and why authors fixed upon 60 CE for the end of Felix's term in Judea. The only conclusion one may draw is a desire upon the authors' part to shoehorn the known historical dates for events recorded in the New Testament into Paul's timeline found in *Acts* and his epistles. No substantial evidence exists for dating the arrest of Paul to anything other than

---

[252] *Acts* 24:27.

[253] <u>Antiquities</u> XX 8:8.

[254] <u>Journal of Theological Studies, Volume 3</u> By Oxford Journals (The Clarendon Press 1990) at page 120; <u>Bibliotheca Sacra, Volume 55</u> edited by Wright and Holbrook (Bibliotheca Sacra Company 1898) at page 2480; <u>The Acts of the Apostles: The Greek Text with Introduction and Commentary</u> By Frederick Fyvie Bruce (Wm. B. Eerdmans Publishing Co. 1990) at page 56.

[255] See <u>The Illustrated Guide to the Bible</u> By J. R. Porter (Oxford University Press 1998) at page 235; <u>The Book of Acts in Its Palestinian Setting</u> By Richard Bauckham (Wm. B. Eerdmans Publishing Company 1995) at page 25; <u>Dictionary of the apostolic church, Volume 1</u> By James Hastings, John Alexander Selbie, John Chisholm Lambert (Scribners 1916) at page 278; <u>A history of the Jewish people during the Maccabean and Roman periods</u> by James Stevenson Riggs (BiblioBazaar 2009) at pages 257-58.

54 CE (i.e., two years before Festus became prefect of Judea). The below table summarizes the dates established for the activities of Paul.

Paul's First Missionary Journey to Galatia (Terminated in 44 CE).		
44 CE	Paul's second trip to Jerusalem. Herod Agrippa dies.	
46 CE	Famine starts in Judea.	Paul's Second Missionary Journey (44 CE – 51 CE)
49-50 CE	Paul goes to Corinth finding Aquila and Priscilla who arrived there after expulsion from Rome by Claudius.	
51 CE (summer)	Paul hauled before Roman tribunal of proconsul Lucius Junius Gallio Annaeus (brother of Seneca) in Corinth.	
52 CE	Council of Jerusalem	
Paul's Third Missionary Journey (52-54 CE)		
54 CE	Arrest of Paul in Jerusalem by Felix.	
56 CE	Paul deported by Festus from Judea bound for Rome.	

Dating Paul's Conversion

We can now work backward from the dates listed in Paul's timeline above to estimate when Paul converted to the Nazarene movement. The below chart adds a fuller list of historic events into the timeline of Paul's activities. The earliest entries on this chart give us a floor for the conversion. Accepting Paul's statement from *Galatians* that he stayed in Arabia for 3 years after seeing the light on the road to Damascus places his conversion before 41 CE (second trip to Jerusalem in 44 CE less three years). The date of Paul's conversion was probably several years prior to 41 CE in order to account for the unknown interval between Paul's first and second post-conversion visits to Jerusalem. I'm inclined to place the conversion of Paul shortly after the execution of Stephen in 38 CE. Working backward from the second trip to Jerusalem in 44 CE, we need three years for Paul's sojourn in Arabia and an undefined interval between the first and second trips to Jerusalem. If Paul converted in 38 CE, then his first trip to Jerusalem came in 41 CE leaving a three year interval between the first and second trips to the Jewish capital. This is a fuller list of historical dates relating to the career of Paul.

36 CE	Crucifixion of Jesus.
37 CE	Pontius Pilate relieved of duties in Judea and returns to Rome. Death of Tiberius, Caligula becomes emperor. Herod Agrippa becomes ruler over former territories of Herod Philip.
38 CE	Stephen stoned to death in Jerusalem by order of the Sanhedrin. Paul's conversion.
39 CE	Herod Antipas removed by Caligula. Herod Agrippa becomes king of the Jewish kingdom.
41 CE	Caligula assassinated. Herod Agrippa assists Claudius in securing Roman throne. Paul's first trip to Rome to meet Peter and James; begins first missionary journey.
43 CE	Herod Agrippa executes James ben Zebedee.[256]
44 CE	Paul's second trip to Jerusalem. Herod Agrippa dies.
46 CE	Famine starts in Judea.
49-50 CE	Paul goes to Corinth finding Aquila and Priscilla who arrived there after expulsion from Rome by Claudius.
51 CE (summer)	Paul hauled before Roman tribunal of proconsul Lucius Junius Gallio Annaeus

---

[256] *Acts* 12:1. I assume this event occurred in the last year of Herod Agrippa's reign as it is related in the text just prior to the death of Agrippa.

	(brother of Seneca) in Corinth. Paul leaves Greece for Judea.[257]
52 CE	Council of Jerusalem.
54 CE	Arrest of Paul in Jerusalem by Felix.
56 CE	Festus succeeds Felix as prefect of Judea and deports Paul to Rome.[258]
57 CE	Paul arrives in Rome after ship wreck in Malta.
59 CE	Paul's two-year Roman house arrest recorded in *Acts* ends; however, *Acts* does not contain the outcome of Paul's trial before Nero nor the remainder of the events of Paul's life.
64 CE	Great fire of Rome for which Nero used Christians as a scapegoat.
65 CE	Nero orders Seneca to commit suicide.
64-68 CE	Paul executed by Nero (according to Eusebius).
68 CE	Nero commits suicide.

Conflict Between Paul and James the Just

It's safe to say that Paul of Tarsus and James the Just had their doctrinal differences prior to the execution of James by the Sanhedrin in 63 CE. The outer controversy dealt with the application of Jewish law to Gentile converts. Paul sought an exemption for the Gentiles from Jewish religious laws and James eventually authorized limited exemptions. Several incidents highlight the deep nature of this conflict. In *Galatians*, Paul records his own insubordination against the order of James that Jewish Christians not share meals with gentiles. For context on why

---

[257] *Acts* says Paul sailed for "Syria" but I believe they use the word to indicate the Roman province of Syria (which included Judea), not the modern-day country of Syria. *Acts* 18:18.

[258] We date this event from a change in Roman prefects in Judea. *Acts* tells us Paul was first tried before the Roman prefect Felix and, then, new charges were brought when Porcius Festus succeed Felix in office. See *Acts*, Ch. 25. We know from external sources that Festus succeeded Felix as prefect of Judea in 59 or 60 CE.

James may have issued such an order, *Jubilees* contains the following command supposed to have come from the mouth of Isaac to Jacob, ""Separate thyself from the nations [i.e., non-Jews], and eat not with them."[259] Peter and Barnabas, upon receiving the charge of James, acquiesced to his authority but Paul rebelled going so far as castigating his two church elders for following the edict of James. Paul flat out calls Peter a hypocrite in *Galatians*.[260] It's a serious charge made against a superior in the church hierarchy. We also see Paul's theology at work in *Galatians*, that faith and not obedience to the law leads to justification. Much more on this topic is found in Chapter 8 herein.

Paul takes another backhanded swipe at the church leaders in Jerusalem a few lines before he calls Peter and Barnabas hypocrites.

> As for those <u>who seemed to be important</u>—whatever they were makes no difference to me; God does not judge by external appearance—those men added nothing to my message. ... James, Peter and John, those reputed to be pillars, gave me and Barnabas the right hand of fellowship ... .[261] [Emphasis added.]

This passage says that the church leaders in Jerusalem (of which James was the head) only seemed to others to be important. To Paul, the perceptions of others "made no difference" as they held no real authority in his eyes. In Paul's *Letter to the Romans*, we find another smear on James when Paul carps against vegetarians.

> Accept him whose faith is weak, without passing judgment on disputable matters. One man's faith allows him to eat everything, but <u>another man, whose faith is weak, eats only vegetables.</u>[262] [Emphasis added.]

---

[259] *Jubilees* 22:16.
[260] *Galatians* 2:11-16.
[261] *Galatians* 2:6, 9.
[262] *Romans* 14:1-2.

Eusebius records that James the Just was a vegetarian. The most logical reading of this passage from *Romans* is Paul calling out James and his fellow Jerusalem Nazarenes who were vegetarians as being weak of faith, a serious slur on their character. In light of such statements, one must accept that Paul held the leaders of the Nazarene church, including James and Peter, in barely concealed contempt.

James Ordered Paul To Undergo Seven Day Purification Ritual

The Bible records one last trip of Paul of Tarsus to Jerusalem to meet with church leaders. It occurred after the Council of Jerusalem (52 CE). James sat as the head of the elders during this meeting; therefore, the date must have been prior to 63 CE. Paul opens the meeting with an account of his recent activities with the Gentiles. James replies by blasting Paul's conduct ordering him to undergo Nazarite purification to demonstrate his obedience to Jewish law. James also orders Paul to pay the expenses of the ritual for four additional church members as a penalty for his conduct.

> "You see, brother, how many thousands of Jews have believed, and all of them are zealous for the law. They have been informed that you teach all the Jews who live among the Gentiles to turn away from Moses, telling them not to circumcise their children or live according to our customs. What shall we do? They will certainly hear that you have come, so do what we tell you. There are four men with us who have made a vow. Take these men, join in their purification rites and pay their expenses, so that they can have their heads shaved. Then everybody will know there is no truth in these reports about you, but that you yourself

are living in obedience to the law."[263]
[Emphasis added.]

On this occasion, Paul obeyed James and submitted himself to ritual purification under Jewish law.

The End of Paul's Life

"What happened to Paul after his Roman imprisonment? The evidence of *Titus* and 1 and 2 *Timothy* provides an answer. * * * Several geographic references in the Pastorals (1 Tim 1:3; 2 Tim 1:17a; 2:12; 4:13, 20; Titus 1:5; 3:12), not easily reconciled with *Acts*, point to a fourth missionary journey of Paul."[264] Eusebius maintains Nero executed Paul. We know Nero died in 68 CE. Thus, if we believe Eusebius, Paul must have died before 68 CE. What caused Nero to execute Paul after the long Roman house arrest? The most logical event to associate with Paul's execution is Nero's persecution of the Christians after the great fire of Rome in 64 CE. Dating Paul's death between 64 and 68 CE fits with ancient Christian tradition on Paul. However, we are left with conjecture regarding the activities of Paul between 59 CE and his purported execution in 64-68 CE. My personal opinion is that he almost assuredly left Rome during this interval, destination unknown. Paul has always been something of mystery so it's fitting his last years are nebulous to history.

---

[263] *Acts* 21:20-24.
[264] *Paul Goes to Rome* by Dr. James Harrison, Wesley Institute.

Chapter 8
The Jesus Movement
Origins and Theology

This chapter explores the Jewish and non-Jewish origins of the theology taught by Jesus. Contrary to Paul's claim that Jesus came to obliterate the law of Moses, Jesus himself said something quite different. The words of Jesus quoted in Chapter 1 herein bear repeating, "Think not that I am come to destroy the law, or the prophets: I am not come to destroy, but to fulfill."[265] That said one must accept that certain elements of Jesus' teaching and practices innovated upon established Jewish law of the day, especially in regard to the status of women. Is there another Jewish sect whose tenants match up with those taught by Jesus? John the Baptist is generally regarded to have been influenced by the Essene sect of Judaism. Many scholars also contend Jesus came from an Essene school but there is no solid match. This chapter analyzes the teachings of Jesus against known Essene teaching and that of an Egyptian sect called the Therapeutae by Philo. Further, we'll examine a theological split between James the Just and Paul of Tarsus on the role of faith and works.

<u>Nazareth</u>

Pontius Pilate ordered a board nailed above the cross of Jesus, which read "Yeshua Nazarene King Jews". *Matthew* suggests

---

[265] *Matthew* 5:17.

the term "Nazarene" referred to Jesus' upbringing in the small town of Nazareth in Galilee.[266] If the town of Nazareth existed in the time of Jesus, it must have been extremely small such that it escaped mentioned in all written works existent in the time of Jesus.[267] We know of an ancient town about three kilometers from present day Nazareth called Japhia (destroyed in 67 CE during the Jewish revolt against Rome) but no mention of Nazareth is found in the Old Testament, Talmud, or writings of Josephus. Strange, either the town of Nazareth did not exist before the time of Jesus or Nazareth was so small in this period that no historical mention of it exists outside of the New Testament.

Acts of the Apostles presents a different view of the term Nazarene. Paul is said to be a "ringleader of the Nazarene sect".[268] Few if any of the twelve apostles nor Paul of Tarsus are identified as natives of the town of Nazareth yet, after the death of Jesus, his movement was publicly known as the "Nazarene sect". Reason dictates that when Pontius Pilate used the term "Nazarene", he referred to a religious sect (not a small village in Galilee). Further, by identifying Jesus as a Nazarene while he hung on the cross, Pilate sent a shot across the bow of the followers of Jesus then known as Nazarenes warning them against insurrection or risk the same punishment.

I submit the term "Nazarene" refers to a splinter group from the Essene movement. If we combine the terms "Nazarite" and "Essene", we get Nazarene. The term Nazarene has nothing to do, per se, with a small village in Galilee by a similar name other than the possibility that Nazareth was founded by a group of Nazarene monks seeking solitude and purification in rural Galilee.

Nazarites

The term Nazarite comes to us from fragmentary references in the Old Testament.[269] The main injunctions for those

---

[266] *Matthew* 2:23.

[267] See The Myth of Nazareth: The Invented Town of Jesus by Rene Salm (American Atheist Press 2008).

[268] *Acts* 24:5.

[269] Josephus also mentions the Nazarites. See Antiquities IV 4:4 (72).

under a Nazarite vow seems to have been: 1) do not take wine or anything made from grapes, 2) do not touch the dead, and 3) do not cut the hair on your head. Nazarite priests were dedicated to God and considered especially holy. The best-known Nazarite of the Old Testament was Samson. Unusual for Judaism, women were allowed to take Nazarite vows.[270] Given the prominent participation of women in the Nazarene movement, this marker helps connect Nazarite principles with Jesus. Further, *Acts* records Paul being ordered by James the Just to undergo a Nazarite purification ritual (having his head shaved and separating himself from the community in prayer).[271]

<u>Comparing Nazarene Sect Of Jesus With the Essenes</u>

Josephus and Philo extensively described the Essenes allowing us to create a detailed list of their tenants. The below chart presents a side-by-side comparison of the recorded description of the Essenes against the teachings of Jesus as found in the New Testament. The shaded points show variance between the Essenes and the teachings of Jesus.

Essenes per Josephus & Philo	Teachings of Jesus
Main tenants: love of God, love of virtue, and love of mankind.[272]	Two greatest commandments are love God with your whole heart and love your neighbor as yourself.[273]
Abstain from covetousness of money.[274]	"It is easier for a camel to pass through the eye of a needle than a rich man to reach the kingdom of God."[275]

---

[270] <u>See</u> JewishEncyclopedia.com.
[271] *Acts* 21:20-24.
[272] Philo, *Every Good Man is Free* (83).
[273] *Matthew* 22:37-39.
[274] Philo, *Every Good Man is Free* (84).
[275] *Matthew* 19:21.

Condemn masters as corrupting the principle of equality.[276]	"Whoever wishes to be great among you must be your servant, and whoever wishes to be first among you must be your slave."[277] See also Jesus washing feet of the apostles.
Eat communal meals.	Last supper (example of Nazarene communal meal).
Hold a common purse treating all revenue and expenses communally.	Judas held common purse for the disciples of Jesus.[278]
They carry nothing with themselves when traveling.[279]	"Take nothing for the journey-- no staff, no bag, no bread, no money, no extra tunic."[280]
They bathe in cold water.	Baptism ritual.
They inquire after roots and medicinal stones as may cure.[281]	Jesus was a healer.
Swear not to communicate the doctrines of the sect to others.	"Do not give what is holy to dogs nor throw pearls before swine."[282]
Be ministers of peace and abstain from craft connected with war.	Blessed are the peacemakers. Mt. 5:9.
Do not sacrifice animals.	"I desire compassion, not sacrifices."[283]
Rejected slavery.	A slave is not above his master.[284]

---

[276] Philo, *Every Good Man Is Free* (79).
[277] *Matthew* 20:26-28.
[278] *John* 13:29.
[279] Jewish Wars II 8:4 (125).
[280] *Luke* 9:3.
[281] Jewish Wars II 8:6 (136).
[282] *Matthew* 7:6.
[283] *Matthew* 12:7.
[284] *Matthew* 10:24.

They neglect marriage.[285]	Simon Peter was married. Mt. 8:14
Do not place oil on their bodies.	Jesus was anointed with oil.
No female members, nor children.	Women traveled with Jesus.
Stricter than other Jews in observance of Sabbath.[286]	Jesus preached a relaxed observance of the Sabbath law.
Obey government officials.[287]	Jesus was crucified for insurrection against Rome.

It's tempting to focus upon the close similarity between the two movements demonstrated in the points at the top of the list and downplay the opposition of the last six items. I'll not fall into that trap. The Essene prohibition against women members, according to Philo, bordered on the pathological.

> [N]o one of the Essenes ever marries a wife because woman is a selfish creature and one addicted to jealousy in an immoderate degree, and terribly calculated to agitate and overturn the natural inclination of a man, and to mislead him by her continual tricks.[288]

Jesus, on the other hand, was frequently recorded in the company of woman who were presented in the NT as an integral part of his movement. Also, the apostle Peter had a wife.[289] Jesus taught an "easy yoke" approach toward Jewish dietary and Sabbath laws that was antithetical to Essene doctrine. Clearly, Jesus was not an orthodox Essene as described by Philo (a contemporary of Jesus). Nor could he be considered a Pharisee. Recall Jesus railing against the "doctors of the law" (a/k/a the Pharisees).

---

[285] Jewish Wars II 8:2 (120-21) and Philo, Hypothetica (11:14).
[286] Jewish Wars II 8:9 (147).
[287] Jewish Wars II 8:7(140).
[288] Philo, Hypothetica (11:14).
[289] Matthew 8:14.

Given these differences, at most one may conclude that the Nazarene movement was influenced by the Essenes but they were not orthodox Essene Jews. Jesus innovated upon Jewish tradition. But where do we find the source for his peculiar brand of Judaism?

The Therapeutae

When casting a net beyond the Essenes, Pharisees, and Sadducees looking for theology reminiscent of the teachings of Jesus, one need not look far to find comparable concepts. Below is Philo's description of women participating in a Therapeutae feast.

> And the women also share in this feast, the greater part of whom, though old, are virgins in respect of their purity not through necessity … but out an admiration for and love of wisdom, with which they are desirous to pass their lives [and] on account of which they are indifferent to pleasures of the body, desiring not a mortal but an immortal offspring.[290]

Zoroastrians also taught their scriptures to women and allowed them to participate in religious life (although subordinate to men). Women studying scripture as fellow seekers of wisdom was something totally foreign to Judaism of the first century of the Common Era.[291] Knowing that Jesus initially lived in Egypt where the Therapeutae were based and that Zoroastrian priests (i.e., the Magi) venerated him as a king at birth gives us at least circumstantial facts to infer that Jesus borrowed from these religions in constructing his new brand of Judaism.

Backtracking to the above quote from Philo on the Therapeutae, one is struck by the fact that female community members were virgins. Philo takes pains to explain that this was by choice and not forced upon the women as with the Vestal Virgins

---

[290] Philo, On The Contemplative Life (68).
[291] Simeon ben Azzai was the first prominent rabbi to even suggest women should be taught the Torah in the 2nd century of the Common Era. His suggestion was fiercely opposed for centuries.

in Rome. "Several recent writers on the history of women's religion have made the ... point that in ascetic religious formations [including the Therapeutae], women ... achieve autonomy and power that they seem to have nowhere else in late antiquity. * * * Virginity was considered to make it possible for women to be 'as men,' or even for the distinction of gender to be abolished entirely, and this abolition was a major goal of sexual renunciation for women."[292] This concept connects with Philo's description of the first Adam: "But the man who came into existence after the image of God is what one might call an ... object of thought, incorporeal, neither male nor female, by nature incorruptible."[293] In Philo's view, the ideal human was androgynous. Consider then the words of Jesus: "There are eunuchs that made themselves eunuchs for the kingdom of heaven's sake. He that is able to receive it, let him receive it."[294] Further, we know early Christians practiced self-castration. The best known example was the Church father Origen of Alexandria, a prominent Christian priest and scholar born in the second century who castrated himself based upon the words of Jesus found in *Matthew* (quoted above). See also Paul's exhortation to abstain from sex and only marry if carried away by passion.

> It is good for a man not to have sexual
> relations with a woman. To the unmarried
> and the widows I say that it is good for them
> to remain single as I am [i.e., celibate]. But if
> they cannot exercise self-control, they should
> marry. For it is better to marry than to burn
> with passion.[295]

The emphasis upon celibacy is a prominent parallel between the Therapeutae and early Christianity. To summarize, two prominent features of the Therapeutae are found in the Nazarene movement: (a) acceptance of women members and (b) emphasis upon celibacy. The connection between early Christianity and the Therapeutae

---

[292] Carnal Israel by Daniel Boyarin (University of California Press 1993) at page 167.
[293] Philo, On the Creation (134).
[294] *Matthew* 19:12.
[295] 1 *Corinthians* 7:1&8.

was not lost on Church historian Eusebius. In fact, Eusebius gushingly described the Therapeutae as proto-Christians.[296]

The Celibate Jesus

In light of this evidence, I conclude that Jesus in all probability led a celibate life in the mold of the Essenes and Therapeutae. The concept of celibacy was never associated with Jewish kings or the Levite priesthood. Jewish kings were known for multiple wives (and concubines) liberally obeying God's commandment to Noah, "Be fruitful and multiply."[297] All Jewish kings were required to be married and Jesus claimed the Jewish throne. Thus, it is inconceivable to me that Jesus stormed the Jewish countryside drumming up popular support for his aspirations to the throne without a royal wife at his side. The average Jew of Jesus' day was vested in the concept of procreation (as found in modern Rabbinic Judaism).

Did Jesus sell out his principles in order to seek the throne by marriage to Mary Magdalene? I see Jesus as a man of principal unwilling to sacrifice a core belief merely to advance a political career hoisted upon him by his parents. One solution to the apparent conflict lies in a political yet celibate marriage. I believe this was the nature of the marriage between Jesus and Mary Magdalene. They came together in pursuit of a common goal, the restoration of the Hasmonean dynasty. It was a marriage founded upon respect and love, the true agape. Further, as it was a chaste relationship, Jesus had no biologic children meaning no direct descendants of Jesus walk the earth today.

Jesus on Jewish Law

Jesus said he did not come to abolish the law, only to fulfill it.[298] However, his emphasis in the corpus of Jewish law focused on but two Jewish commandments.

> "Teacher, which is the great commandment in the Law?"

---

[296] *The History of the Church* II:17-18.
[297] *Genesis* 1:28.
[298] *Matthew* 5:17.

> And He said to him, "You shall love
> the Lord your God with all your heart, and
> with all your soul, and with all your mind.
> This is the greatest and foremost
> commandment. The second is like it, 'You
> shall love your neighbor as yourself. On
> these two commandments depend the whole
> law and the Prophets."[299]

On the face of it, the above is very straight forward. The Gospels record Jesus exhorting followers with, "Take my yoke upon you ... for my yoke is easy and my burden is light."[300] He loosely interpreted Jewish law on such issues as the Sabbath and dietary law. For example, Jesus said, "It is not what enters into the mouth that defiles the man, but what proceeds out of the mouth, this defiles the man."[301] Despite the promise of an easy yoke, the simple rules laid down by Jesus were not to be achieved without difficulty. Jesus acknowledged that one must enter through the "narrow gate" for the wide gate led to destruction.[302] Recall that Jesus preached the renunciation of wealth.

The Parables of Jesus

It is well established that Jesus used allegorical parables when preaching to the public. A passage from *Matthew*, Chapter 13 regarding the parable of the wheat and the tares brings home this point. After Jesus told this parable to the general public, the disciples cornered him inside a home away from the crowd requesting that he explain the parable to them. Jesus responded as follows setting forth the meaning of each allegory contained in the parable.

> And He said, "The one who sows the good
> seed is the Son of Man, and the field is the
> world; and as for the good seed, these are the
> sons of the kingdom; and the tares are the

---

[299] *Matthew* 22:36-40.
[300] *Matthew* 11:29-30.
[301] *Matthew* 15:11.
[302] *Matthew* 7:13.

> sons of the evil one; and the enemy who
> sowed them is the devil, and the harvest is
> the end of the age; and the reapers are angels.
> So just as the tares are gathered up and
> burned with fire, so shall it be at the end of
> the age."[303]

One cannot understand the teaching of Jesus without a firm grasp of his parables. In my view, the *Parable of the Prodigal Son*[304] stands at the heart of Nazarene theology. We all know the story of the younger son who leaves his father's home for a distant land where he squanders his inheritance ending up wallowing in the pig sty eating food meant for the animals. He comes to his senses returning home to his father begging for forgiveness. The father graciously welcomes him home putting a ring on his finger. But what does it mean?

Obviously, the father in the parable is God and his home is the kingdom of God. The key to understanding the parable lies in the last line. The father says in response to a question from the older son, "But we had to celebrate and be glad, because <u>this brother of yours was dead and is alive again</u>; he was lost and is found." Emphasis added. Thus, when the younger son went to the foreign land he was dead but became alive again when he returned home. Said another way, the prodigal son passed from death to life upon his return home to kingdom of God from his sojourn in a foreign land.

How does one pass from death to life? The *Gospel of John* grants us insight on the topic. Jesus said, "Truly, truly, I say to you, he who hears my word, and believes him who sent me, has eternal life, and does not come into judgment, but has passed out of death into life."[305] The *Epistle of John*, believed to have been written by the same author as the Gospel, expounds further on the passage from death to life--"We know that we have passed out of death into life, because we love the brethren. He who does not love

---

[303] *Matthew* 13:37-40 (New American Standard).

[304] *Luke* 15:11-32.

[305] *John* 5:24.

abides in death."[306] The doctrines of Jesus always circle back to the overriding importance of love. Notice that this quote from the *Epistle of John* places emphasis upon love of your brethren, not love of God or Jesus Christ. We see the same formulation in the *Epistle of James* (discussed below). The foregoing discussion begs the question of how one passes from allegorical life to death in the first place. What is the symbolism of the foreign land to which the prodigal son travels? My view on the subject favors a Gnostic spin on the question best left for a separate work.

Why did Jesus speak in parables? He said, "Do not give what is holy to dogs, and do not throw your pearls before swine."[307] Jesus had an outer message for the masses and inner teaching (pearls) reserved for those with ears to hear.

Son of God

The phrase "Son of God" appears 25 times in the four NT Gospels, rarely spoken by Jesus himself. Did Jesus call himself the Son of God? Yes. Luke contains the following exchange between Jesus and the chief priest of the Sanhedrin--"And they all said, 'Are You the Son of God, then?' And He said to them, 'Yes, I am.'"[308] Does this phrase infer Jesus was a God and not a man? Despite the Sanhedrin convicting Jesus of blasphemy, I think not. When a "certain ruler" refers to Jesus as "good rabbi", Jesus rebukes the ruler for addressing him in this way because "No one is good except God alone."[309] The phrase Son of God specifically refers to Adam, the first man. See *Luke* 3:38. Adam was man of flesh and bone, although we associate supernatural qualities with him as Adam's body was said to have been fashioned by God himself. The phrase Son of God does not appear in the Torah or elsewhere in the Old Testament so it's difficult to pin down exactly what Jesus meant by the phrase other than to connect himself with Adam.

Paul calls Jesus the "last Adam" signifying the dawn of a

---

[306] 1 *John* 3:14.
[307] *Matthew* 7:6.
[308] *Luke* 22:70.
[309] *Luke* 18:18-19.

162

new age of man ushered in by Jesus.[310] Another way to look at the connection of Jesus with Adam is the concept of Adam as the perfected man, one free from sin. "The general consensus has been that (Adam) is perfect man in full possession of all human faculties, in perfect harmony of body and soul, and in a right relation to God, to woman, to himself, and to the natural world around him."[311] In this construction, Jesus was man perfected, thus, another Adam and a Son of God.

Son of Man

The phrase "Son of Man" appears 80 times in the NT Gospels, most often from the lips of Jesus himself. Other than the term Christ, it was the preferred way that Jesus referred to himself. Unlike Son of God, the phrase appears numerous times in the Old Testament helping us to place the usage by Jesus into context. The first usage of the phrase in the OT reads, "God is not a man, that he should lie, nor a Son of Man, that he should repent."[312] I take this reference from *Numbers* to mean that a Son of Man is one born with the mark of original sin. Notice also that both "man" and Son of Man are referred to in the same verse indicating that these are two separate classes. *Job* states, "How much less man, that maggot, and the Son of Man, that worm!"[313] Again, man and Son of Man are separately referred to. Man is cursed as a maggot, Son of Man slightly less so as a worm. Next we find a reference in *Psalms*, "Let your hand be upon the man of your right hand; Upon the Son of Man whom you made strong for yourself."[314] Here, the Son of Man is one made strong by God seated at his right hand.

The most prominent usage of the phrase Son of Man in the Old Testament comes from the *Book of Ezekiel*. Therein, God addresses the prophet Ezekiel thusly, "Then he said to me, 'Son of

---

[310] See The Theology of Paul the Apostle by James D. G. Dunn (Wm. B. Eerdmans Publishing Company 2006) at pages 241-42.

[311] International Standard Bible Encyclopedia by Geoffrey W. Bromiley (Wm. B. Eerdmans Publishing Company 1995).

[312] *Numbers* 23:19.

[313] *Job* 25:6.

[314] *Psalms* 80:17.

Man, stand on your feet that I may speak with you!'"[315] What follows in the text are a long list of instructions from God to the prophet. Interestingly, one of God's instructions reads, "Son of Man, propound a riddle and speak a parable to the house of Israel."[316] Jesus also spoke in parables and riddles to the house of Israel. Nothing in this text leads to the conclusion that God appointed Ezekiel as king. He was strictly a messenger from God.

Was Jesus merely a prophet from God to the Jewish people? Jewish Prophets of the Old Testament were important figures in the administration of the kingdom as they selected the king (upon divine guidance from God) and spoke out against the king when he strayed from God's will; however, they were not direct rulers. The OT formulation of the "son of man" as a prophet does fit my theory of Jesus as a Hasmonean claimant to the Jewish throne. The NT Gospels present Jesus as one who was prophesied by the prophets, although he does occasionally make prophesy himself.

> Then He took the twelve aside and said to them, "Behold, we are going up to Jerusalem, and all things which are written through the prophets about the Son of Man will be accomplished.[317]

Notice that the Son of Man is the object of prophesy in this quote from *Luke*. Is there another pre-existent model for the Son of Man that could have been the template for Jesus? Yes, the *Book of Enoch* contains such a formulation for the son of man. *Enoch*, although not canonical for Pharisaic Jews or mainstream Christianity, stands as an interesting contributor to our understanding of the origins of Christianity.

> Enoch (in common with Elijah) occupies this singular position among the Old Testament men of God, that when removed from the earth he was carried directly to heaven. A

---

[315] *Ezekiel* 2:1.

[316] *Ezekiel* 17:2.

[317] *Luke* 18:31.

man of his stamp could not but appear peculiarly well fitted to serve as a medium through which to communicate to the world revelations regarding divine mysteries, seeing that he had been deemed worthy of immediate intercourse with god. Accordingly, at a somewhat early period, probably as far back as the second century before Christ, an apocalyptic writing appeared reporting to have been composed by Enoch, which work * * * was afterwards a great favorite in the Christian Church. As is well known, it is quoted in the *Epistle of Jude* (14, 15), while many of the [church] fathers use it without hesitation ... as containing authentic divine revalation.[318]

The *Book of Enoch* prominently discusses the Son of Man. Therein, the Son of Man is a messiah figure possessed of righteousness sent by God to smite the powerful, punish the sinners and perform God's will. Specifically, he expels unjust kings from their thrones. Most importantly for our discussion, there is no connection between the Son of Man and King David in *Enoch*.

This is the Son of Man who has righteousness and with whom righteousness dwells, and who revealeth all the treasures of that which is concealed, because the Lord of spirits has chosen him * * *. And this Son of Man, whom thou hast seen shall [rouse] the kings and the mighty from their couches, and the powerful from their thrones, and shall loose the reins of the strong, and will break the teeth of the sinners. And he shall hurl the kings from their thrones, and drive them

---

[318] A History of the Jewish People in the Time of Jesus Christ, Volume 3 By Emil Schürer (T. & T. Clark 1886) at pages 54-55.

out of their kingdoms, because they magnify him not nor praise him, nor thankfully acknowledge whence the kingdom is lent to them.[319]

When Jesus declared himself to be the Son of Man, the above-description from *Enoch* is what I believe to have been the meaning he attached to these words. The Son of Man was not a passive elderly prophet dispensing wisdom. He both conveyed God's message but, also, expeled unjust kings from their kingdoms. This was a man of action.

My Kingdom Is Not of This World

I see Jesus as a religious reformer who also sought to regain the lost Hasmonean throne as an earthly king. On the face of it, his central message of peace and love appears incompatible with the goal of acquiring temporal power. However, if you accept that Jesus proclaimed himself to be the messiah then it's not a stretch to also accept that a Jewish messiah was, by definition, a king. Against that backdrop, we have an opposing statement from Jesus on this issue found in the *Gospel of John* (and only *John*). While under arrest, Pontius Pilate questioned Jesus upon the nature of his crime. The clear implication of the exchange was that a charge of sedition had been made by the chief priests against Jesus. He responded as follows.

Jesus answered, "My kingdom is not of this world. If my kingdom were of this world, then my servants would be fighting so that I would not be handed over to the Jews; but as it is, my kingdom is not of this realm."[320]

Did Jesus claim to be an earthly king? I believe the answer to this question is "yes" but the proof behind that conclusion is open to debate as reasonable minds could reach different conclusions.

Here is my view. The *Gospel According to Thomas* contains an interesting twist on the well-known NT passage where the

---

[319] A Cyclopædia of Biblical Literature, Volume 1 by John Kitto and William Lindsay Alexander (Adam and Charles Black 1876) at page 796.
[320] *John* 18:36.

Pharisees ask Jesus whether or not the Jews should pay taxes to Caesar.

> They showed Jesus a denarius and said to him, "The agents of Caesar demand taxes from us." Jesus replied, "Give the things of Caesar to Caesar, give the things of God to God, and <u>give to me that which is mine</u>."[321]
> [Emphasis added.]

The underlined portion of the quote is added by *G of T*. What earthly thing could Jesus have demanded as his? It was something that did not belong to Caesar nor to God (i.e., the kingdom of God). I believe Jesus referred to his birthright, the Hasmonean throne. God declared the Jewish lands belonged to the Jewish people, not the Romans. Jesus was there in Jerusalem to reclaim the Jewish kingdom for his people.

On the eve of his last trip to Jerusalem, Jesus told a parable in Jericho often referred to as the *Parable of the Minas*.[322] Jesus most often used allegory in his parables to convey spiritual messages. In this instance, I think the allegory contained a political message. Why would Jesus use parables to speak of political matters to the people? At this time, he was in Judea on his way to Jerusalem for his last Passover. Herodian or Sanhedrin spies certainly interspersed themselves within the crowd. How do we know this? Josephus recorded Herod having a large spy network[323] and, at the trial of Jesus before the Sanhedrin, prior public statements of Jesus were read in court as evidence. We may infer that the Sanhedrin had been building a case against Jesus for some time by employing spies to record his public statements.

The central character in this parable was a nobleman who went to a distant country to receive a kingdom for himself; however, certain citizens of this kingdom he claimed "hated him" and opposed his bid for the throne. Jesus tells the crowd that after the nobleman obtained the throne, he slew those that opposed

---

[321] *Gospel of Thomas*, Logion 100.
[322] *Luke* 19:11-28.
[323] <u>Antiquities</u> XV 10:4 (366).

him. Most agree the nobleman going to claim his kingdom was Jesus but believe the parable referred to a time when the world ends and the kingdom of God was at hand. My interpretation is that Jesus told the Judeans who opposed his kingship (i.e., the Herodians) that he will slay them when he obtains the throne if they persist in their resistance. Either it was a bluff or Jesus believed his mission's chances of success were high.

Jesus arrived in Jerusalem to claim the throne with his wife (Mary Magdalene) and his mother along with many other women of his party. I find it hard to believe he would bring the women of his family along on this venture if he expected to end up nailed to a cross. To borrow the words of Robert Burns, "The best laid plans of mice and men often go awry." Something went terribly wrong during that fateful last Passover. Jesus aborted his quest for the throne to save his followers from destruction sending Judas to cut a deal with the chief priests. Even though Jesus sacrificed himself for the welfare of his followers, he still fervently prayed to God immediately prior to his arrest asking God to allow the cup to pass.[324] This was not a suicide mission. Jesus desired to live.

That brings us back to the passage from *John 18*. The Sanhedrin had already convicted Jesus of blasphemy and turned him over to Pilate on the charge of sedition when these words were spoken. Pilate was questioning Jesus about his crime and, very understandably, Jesus did not wish to die a horrible death on the cross. He admitted he was a king but said his kingdom was not of this world. Thus, Jesus claimed innocence of the charge of attempting to overthrow Roman rule of the Jewish kingdom. Who would not bend the truth under those circumstances? The Romans executed Jesus on the charge of sedition for claiming to be the true Jewish king, thus usurping Roman authority to name Jewish kings. This was evidenced by the inscription Pilate placed on the cross (also recorded in *John*). Thus, I discount this statement of Jesus as having been made under duress while facing the imminent threat of crucifixion.

---

[324] *Matthew* 26:39.

Faith (Paul) v. Works (James)

As much as I would love to leave Paul of Tarsus in the rear view mirror, it's not possible to discuss the founding principles of the Nazarene movement without touching upon a central doctrinal question that plagues Christianity to this day. James the Just and Paul of Tarsus disagreed on that which was necessary for "justification". It's another word for perfection and signifies that one is fit for entry into the kingdom of God. This was an important theological battle in the early church. Paul emphatically declared faith alone does the job in his *Epistle to the Galatians*.

> We, who are Jews by nature and not sinners from among the Gentiles, (yet) who know that <u>a person is not justified by works of the law but through faith in Jesus Christ</u>, even we have believed in Christ Jesus that we may be justified by faith in Christ and not by works of the law, because by works of the law no one will be justified.[325] [Emphasis added.]

The brother and successor of Jesus proclaimed exactly the opposite in his epistle. "What good is it, my brothers, if someone says he has faith but does not have works? Can that faith save him? ... [F]aith of itself, if it does not have works, is dead."[326] The two are in direct conflict. James says good works were required for justification, Paul maintains faith alone was sufficient.

I view the doctrinal battle between Paul and James to have been waged progressively. Paul launched the first salvo in *Galatians*, then a response came from James in his general epistle, and, finally, a reply from Paul in *Romans*. Before getting into the theology of *Galatians*, we need to first understand what Paul meant by the term "Galatians" and, second, date the letter to properly place it into the events of *Acts*.

---

[325] *Galatians* 2:5-16.
[326] *Epistle of James* 2:14-18.

Paul's use of term "Galatians"

Confusion exists over Paul's use of this term. There was an ancient kingdom known as Galatia in the north of Asia Minor near the Black Sea. According to *Acts'* record of his missionary journeys, Paul never traveled to a city belonging to the ancient Galatian kingdom. The closest he got was Dorylaeum during his second missionary journey. After the death of the last Galatian king in 25 BC, it became a Roman province.

> In Paul's day the province of Galatia was an enormous province, usually governed by a legate rather than a consul from the Senate, until at least the time of Nero. This is what made it a praetorian province. It bordered the Black Sea in the north and the Mediterranean Sea in the south, and in theory when Paul addressed persons as Galatians, if he used the Roman provincial designations, he could be addressing people anywhere in this region. Strabo in his discussion of Galatia confirms the province included old Galatia, Pisidia, Lycaonia, parts of Pamphylia, and Cilicia Trachea.[327]

Given that no mention of cities belonging to the old kingdom of Galatia are mentioned in either *Acts* or Paul's letters, it's inconceivable to me that Paul used the term "Galatians" as referring to those persons who were ethnically Galatian from the old kingdom of Galatia. The obvious conclusion is that Paul used the term Galatians in the Roman sense as referring to residents of a Roman province by the same name. This point has significance for the Paul timeline. Paul's first missionary journey was almost exclusively conducted within the greater Roman province of

---

[327] Grace in Galatia: a commentary on St. Paul's Letter to the Galatians By Ben Witherington (Wm. B. Eerdmans Publishing Company 1998) at page 3.

Galatia, meaning the "Galatians" (i.e., residents of the Roman province of Galatia) were among Paul's earliest converts.

Dating Galatians

The *Epistle to the Galatians* mentions Paul's second trip to Jerusalem, therefore, the letter was written after this event. I previously dated Paul's second trip to Jerusalem to 44 CE (see Chapter 7). One of the main themes of the letter was the verbal flogging of Christians who gave in to the demands of the so-called Circumcision Party to obey Jewish law regarding circumcision and diet. At the Council of Jerusalem, James granted an exemption for Gentile converts from complying with some Jewish laws including circumcision and dietary rules. Paul's self-described mission was converting Gentiles. It defies reason to argue *Galatians* was written after the Council of Jerusalem. Why would Paul fail to mention the council in *Galatians* if it already occurred? Why would he continue to beat a dead horse on an issue previously settled by the Nazarene leaders at the council? There is no response to these points. Also, Paul identified the Judaizers he attacked in *Galatians* as "men from James".[328] Paul attended the Council of Jerusalem and, apparently, leveled the same charge there. The written verdict of the Council recorded in Chapter 15, verses 23-29 of *Acts* contains what appears to be a correction of the record—"Since we have heard that some of our number to whom we gave no instruction have disturbed you."[329] James, in essence, disavows the actions of members of the Circumcision Party who caused a stir among Paul's converts in Galatia. Thus, Paul would not identify the Judaizers as "from James" <u>after</u> the Council of Jerusalem. Combining these two facts, I feel confident dating *Galatians* to before the Council of Jerusalem.

At a minimum we can date *Galatians* to after 44 CE and before the Council of Jerusalem, which I previously dated to 52 CE (see Chapter 7). Evidence exists allowing us to further narrow the range of dates. Some scholars view *Galatians* as Paul's brief against the Circumcision Party written just prior to the Council of

---

[328] *Galatians* 2:12.
[329] *Acts* 15:24.

Jerusalem. Further, they see parallels between the arguments attributed to Peter at the conference (see *Acts* 15:7-11) and the text of *Galatians*.[330] I agree with this analysis. In the opening lines of *Galatians*, Paul was amazed the people of Galatia were so quick to desert him for a "different gospel" given to them by the Judaizers.[331] The second missionary trip was the last time the NT records Paul stopping in cities of the Roman province of Galatia. Paul's *Galatians* is full of boast and pomposity. I personally do not see Paul writing with such confident vim and vigor after the hearing before Gallio at Corinth. Why? Paul ended a Nazarite vow just after leaving Greece during which stay he appeared before proconsul Gallio.[332] One undertook the Nazarite vow to show humility and respect for Jewish law. For these reasons, I date *Galatians* to just after Paul's arrival in Greece after having passed through Galatia on his second missionary journey but before the hearing in Gallio's court. Relying on evidence discussed in the previous chapter regarding the expulsion of Aquila and Priscilla from Rome, I date Paul's arrival in Corinth to 50 CE. Paul appeared in court before Gallio in the summer of 51 CE, thereafter departing for Judea and the Council of Jerusalem. Thus, Paul wrote his famed *Epistle to the Galatians* in later 50 or early 51 CE.

Pauline Doctrine on Faith (*Galatians*)

The *Epistle to the Galatians* stands as a stripped-down, full throat pronouncement of the central Pauline theology. It constituted a cannon shot fired at the Nazarene "Judiazers" and their law. Here are the highlights.

- **Anyone who gives you a gospel other than Paul's is accursed.** (1:9)
- Paul received his gospel not from a man, nor was it taught to him, but through mystic revelation from Jesus Christ.

---

[330] New Testament Survey by Merrill Chapin Tenney (Wm. B. Eerdmans Publishing Company 1985) at page 270.
[331] *Galatians* 1:6-7.
[332] Paul "had his hair cut, for he was keeping a vow." *Acts* 18:18. One under a Nazarite vow did not cut his or her hair until the vow ended when the hair was offered as a sacrifice.

(1:12)

- Paul assures his readers he is not lying. [Why bother making such a statement unless your reputation is questionable and under attack?] (1:20)
- Paul says those of "high reputation" in the Jerusalem church contributed nothing to him. (2:6)
- The leaders in Jerusalem only asked he and Barnabas to give to the poor. (2: 10)
- **Peter committed hypocrisy in Antioch, for which Paul opposed him to his face.** (2:11-13)
- Jews know that man is not justified by the works of the law but through faith in Jesus Christ. No flesh is justified by works of the law. (2:15-16)
- If righteousness comes through the law, then Christ died needlessly. (2:21)
- Did you receive the spirit through works of the law or by hearing with faith? (3:2)
- **For as many as are of the works of the Law are under a curse.** * * * Now that no one is justified by the Law before God is evident; for, "the righteous man shall live by faith." (3:10-11)
- Christ redeemed us from the curse of the law. (3:13)
- Now that faith has come, we no longer live under the law. (3:23-25).
- Christ set you free, do not return to slavery. If you receive circumcision, Christ will be of no benefit to you. (5:1-2)
- Circumcision means nothing but, rather, faith working through love. (5:5)
- Walk by the spirit and you will not carry the desire of the flesh. If you are led by the spirit, you're not under the law. (5:16,18)
- "And let the one who was taught the word share all good things with him who teaches." (6:6)

Reading *Galatians* in historic context, I view it as the rantings of a brash junior member of the Nazarene church who presupposed his position based upon his royal birth. Paul condescended to James and the other leaders in Jerusalem as those of "high reputation" who contributed nothing to him, meaning James and the others possessed nothing he could learn from. He accused Peter of hypocrisy to his face. <u>He declared there to be no other gospel but the one he taught</u>. Those of works (i.e., the circumcision party) were under a curse. Those who taught a gospel other than Paul's were "accursed". Essentially, Paul named himself the one true prophet of the God Jesus Christ placing himself superior to James the Just, Peter, Barnabas, and all the other church leaders. I see Paul as drunk on his own perception of power in *Galatians*. Not too many years in the past, Paul had been out killing Nazarenes on behalf of the Sanhedrin. Fast forward perhaps a decade and Paul then sees himself as the one true recipient of the teachings of Jesus Christ above the man's own brothers and long-term followers. *Galatians* displays an astounding level of arrogance.

<u>Dating the Epistle of James</u>

We turn now to the other side of the debate. The *Epistle of James* gives us a clue to date of its authorship. It is addressed to the Jewish Diaspora outside of Jerusalem and, directly after the salutation, discusses trials and tribulations of life. No other epistle in the New Testament contains a prominent discussion of this doctrine. What large scale trials and tribulations of the Jewish Diaspora could have prompted James to address this issue at the beginning of his epistle? I believe James refers to the expulsion of Jews from Rome by Claudius in 49 CE, meaning it was written after this date. My thesis is that the *Epistle of James* was written as a rebuttal to *Galatians*; therefore, it must have come after 51 CE. But given the reference troubles in the Diaspora, I date the *Epistle of James* to 51 CE and directly after the publication of *Galatians*.

<u>James Rebukes Paul</u>

Christian scholars, in my view, go out of their way attempting to reconcile the writings of Paul and James so as to avoid conflict between the two. The energy is misspent. The

174

Epistle of James is best viewed as a rebuttal of *Galatians*. If one puts aside *Romans* and other later epistles of Paul focusing solely on *Galatians* and the *Epistle of James* by placing one against another, the contrast quickly comes into focus.

Paul's Epistle to the Galatians	Epistle of James
Rich Men	
Paul was a rich man of high birth.	"But let the brother of humble circumstances glory in his high position; and let the rich man glory in his humiliation. * * * [T]he rich man in the midst of his pursuits will fade away." 1:9-11.
Lying	
"I assure you before God I am not lying." 1:20.	"[D]o not be arrogant and so lie against the truth." 3:14.
Good Things	
"The one who is taught the word is to share all good things with the one who teaches him." 6:6 (New American Standard). Paul tells his students to share "all good things" with him. One can only assume this means material "good things". Paul sees himself as the sole earthly fount of spiritual wisdom.	"Every good thing bestowed and every perfect gift is from above, coming from the Father of lights." 1:17.
Slow to speak	
As one who rebukes church members senior to himself, Paul was slow to hear and quick to speak. Pre-conversion, he displayed anger in his	"[B]e quick to hear, slow to speak and slow to anger." 1:19.

persecution of the Nazarenes.	
Liberty from the law	
Christ set us free from the law. 5:1-15; see also, "our liberty [from the law] which we have in Christ Jesus." 2:4.	"Do not merely listen to the word, and so deceive yourselves. Do what it says. Anyone who listens to the word but does not do what it says is like a man who looks at his face in a mirror and, after looking at himself, goes away and immediately forgets what he looks like. But the man who looks intently into the perfect law that gives freedom (liberty), and continues to do this, not forgetting what he has heard, but doing it, he will be blessed in what he does." 1:22-25.
The religion of those who boast is worthless	
"[I]f any man is preaching to you a gospel contrary to that which you received from [me], let him be accursed." 1:9.	"If anyone thinks himself to be religious, and yet does not bridle his tongue * * *, this man's religion is worthless." 1:26.
Favoritism for the rich	
Paul was not only rich but, also, appeared to court the wealthy to become Christians.	Do not show favoritism to a rich man "with a gold ring and dressed in fine clothes * * * [paying] special attention to the one in fine clothes." 2:2-3.
Failure to follow the whole law	
Paul was famous for abrogating the law choosing only to follow the "love your neighbor" maxim.	"For whoever keeps the whole law and yet stumbles in one point, he has become guilty of all." 2:10.
Faith without works is dead	
"For as many as are of the works of the law are under a	'[F]aith, if it has no works, is dead." 2:17; restated same

curse. * * * [N]o one is justified by the law." 3:10-11.	point at 2:26.
Example of Abraham	
"Even so Abraham believed God, and it was reckoned to him as righteousness. Therefore, be sure that it is those who are of faith who are sons of Abraham." 3:6-7.	"Was not Abraham our father justified by works when he offered up Isaac his son on the altar? You see that faith was working with his works, and as a result of the works, faith was perfected. * * * You see that a man is justified by works and not by faith alone." 2:20-24
Judgment of teachers	
Paul refers to himself as a teacher. 6.6.	"Let not many of you become teachers, my brethren, knowing that as such we will incur a stricter judgment." 3:1.
Sin of boastfulness	
Paul boasts that his gospel is the only true one, having been revealed (not taught) to him by Jesus Christ. 1:9 and 11-12. Paul also boasts of having rebuked Peter "to his face" for hypocrisy. 2:11-13.	"So also the tongue is a small part of the body, and yet it boasts of great things. * * * And the tongue is a fire, the very world of iniquity; the tongue is set among our members as that which defiles the entire body." 3:5-6.
Friendship with the world	
Paul was a Herodian prince with friends in high places. Preferential treatment from proconsul Gallio is but one example.	"[F]riendship with the world is hostility toward God? Therefore whoever wishes to be a friend of the world makes himself an enemy of God." 4:4.
Submit to God and cleanse yourself	
Paul underwent a Nazarite vow just after his appearance before Gallio in Greece and, again, during his last reported trip to	Submit therefore to God. * * * Cleanse your hands, you sinners; and purify your hearts, you double-minded. * * *

Jerusalem. One undertakes these vows to demonstrate submission to God and humbleness.	Humble yourselves in the presence of the Lord." 7-10.
Wisdom	
Paul makes faith the centerpiece of his theology. He never mentions wisdom.	"Those who lack wisdom, ask for it from God with faith." 1:6. Does James infer those who rely on faith lack wisdom? A reasonable view.

In my eyes, the evidence supporting the position that the *Epistle of James* was written as a polemic against Paul is powerful. Without using his name, James condemns the theology and actions of Paul. I found the second entry on the list (Lying) particularly interesting. In my experience, a witness who proclaims he is not lying does so in response to repeated accusations that he is a liar. The NT records two instances where Paul was hauled before courts and accused of violations of the law. One can infer lying was among the charges hurled at Paul. In *Galatians* we find Paul attempting to shed the tag of liar. James reasserts that Paul was a liar in my reading of the *Epistle of James*.

Verdict of Scholars upon the Theological Battle Royale

Scholars have struggled with this issue for millennia. Writing in the sixteenth century, Martin Luther basically urinated on the *Epistle of James* declaring it unapostolistic chiefly because it contradicted Paul but, also, for failing to speak of the passion of Jesus.[333] Who did this James the Just fellow think he was anyway disagreeing with Paul? Luther kicked off a wave of scholarly irrationality on the issue covering the last 500 years. The argument of esteemed Christian scholars center around two main tenants: (a) James and Paul use the term "works" differently so they really are not in disagreement and (b) James, if he truly attacked the doctrine

---

[333] See A commentary on the Epistle of James by Sophie Laws (A. and C. Black 1980) at page 1.

of Paul, was a slow-witted snot who just didn't understand Paul. One of the more pernicious attacks I've read straddles both points.

> [I]f James is opposing Pauline thought, then he clearly does not understand Paul. Paul always speaks of "the works of the law," meaning the markers of Judaism, especially circumcision and dietary laws, <u>never of works per se</u>. * * * Thus James must at least be misunderstanding Paul, as Joachim Jeremiah pointed out years ago. If he had had direct contact with Pauline thought as expressed in *Romans*, we would indeed have to say, "Frère Jacques, dormez-vous?"[334] [Emphasis added.]

Translating the French phrase borrowed from the children's' song, it reads "Brother John [James], are you sleeping?" The above passage calls out James the Just as stupid for not understanding the writings of the august Paul of Tarsus, former executioner of Christians, late convert to the movement. I must admit to being horrified upon reading these raw words. The pronouncements of Paul most often held up in rebuttal to James by academics come from Paul's *Epistle to the Romans*. The easy response to the critics is that James had not read *Romans* because it hadn't been written at the time James authored his epistle. James wrote specifically to rebut the outrageousness of *Galatians*. Paul wrote *Romans* as a reply to *Galatians*.

Beyond the cheap-shot of James sleeping on Paul, the above-quoted attack also infers that Paul and James use the word "works" differently. We have the quizzical phrase that Paul does not speak of works "per se". Say what? The Latin term "per se" is often used in the American legal profession. It literally means "as such" and connotes "without further explanation". I believe the author's point was that Paul never speaks of works in the general sense but only specifically. The argument is that when Paul

---

[334] <u>James the Just and Christian Origins</u> by Prof. Bruce Chilton (Brill Academic Publishers 1999) at page 52. The "Frère Jacques" reference comes courtesy of Klaus Haacker.

trivializes "works", he refers to works in accordance to Mosaic laws that he, Paul, disagrees with ("especially circumcision and dietary laws"). The upshot of this defense is that Paul asserts that justification is not to be had by observance of lesser Jewish laws such as circumcision and dietary laws. James the Just was unable to fathom the nuance with which Paul used the terms "works" and "laws", leading to his gross error. Supporters of this position point to *Romans* Ch. 4 where, in the midst of railing against works as worthless, Paul mentions circumcision.[335] They argue that Paul only disliked some Jewish laws, not all religious laws.

What works of law would Paul agree lead to justification? Why bother with this entirely tortured argument that Paul valued some unspecified works of law unless the views of Paul and James on the issue intersected at some point? The answer is they never intersect. There is no law (or laws) whose observance Paul agrees lead to justification. A man "is not justified by the works of the law but through faith in Christ Jesus."[336] A pagan could love his neighbors to death but will never be justified by said act in Paul's judgment. For that, Paul required faith in Jesus Christ. He referred to this principle as "the law of faith,"[337] essentially meaning that faith supplanted and swallowed up the law. Paul had but one law—faith. For Paul, good deeds were merely a byproduct of faith. For James, a man could believe in God with all his heart but without love, humility, and detachment from the allure of the physical world his faith was worthless.

Defense of James

What was the main thrust of the *Epistle of James*? To do good works in accordance with the royal law, love your neighbor as yourself. And how did one put this law into action? James said to be humble and renounce the material world as failure to do so led to destruction. James castigated material wealth and boastfulness many times in his epistle. Stringing together the major points of

---

[335] To be fair to Prof. Chilton, he's not certain James addressed Paul directly in his epistle. His defense of Paul against James was given on a "what if" basis.
[336] *Galatians* 2:16.
[337] *Romans* 3:27.

the epistle, it follows that one cannot love your neighbor as yourself if he or she also was boastful, in "friendship with the world" or possessed material wealth. In renouncing worldliness and by performing good works one became a "doer of the law". These principals were also taught by Jesus. Recall his famous saying, "It is easier for a camel to pass through the eye of a needle than a rich man to reach the kingdom of God."[338] We also have the story of the rich man who came to Jesus asking what else must he do in addition to obeying the commandments and Jesus told him to sell all his possessions and give to the poor.[339] In the *Beatitudes* (*Matthew*, Ch. 5) Jesus set forth examples of how one put love in action—blessed are the poor in spirit, blessed are the gentle, and blessed are the peacemakers.

Has Paul complied with the law by reciting the platitude in his letters that he loved his brothers in Christ? Not according to James. An important step was missing. "[F]riendship with the world is hostility toward God. Therefore whoever wishes to be a friend of the world makes himself an enemy of God." *James* 4:4. The same concept comes from the mouth of Jesus in the *Gospel of Thomas*: "If you do not abstain from the world you will not find the kingdom."[340] Paul consorted with the wealthy and powerful, which is not in keeping with the teachings of James (nor, in my view, Jesus). "For whoever keeps the whole law and yet stumbles in one point, he has become guilty of all." *James* 2:10. James had not slept on Paul. The brother of Jesus called out a boastful, arrogant and wealthy man of high birth who was in friendship with the material world and those possessing power. Circumcision and dietary laws were mere red herrings having little to no bearing upon the underlying dispute between Paul and James.

Jesus and the Pharisees

Finally switching topics away from Paul of Tarsus, Rabbi Harvey Falk argues in his book Jesus the Pharisee[341] that Jesus was

---

[338] *Matthew* 19:24.
[339] *Matthew* 19:16-21.
[340] Logion 27.
[341] Paulist Press, 1985.

in fact a member of the Hillel Pharisaic school of Judaism. It's an interesting premise, even though I disagree. His central thesis is that "Jesus never intended to abolish Judaism, only to establish a new religion for the Gentiles based upon the ancient Noahide Commandments transmitted by Moses at Mount Sinai."[342] The seven Noahide laws were against idolatry, murder, theft, sexual promiscuity, blasphemy, and eating flesh cut from a living animal while the seventh required setting up courts of justice. These commandments, if followed, were an avenue under Jewish law for non-Jews to live a righteous life and thereby gain a place in the Jewish heaven (the world to come). Jews by birth, however, were required to follow the whole of the Mosaic law. At the Council of Jerusalem (around 52 CE), the early Christian Church adopted this two-tier approach to Jewish law for Gentile converts. The Jewish laws enforced upon early Christian Gentile converts bear striking resemblance to the Noahide Commandments. I'm with Rabbi Falk up to this point.

After noting the similarities between Essene writings found in the Dead Sea Scrolls and Christian texts, Rabbi Falk states that he "discovered a passage in the Jerusalem Talmud recording that Menahem the Essene and one hundred and sixty disciples had left the Jewish community about 20 BCE on a mission to the Gentiles."[343] The Talmud and Maimonides "indicate that Moses obligated the Jews to spread knowledge of the Noahide Commandments to the Gentiles."[344] The Rabbi then takes a shot at connecting Rabbi Hillel, president of the Sanhedrin and founder of an important rabbinic school, with the Essenes. It's a tenuous connection but, given how little is known about the Essenes, a position not easily confirmed or denied. The long and the short of Rabbi Falk's theory is that he views Jesus as having operated within Jewish law as an emissary to the Gentiles while affiliated with the Hillel school.

Further, when the NT quotes Jesus railing against "Pharisees", Rabbi Falk maintains Jesus was actually speaking

---

[342] Ibid at page 4.
[343] Ibid at page 6.
[344] Ibid at pages 51-52.

against members of the Pharisaic school of Shammai who were the bitter rivals of Bet Hillel. Such an argument helps explain why the NT records Jesus on somewhat friendly terms with some Pharisee rabbis going so far as to dine with them in their homes.[345] Hillel gave the whole of the Torah as, "That which is hateful to you do not unto your fellow man." His was the more liberal of the two Pharisaic schools. Hillel's grandson, Gamaliel, is named as the teacher of Paul of Tarsus[346] and stands as the only rabbi given favorable treatment in the NT (outside of Jesus and John the Baptist).

It is difficult to connect Jesus to the school of Hillel beyond a few similarities in their sayings. In particular, Jesus' treatment of women went well beyond what any Pharisaic school of its day would have sanctioned. Also, those instances recorded in the NT where Jesus dined with Pharisees reveal a wary antagonism between Jesus and his hosts.[347] Remember further that the Pharisees numerically dominated the Sanhedrin and this body convicted Jesus of blasphemy in short order. In my view, the most that can be said is that one group of Pharisees (which I am willing to accept were from the school of Hillel) attempted to engage Jesus in respectful discourse on his view of Jewish law while still being in fundamental disagreement. However, I find this line of reasoning important to aid readers of the NT in seeing Jesus as a Jewish rabbi debating points of law with competing rabbis. This view of Jesus is completely at odds with Paul's claim made in *Galatians* that Jesus came to set all mankind free from the curse of Jewish law.

---

[345] See *Luke* 14:1.
[346] *Acts* 22:3.
[347] See *Luke* 11:37 where Jesus condemns his Pharisee lunch companions.

Chapter 9
Antipater ben Herod
(The Father of Jesus)

The story of Antipater ben Herod is a fantastic Greek-style tragedy. The eldest son of one of the most powerful rulers in the Roman world was exiled at age five with his mother to Rome upon Herod's marriage to his Hasmonean queen. Herod recalled Antipater and his mother (Doris) twelve years later after executing Mariamne bat Alexander, Herod's Hasmonean wife. Antipater rose up through the ranks of Herod's sons to the exalted position of coregent (essentially co-king). He became crown prince after Herod executed his Hasmonean sons (Aristobulus and Alexander) in 7 BCE. Thereafter, Antipater stood first in line of succession to Herod's throne. Although Josephus never specifically states that Antipater also became coregent, it's rather obvious from the description of his powers given by Josephus that this was the state of affairs in the last days of Herod's reign. See *Supplement 4* at the end of this book. Herod executed his eldest son five days before his own death. The king prosecuted and convicted Antipater of the charge of conspiracy to commit patricide (i.e., the killing of one's own father). Why would Antipater risk losing everything to assassinate his father when he was already coregent and named as prime heir in Herod's will? At this time Herod was in very poor health and expected to die at any moment. The story of Antipater as told by Josephus defies logic.

Reassessing Antipater in light of the identity of his royal wife Mariamne bat Antigonus (Mary the mother of Jesus) I conclude Prince Antipater was framed by his father Herod, who lacked the authority to execute his son. The motive for wishing his son and heir dead was Antipater's secret marriage to the daughter of Antigonus, Herod's mortal enemy. Josephus only mentioned the daughter of Antigonus in one instance during the trial of Antipater.[348] Herod systematically exterminated the Hasmoneans over his entire thirty-four year reign as king. Then, at the end of Herod's life, Antipater married the only surviving daughter of Antigonus who must have been in hiding all those many years. Herod surely would have killed her had he known of her existence. This marriage irretrievably severed the relationship between father and son as it undid all of Herod's plans for his future dynasty. Herod brought charges against Antipater before Publius Quinctilius Varus, then Roman governor of the Syrian province. The trial was held in Jerusalem with a stenographer transcribing the evidence, which Varus sent to Caesar Augustus accompanied by his own report and recommendation for disposition of the case. It was Augustus who held the final say upon the fate of Antipater and his verdict contained a twist not apparent from a superficial reading of Josephus.

Herod's Hasmonean Extermination Program

Herod's father (another Antipater) was Idumean and a commoner. Herod's mother, however, was Nabatean and "daughter of one of their eminent men."[349] The ancient Nabatean kingdom occupied the desert region to the east of Judea with Petra its capital. In today's parlance, we would call Herod an Arab. He most likely possessed a few drops of Jewish blood from his Idumean side given the historical interbreeding between Judea and Idumea but not enough to alter the view of Herod as an ethnic Arab. The Hasmoneans conquered Idumea forcibly converting its inhabitants to the Jewish faith a few generations prior to the birth

---

[348] Antiquities XVII 5:2 (92).
[349] Antiquities XIV 7:5 (121).

of Herod. Thus, he was born into the Jewish religion. The *Book of Deuteronomy* contains a special rule for conversion of Idumeans (a/k/a Edomites) such as Herod stating that they may not "enter the assembly of the Lord" until the "sons of the third generation" after conversion to Judaism.[350] Although ethnically Arab, Herod probably qualified to enter the Jewish assembly of the Lord by being born in the third generation after the Hasmoneans converted his Idumean forefathers. The point being that Herod's Jewish credentials were weak, much less so for the office of Jewish king.

The partnership between the Romans and Herod extended back to Herod's father Antipater, whose initial political patron was Pompey Magnus (and later Julius Caesar). Hyrcanus II, a weak Hasmonean ruler, stood as the titular leader of the Jewish kingdom near the end of the Hasmonean dynasty but Antipater the Idumean held the real power as de facto Roman client rule. Antipater the Idumean was poisoned perhaps in retaliation for the assassination of Aristobulus II (a Hasmonean rival of Hyrcanus). The most likely party behind the assassination of Herod's father was Antigonus, the only surviving son of Aristobulus II. Soon thereafter the Herodian apple cart tumbled over and all hell broke loose in 40 BCE. Antigonus overran the Jewish kingdom at the head of a Parthian army taking advantage of a Roman civil war following the assassination of Julius Caesar. The first phase of this war left Herod's elder brother Phasael dead. [351] Herod narrowly escaped capture himself while fleeing Judea for his life. Antigonus crowned himself Jewish king and high priest banishing Hyrcanus II (his uncle) to Babylon inside Parthia.

After fleeing Judea, Herod completed a dangerous winter crossing to Rome accompanied by a small body of men. He landed in Italy depleted of resources. This was the low point of his entire political career. But fortune smiled on Herod ben Antipater. When the Romans looked around Palestine for allies in 40 BCE they found Herod and his younger brothers Joseph and Pheroras as the last men standing. Marc Antony became Herod's new

---

[350] *Deut.* 23:7-8.

[351] Herod's elder brother Phasael killed himself while imprisoned by Antigonus.

political patron nominating him king of the Jewish kingdom, which the senate rubber-stamped. The Romans needed a nominal Jewish king who they could send to war against Antigonus and the Parthians in Palestine after their Hasmonean ally (Hyrcanus) was shipped to exile in Parthian territory.

Replenished by Rome but receiving precious little in the way of troop support, Herod rose from the ashes counterattacking Antigonus. What appeared the previous year to have been his crushing defeat flipped the next spring to Herod on the attack. However, his younger brother Joseph died on the field of battle against Antigonus, having attacked Jewish-Parthian forces under Antigonus in Judea on his own initiative while Herod was north assisting Antony in another theatre of battle. Herod overcame this setback eventually capturing Jerusalem in 37 BCE. Upon capturing the capital, Herod immediately began exterminating the Hasmoneans except for a select few who became members of his family. He transported Antigonus in chains to Antioch and bribed Marc Antony to execute the former king. Josephus quotes Strabo's explanation for the reasoning behind the beheading of Antigonus as follow:

> [F]or by no torments could [the Jews] be forced to call him king, so great a fondness they had for their former king; so he thought that this dishonorable death would diminish the value they had for Antigonus's memory, and at the same time would diminish the hatred they bare to Herod."[352]

This quote from Strabo (found in Josephus) lays bare the crux of Herod's political situation after capturing Jerusalem. The Jewish people had no inclination to receive Herod as king and fervently desired the return of Antigonus to rule them. Further, even after the execution of Antigonus, Herod feared "Antigonus's memory." For this reason, Herod found it necessary to exterminate his entire family to ensure that no relative of

---

[352] Antiquities XV 1:2.

Antigonus came forward to claim the hearts of the Jewish people by resurrecting the memory of Antigonus.

Herod desperately wished to be accepted as a Jewish king and the key to this strategy was his marriage to a Hasmonean princess, Mariamne bat Alexander who was the granddaughter of two Hasmonean kings (Hyrcanus II and Aristobulus II). The ploy was not as great of a stretch as one may imagine. Remember that King David had been born a commoner, the youngest son of a Judean shepherd named Jesse. The Bible tells us God led the prophet Samuel to select David from among Jesse's sons. David then consolidated his claim to power by marrying the daughter of the current king (Saul), whose kingdom David eventually seized by force. If the Jewish people believed God controlled all things, then they would beleieve Herod was favored by God or so the reasoning went. He sat on the Jewish throne married to the granddaughter of two Jewish kings lending his reign an air of legitimacy it completely lacked without Mariamne.

In my view Herod hatched a plan from the inception of his dynasty to utilize Hasmonean blood to infuse Jewish nobility into his own family tree. But the plan didn't stop there. The Hasmoneans represented a risk to Herod's throne. Had not the Parthians backed Antigonus with an army leading to the deaths of Herod's two brothers (Phasael and Joseph)? Herod could not risk leaving Hasmonean royals still drawing breath. He tried to assassinate all Hasmoneans of royal lineage after fathering children by his queen, Mariamne bat Alexander. The below-table lists all Hasmoneans known to have survived Herod's capture of Jerusalem in 37 BCE.

Hasmoneans post 37 BCE	Fate
Aristobulus ben Alexander (Brother of Mariamne)	Became high priest (36 BCE); Assassinated by Herod (36 BCE).
Hyrcanus II (Grandfather of Mariamne)	Executed by Herod (30 BCE).
Mariamne bat Alexander	Married Herod (38 BCE); Executed by Herod (29 BCE).
Alexandra bat Hyrcanus	Executed by Herod (28 BCE).

(Mother of Mariamne)	
Sons of Babas[353]	Executed by Herod (28 BCE).
Unnamed daughter of Antigonus (Wife of Antipater)	Fate unknown.

Do you see the pattern? The Hasmoneans within Herod's family were window dressing. He only desired their bloodline then executed the royals after siring his own children of Hasmonean descent. Herod even went so far as to execute his own Hasmonean sons (Aristobulus and Alexander) after they had fathered children. Herod had no intention of allowing a 50/50 Hasmonean-Herodian king to sit upon his throne. He planned for his blood to predominate within the Jewish royal family after his death.

Antipater was Herod's only son from his own ethnic homeland of Idumea. Josephus records Antipater with two Hasmonean wives at the time of his execution: (a) Mariamne bat Aristobulus (his young niece) and (b) the unnamed daughter of Antigonus. When Antipater became coregent this repeated the archetype Herod established—Idumean king with Hasmonean queen. But Herod planned for the Hasmonean queen to also be his descendant, making his blood predominate within the royal family. I see it as fulfilling Herod's long-held master plan for his dynasty. Yet something went terribly wrong in Herod's final days. The only possible source of the fallout between Herod and his son Antipater was the son's marriage to the daughter of Antigonus. Why was that a problem? Because it could have led to the resurrection of the Hasmonean dynasty. The progeny of Antipater ben Herod and the daughter of Antigonus (if allowed to live) could have been viewed by the Jewish people as the continuation of the royal line of Antigonus with history regarding Herod as an Idumean interloper who merely disrupted the august Hasmonean

---

[353] The "sons of Babas" were Hasmoneans found living in territory controlled by Costobarus, brother-in-law of Herod and then governor of Idumea. Herod also killed his brother-in-law for granting safe haven to the sons of Babas. Antiquities XV 7:10 (259-266).

dynasty. If the marriage produced children, then Antigonus' blood would stand on equal footing with that of Herod in the third Herodian generation to sit on the throne (assuming Antipater succeeded his father and passed on the throne to his own son). Herod intended for his own blood to grow in proportion with each succeeding Herodian generation. Antipater's marriage to the daughter of Antigonus threatened to undo the legacy Herod planned for himself. Wracked by illnesses of every imaginable sort, Herod soldiered on in his last days with the sole object of securing his place in history. Antipater threatened to ruin his father's plans and died because of it.

Antipater's Second Hasmonean Wife

Why did Antipater marry a second Hasmonean wife? It's a vexing question given the risk Antipater undertook by wedding the daughter of Antigonus, an act he surely knew would cause Herod to blow like a volcano should he find out. Herod spent his entire reign executing pure-blooded Hasmoneans and severely punished those who failed to adhere to this policy. For example, he executed his brother-in-law (Costobarus) for merely harboring Hasmoneans in Idumea. And the royal princess wed by Antipater wasn't just any Hasmonean; she was a daughter of Antigonus. He caused the deaths of Herod's brothers Phasael and Joseph and was likely behind the assassination of Herod's father. On top of that, Antigonus was the last Hasmonean king. The bloodline of Antigonus' daughter held the last hope for resurrecting the Hasmonean dynasty that Herod worked his entire life erasing from Jewish consciousness. Why did Antipater marry this woman knowing the action was so dangerous? Why not just wait for Herod to die?

I've probably spent more time contemplating this issue than any surrounding the Herodians. Let us slip into Antipater's shoes attempting to fathom the motivation for his decision. Antipater became crown prince and coregent most likely in 6 BCE after the execution of his Hasmonean brothers the prior year. At this point, Antipater jointly ruled with Herod. But one year later in 5 BCE Antipater fled the Jewish kingdom for Rome fearing for his own safety in Herod's court. How and why did Antipater's status change so rapidly? First, there was blowback from Antipater's role in the execution of his Hasmonean brothers. The Jews had not taken the execution of their Hasmonean princes lightly. Antipater, as the major beneficiary of their death, was seen as the primary driving force behind their execution.

> [I]ntolerable hatred fell upon Antipater from the nation, though he had now an indisputable title to the succession, because they all knew that he was the person who contrived all the calumnies against his brethren.[354]

Josephus singles out Antipater for scorn to a degree unmatched by his recorded actions. Antipater was but one of many voices whispering evil words into Herod's ear regarding his Hasmonean brothers. Salome bat Antipater (Herod's sister) appears to have been a prime mover in this palace intrigue as well. Ultimately, Herod made the call to terminate the lives of his sons. Those out of power eternally lust for power in any ancient royal court. Once Antipater became top dog, those family members not within his inner circle conspired against him. Antipater allied himself with his uncle Pheroras. His aunt Salome acted as the ringleader of the Herodian opposition camp.

Antipater departed for Rome and partied with the elite at Caesar's court for an entire year waiting for his father to die. Yet Herod tenaciously clung to life while the anti-Antipater forces gathered strength in Jerusalem. The first sign of trouble for Antipater was Pheroras' mysterious death with indications from the servants that he had been poisoned. Unbeknownst to Antipater, Herod conducted his own investigation by torturing the servants of Pheroras ostensibly to find the killer of his brother. Instead, the torture examination inexplicably uncovered a plot by Antipater to poison Herod. Funny thing about torture, the witness under examination says whatever the examiner desires. Essentially Antipater stood convicted via torture induced testimony while still

---

[354] Jewish Wars I 28:1.

in Rome. How did Herod gain Antipater's voluntary return to Jerusalem under such circumstances? That's the money question!

Josephus reports in Antiquities that Herod wrote to his son in Rome complaining about his mother (Doris).[355] Reading between the lines, Herod threatened to banish Doris from the kingdom. Further, Herod promised "if [Antipater] came quickly, he would lay aside the complaints he had against his mother."[356] Jewish Wars contains additional information that Antipater knew his mother had already been banished before he sailed from Rome.[357] The whole scenario laid out by Josephus doesn't wash. Antipater previously watched his father execute two of his brothers and a laundry list of other family members. He was hunkered down in Rome specifically because he feared for his own safety back home. Then his uncle (and only true ally at Herod's court) mysteriously died, perhaps having been poisoned. Why on earth would Antipater sail for Judea under those circumstances knowing that to do so risked death? To restore his mother's social standing at Herod's court? No way. She had already been banished.

I reason Herod discovered Antipater's secret marriage to the daughter of Antigonus and held her captive in Jerusalem. Antipater had not been able to smuggle her out of the country when he departed for Rome. Antigonu's daughter was the bait used to lure Antipater home. Josephus left unsaid the threat by Herod to kill Mariamne bat Antigonus[358] unless Antipater promptly returned to Jerusalem. Those hard of heart may ask why didn't Antipater allow Herod to kill his wife and thereby save his own life? Antipater clearly thought about the situation long and hard before sailing home. He put into the Cilician port of Celenderis, well north of Judea and not on a direct path home, to ponder the matter.

---

[355] Antiquities XVII 5:1 (83).
[356] Jewish Wars I 31:3 (608).
[357] Jewish Wars I 31:3 (608).
[358] As stated earlier in this work, Josephus never gave the proper name of the daughter of Antigonus who married Antipater. I surmise it was Mariamne based upon the genealogy for Jesus found in Luke 3.

Two factors may have swayed Antipater to decide to sail home into the belly of the beast. First, Antipater "was dismissed with honor by Caesar" upon leaving Rome. Only Caesar could order his death in spite of his father's wishes and Antipater must have trusted that Caesar would not order his execution. Second, the elderly Herod suffered poor health and was near death by all accounts. Josephus described Herod's ailments in the last days of his life as follows:

> The distemper seized upon his whole body, and greatly disordered all its parts with various symptoms; for there was a gentle fever upon him, and an intolerable itching all over the surface of his body, and continual pains in his colon, and dropsical tumors about his feet and inflammation of the abdomen, and a purification of his private member that produced worms.[359]

What was so valuable about the bloodline of Antigonus' daughter that Antipater risked everything to save her? Antipater stood at the head of a long list of Herod's sons. Being named heir in the king's will was but the beginning round in a continual struggle for control of the Jewish kingdom. Mariamne bat Antigonus was the last pure-blooded Hasmonean princess then alive. With her as his queen, Antipater could spawn offspring of the most royal Hasmonean blood unmatched by the competing Herodians. Bloodlines were immensely powerful political tools in this age. She constituted his one shot at becoming a strong Jewish king towering above his siblings. His queen (Mariamne bat Antigonus) would have been exceedingly popular with the Jewish people. Mariamne was Antipater's best hope for gaining the support of the Jewish people for his reign. Without the support of the Jewish people, Antipater would be a weak ruler susceptible to being toppled by the Romans at the behest of competing Herodians. This in fact was the fate of his younger brother

---

[359] Jewish Wars I 33:5 (656).

Archelaus who succeeded Herod as Jewish king. Antipater risked all for the chance to have a long and powerful reign.

<u>Antipater's Execution, The Final Plot Twist</u>

Antipater rolled the dice by returning to Judea in a bid to save his royal wife but came up snake eyes. Herod ordered Antipater arrested the moment his ship docked in Caesarea. Then a show trial ensued before Varus in Jerusalem consisting of a parade of tortured witnesses. Herod bribed Varus so his verdict was never in doubt. However, Antipater's fate was far from decided until the very last moment of his life. Antipater could only be executed with authorization from Caesar Augustus. Of all Herod's sons, Antipater spent the most time in Rome having ingratiated himself to the important persons of the city. It was by no means a foregone conclusion Augustus would approve the recommended sentence of death forwarded to him by Varus. Each day Herod survived during 4 BCE constituted a minor miracle given his afflictions. Forty days was a brisk round trip from Caesarea to Rome.[360] Bad weather (<u>see</u> the journey of Paul of Tarsus to Rome) could easily double that interval.

While awaiting a final verdict from Caesar Augustus, Herod moved to his winter palace at Jericho taking his imprisoned son along as well. Josephus records a series of events occurring while Herod resided at his winter palace awaiting the verdict from Caesar. <u>See</u> *Supplement 2* herein. What we have from Josephus indicates several months elapsed between the trial and the arrival of Caesar's verdict at Jericho. Clearly, Herod survived up to this point solely by force of will power alone given the condition of his health. He was determined to see the death of his eldest son.

Eventually, the long awaited dispatch from Rome arrived in Jericho. Josephus records that "Caesar left it to Herod to act as became a father and a king, and either to banish [Antipater] or to take away his life, which he pleased."[361] The verdict Herod hoped for, no? Immediately after reading the verdict Herod called for a

---

[360] <u>See</u> "Speed Under Sail of Ancient Ships" by Lionel Casson, Transactions of the American Philological Association, Vol. 82 (1951), pp. 136-148.

[361] <u>Antiquities</u> XVII 7:1 (182); <u>see</u> parallel passage at <u>Jewish Wars</u> II 33:7 (661).

knife ostensibly to cut an apple but, instead, tried to plunge the knife into his heart. Only the quick action of Herod's cousin Achiabus prevented the king from killing himself. The sequence of events recorded by Josephus makes absolutely no sense. Obviously the verdict from Caesar was not to the liking of Herod, otherwise he would not have tried to kill himself. Something has been edited out of the text. My reasoned conclusion is that Caesar wished to allow Herod to save face by confirming the verdict with the added option of banishment; however, Caesar must have suggested to Herod his desire that Antipater be banished instead of executed. A request from Caesar Augustus constituted a de facto command. Herod read the correspondence from Caesar as a command that Antipater be sent into exile and, therefore, tried to commit suicide. This is the only scenario that makes sense of what Josephus records.

This strange series of events did not end with Herod's attempted suicide. As word spread through the palace that the king attempted to kill himself (perhaps, in the confusion, some believed he had succeeded), wails and screams of lamentation echoed all the way down to the dungeon in the lower level of the palace. Antipater concluded Herod had died based on the wailing above and tried to purchase his freedom from the guards through the promise of large sums of money. A guard went to the upper floors of the palace and reported the situation down in the dungeon to the king. This sent Herod into a rage. He ordered the immediate execution of Antipater, and then died himself five days later.

I believe there were repercussions from Herod's failure to follow the instructions from Caesar Augustus. Herod's last will named Archelaus king and prime heir; however, none of Herod's sons were awarded the prized title of king by Caesar. This is not conclusive proof that Herod rebelled against Caesar's command relative to Antipater but it does stand as a piece of corroborating evidence. Had Herod honored the request from Caesar that Antipater be banished, Antipater most probably became king upon Herod's death. He was closest to Caesar among Herod's sons. Further, the only will of Herod on file with the Vestal Virgins in

Rome at the time of Herod's death named Antipater king.[362] And if Herod had obeyed the command from Caesar that Antipater live, then not only would Antipater have become king upon Herod's death but his son Jesus would have been his heir. In my view, this is why Pontius Pilate declared Jesus to be a true king of the Jews.

Doris, Mother of Antipater--The Solomon Connection

Antipater's mother Doris received limited attention from Josephus in his histories as opposed to Herod's Hasmonean wife (Mariamne bat Alexander). Herod divorced and exiled her after she bore him one son, then remarried her approximately 12 years later. But why did Herod bother to remarry her after the execution of Mariamne the Hasmonean? Herod had another wife who was the daughter of a Kohanim priest (that Herod elevated to high priest). What about the lineage of Doris made her a high level princess in the eyes of the Jewish people? Herod clearly had no personal attachment for the woman so one can only surmise he remarried Doris due to the strength of her bloodline as political capital for use during his reign.

I believe a real possibility exists that Doris, the mother of Antipater and maternal grandmother of Jesus, was a descendant of King David through his son Solomon. All we know about Doris comes from Josephus and is summarized below--

- "For as [Herod] had formerly married a wife out of his own country of no ignoble blood, who was called Doris, of whom he begat Antipater * * *."[363]

- "For when he came to the government, he sent away her whom he had before married when he was a private person, and who was born at Jerusalem, whose name was Doris * * *."[364] Emphasis added.

---

[362] Herod's final will naming Archelaus king had not yet made it to Rome when Herod died. It was contested by several of Herod's heirs in a probate proceeding adjudicated by Caesar himself.

[363] Jewish Wars I 12:3.

[364] Jewish Wars I:22:1.

- "[Herod] had also married before this another wife, out of a lower family of his own nation, whose name was Doris, by whom he had his eldest son Antipater."[365]
- "So the king having satisfied himself of the spite which Doris, Antipater's mother, as well as himself, bore to him, took away from her all her fine ornaments, which were worth many talents, and then sent her away, and entered into friendship with Pheroras' women."[366] (4 BCE when Doris' son was tried before Varus for conspiracy in murder plot against Herod.)
- "Thendion, the brother of the mother of Antipater, the king's son * * *."[367]
- "After the execution of Aristobulus (6 BCE), his wife Berenice became the wife of Thendion, maternal uncle of Antipater."[368]

The first item above is a bit of a trick statement through utilization of a double negative--"of no ignoble blood". Ignoble means without nobleness. Thus, the phrase literally means 'no, not noble blood'. In plain English, the phrase means Doris was of noble blood. The third statement in our list about Doris is also confusing--"of a lower family". Is this a direct contradiction to the statement from Jewish Wars stating that she was of noble blood? I think not. Right before the contrary phrase found in Antiquities, Josephus discusses Herod's second wife Mariamne of the Hasmonean dynasty. I believe the intended meaning of the phrase from Antiquities is that Doris was from a family lower in status than Mariamne's. The Hasmoneans were the preeminent Jewish family of the day. To summarize, Josephus tells us Doris is of a noble family of Idumea but one of lower status than the Hasmoneans. Note: Remember that Josephus claimed to be a descendant of Hasmonean kings.

---

[365] Antiquities XIV:12:1.
[366] Antiquities XVII:4:2.
[367] Antiquities XVII:4:2.
[368] Antiquities XVII:1:1 and Jewish Wars I:28:1.

Idumean Kingdom

The ancient kingdom of Idumea (also called Edom) lay to the south and east of Judah. Its peoples were thought to descend from Esau, the twin brother of Jacob. However, the Torah names the Idumeans as lower class members of the extended Jewish family. Idumeans were not allowed into the synagogue until the third generation after intermarriage with a Jew.

> You shall not detest an Edomite, for he is your brother. * * * The sons of the third generation who are born to them may enter the assembly of the Lord.[369]

These descendants of Esau and Jacob were ancient enemies foreshadowing the present era conflict between the Arabs and Israelis. King David nearly wiped out the Idumean royal family during his war with that kingdom. "[W]hen David conquered the nation of Edom [Idumea], Joab his army commander went there to bury those who had died in battle. Joab and his soldiers stayed in Edom six months, and during that time they <u>killed every man and boy who lived there.</u>"[370] Emphasis added. Today the United Nations would term the actions of the Jewish forces in Idumea genocide. Only one Idumean princeling named Hadad escaped the slaughter to Egypt, where he married Pharaoh's sister-in-law who later bore him children. After King David died, Hadad returned to Idumea at the head of an army and reclaimed his kingdom. We are told Hadad did "evil" to Solomon after reclaiming his kingdom in Idumea. Hadad "abhorred Israel and reigned over Aram (Syria)."[371] My reading of the Bible references to Hadad are that he captured both the Idumean homeland to the south of Judah and, also, extended his control north into Syria.

The brief biblical account of the conflict between Hadad and Solomon fails to explain how the war ended. Interestingly, the *First Book of Kings* states Solomon possessed an Idumean princess

---

[369] *Deuteronomy* 23:7-8.
[370] 1 *Kings* 11:15-16.
[371] 1 *Kings* 11:25.

among his 700 wives.[372] This is an odd fact for two reasons. First, the decimation of the Idumean royal family by David meant that the only Idumean royalty in existence by the time of Solomon were descendants of Hadad, who was an enemy of Solomon and "abhorred Israel". Secondly, the low status assigned to the Idumeans by the Torah makes intermarriage between Solomon and one of Hadad's daughters or granddaughters seem like political baggage. Why would Solomon take on a wife from a low status tribe that was his enemy? Peace treaties of the ancient world were sealed with marriages between the royal families of enemy combatants. This strikes me as the best explanation for why Solomon took an Idumean wife. Given that Hadad's forces met with success on the battlefield against the Jews, Hadad was in the stronger bargaining position when a treaty was signed between Idumea and the Jewish kingdom. We know Hadad sent a daughter or granddaughter to be the wife of Solomon but, in all probability, Solomon also sent a son or daughter to intermarry with the Idumean royal family. Another possibility is that an offspring of Solomon and his Idumean wife returned to Idumea thereby bringing Solomon's bloodline into the Idumean royal family.

If Solomon had sent one of his children to marry into the Idumean royal family (or offspring from Solomon's Idumean wife returned to his or her people), that high status royal bloodline would have predominated within the Idumean royal family going forward in much the same way the Hasmonean bloodline marked the highest ranking Herodian princes and princesses of each generation. As explained below, the status and treatment of Doris by Herod was anomalous; however, all anomalies resolve themselves if Doris was a descendant of King Solomon.

The Jews later reconquered Idumea under Jewish king Amaziah who slew 10,000 Idumeans during battle at the Valley of Salt.[373] In later generations the Chaldeans conquered Israel and carried off the Davidic royal family to Babylon. The Idumeans took advantage of the situation by expanding their territory north

---

[372] 1 *Kings* 11:1.
[373] 2 *Chronicles* 25:11.

into Judea. Present day Hebron was one of the Judean cities occupied by the Idumeans during this period.[374] Many centuries later, the Jews repaid the favor. Hasmonean king John Hyrcanus conquered Idumea around 130 BCE forcibly converting the Idumeans to the Jewish religion.[375] From that point forward, Idumea ceased to exist as a separate country having become a province of the Jewish kingdom.

Doris the Idumean Princess

The first anomaly in the biography of Doris is her birth in Jerusalem. Why was an Idumean princess born in Jerusalem and not in her own kingdom? Doris's son by Herod (Antipater) was born in 46 BCE. Surely she was a young woman at his birth, perhaps 20 years of age. Let us estimate her birth year as 66 BCE or sixty-four years after Hasmonean king John Hyrcanus captured Idumea. A common practice at this time was for the conquering nation to take the royal family (or at least selected members of the royal family) of the defeated nation hostage to be raised in the capital of the conquering nation. The logical conclusion from these facts is that the Idumean royal family lived in Jerusalem under liberal house arrest from the time of conquest by John Hyrcanus up until at least the birth of Doris. I submit that after 64 years of continual residence in Jerusalem, the Idumean royal family became fully integrated into Jewish life and undoubtedly intermarried with high level Jewish families.

The second anomaly was Herod's selection of Doris as his first wife. At that time, Herod's father Antipater was the prime minister to Hyrcanus II (high priest and puppet ruler of the Jewish kingdom). Antipater held the real power in the Jewish kingdom as a Roman client with enough power to name his sons governors of Jewish territories. Young Herod was governor of Galilee when he married Doris. Herod and his brothers were powerful Idumeans potentates attempting to burnish their Jewish credentials when selecting wives. Surely they married the highest ranking Jewish

---

[374] Ancient History: From The Creation To The Fall of Rome, A.D. 476 by Samuel Griswold Goodrich (Morton and Griswold 1851) at page 156.
[375] Ibid at page 157.

women they could lay claim to. The top prize of the day was a Hasmonean princess; however, Herod did not then possess enough political capital to secure such a high-born wife. His status changed after being named king of the Jewish kingdom by the Romans allowing him to attract a Hasmonean queen. What level of Jewish nobility lay immediately below the Hasmonean line in first century BCE Judea? The David-Solomon bloodline stood as the only other royal Jewish dynasty. But the royals of that family had been removed from Israel to Babylon many centuries prior to Herod's era. On the other hand, if the Idumean royal family had indeed intermarried with Solomon then they perpetuated the only repository of Davidic royal blood in Judea. It would explain the value of Doris as a wife for Herod. If so, Doris was from the #2 Jewish royal family of her day.

Next, why did Herod banish Doris to Rome when he betrothed his Hasmonean wife Mariamne? After his marriage to Mariamne, Herod married a bus full of additional secondary wives who all lived with the king and queen in Herod's palace. None of Herod's wives after Mariamne bat Alexander were of Jewish royal blood. Something was special about Doris such that Mariamne demanded her banishment as a condition of marriage to Herod. Mariamne clearly viewed Doris as a political threat to her position.

Fourth, Herod remarried Doris after he executed his Hasmonean wife. Why bother? Antipater was not crown prince when he and Doris were recalled from Rome and Herod had many other wives at this time. Doris possessed something that Herod's other wives did not—Jewish royal blood. Herod had no Jewish royal blood in his ancestry nor did any of his of his other wives after the execution of Mariamne. From a political point of view, he needed a wife of Jewish royal blood to legitimatize his reign as a Jewish king. When Mariamne died, Doris filled the void with her Davidic royal ancestry.

Consider further that Herod arranged the marriage of his niece Bernice to Doris' brother Thendion. Berenice was a high ranking Herodian, daughter of Herod's sister Salome and the wife of the Hasmonean prince Aristobulus until his death. Her children were the highest ranking Herodian royals of their generation due to their Hasmonean bloodline. She stood as the future queen mother at the time Herod chose Thendion as her second husband. Such a match only made sense if Thendion possessed Jewish royal blood.[376] I recognize the proof is circumstantial with ample room for contrary opinion but I find the evidence compelling.

<u>Herodian Princesses Married Their Uncles</u>

A peculiar custom of the Herodian clan was marriage of high ranking princesses to their uncles. The pattern began when Herod's father Antipater betrothed his only daughter (Salome) to his brother Joseph. Perhaps the Herodians borrowed the custom from the Egyptians. For whatever reason, the pattern continued into the next generation with Herod's sons.

Herodian Prince	Marriage to Niece
Antipater ben Herod	Mariamne bat Aristobulus
Herod Archelaus	Mariamne bat Aristobulus
Herod grandson of Boethus	Herodias
Herod Antipas	Herodias
Herod Philip	Salome bat Herod[377] (daughter of Herodias)

Another interesting twist on this pattern was that only Herod's Hasmonean offspring were married to their uncles, not Herod's other daughters and granddaughters. Each of the women listed above were mixed Herodian-Hasmonean. One noted break in this pattern occurred with Herod's only brother Pheroras. He refused to marry Herod's eldest Hasmonean daughter Salampsio, which precipitated a serious break in their relationship.

<u>The Unnamed Wife of Pheroras</u>

Antipater ben Herod's chief ally in the Herodian court was his uncle Pheroras, brother of Herod and tetrarch of the pocket

---

[376] Berenice's son Herod Agrippa I went go on to be king of territory nearly as extensive as Herod the Great had ruled. Bernice was also the mother of Mariamne bat Aristobulus (Mary Magdalene) and her sister Herodias.
[377] Salome was the grandniece of Herod Philip.

territory of Perea. Pheroras married a woman described by Josephus as his former servant.[378] This unnamed wife of Pheroras presents an interesting story with a possible Hasmonean connection. Although not directly related to Antipater ben Herod, I placed the material in this chapter for lack of a better location. I shall call this unnamed wife of Pheroras "Alexandra of Perea" (a name of my own invention) due to similarities with Hasmonean queen Salome Alexandra (139–67 BCE). I find her marriage to Pheroras exceptional on several levels. Grizzled Herodian warriors such as Herod and Pheroras were not sentimental men. Ravishing servant girls were taken as concubines, not wives. Potentates such as Pheroras always selected wives for political gain. As reported by Josephus, his marriage to Alexandra of Perea produced only political negatives for Pheroras. The supposed love story should have just been a one or two line entry in Josephus; however, Pheroras' wife occupied a far greater role in the Herodian pantheon than one could reasonably ascribe to a former servant girl. So much of the Josephus puzzle contains missing or suppressed pieces. I believe this to be another case.

Herod and Pheroras were the only sons of Antipater the Idumean to survive the war with Antigonus. Herod's highest ranking daughters were the two Hasmonean princesses he sired by Mariamne bat Alexander, Salampsio and Cypros. Jewish marriages of this period were a two step process. First, a betrothal contract was signed between the groom and the senior male of the bride's family. Later, the couple consummated the actual wedding.[379] Herod wished to continue his pattern of high value princesses marrying their uncles by sending his oldest Hasmonean daughter (Salampsio) to Pheroras as a wife even though Pheroras had already married the servant girl. Josephus indicates that Pheroras initially agreed to put away his wife Alexandra of Perea and entered into a betrothal contract to marry Salampsio but "he was overcome with the charms of his wife, to such a degree of madness, that he

---

[378] Antiquities XVI 7:3 (194).
[379] Jewish Marriage in Antiquity by Michael L. Satlow (Princeton University Press 2001) at pages 162-168.

despised the king's daughter to whom he had been betrothed." [380] Pheroras reneged on the contract to marry Salampsio and Herod gave her in marriage to his nephew Phasael instead. Despite the outrage of the first rejection, Herod again tried to brow beat Pheroras into marrying his #2 Hasmonean daughter (Cypros) when she came of age. Again, Pheroras rejected the entireties of the king. These decisions by Pheroras appear highly unusual. Every Herodian prince of standing went to extraordinary lengths to secure a Hasmonean wife. Josephus seems to chalk up the state of affairs to love but I think not. As explained below, the additional tidbits of information about Alexandra of Perea sprinkled by Josephus within his histories indicate she was a woman of high birth with independent standing at court.

Given that Pheroras' wife was the source of the calamity between Herod and his brother, reason dictates she was persona non grata at the king's court. Far from it, Josephus tells us Alexandra of Perea together with her mother and sister domineered the other royal women at Herod's court.

> There was also a company of women in the court, which excited new disturbances; for Pheroras's wife, together with her mother and sister, and also Antipater's mother, grew very impudent in the palace. She also was so insolent as to affront the king's two daughters, on which account the king hated her to a great degree; yet although these women were hated by him, they domineered over others. [381] [Emphasis added.]

A related passage from Antiquities reads, "Pheroras was greatly enslaved to his wife, and to her mother, and to her sister."[382] Notice that not only did Pheroras' wife have a place at Herod's court but, also, her mother and sister! The mother and sister of a servant held positions at Herod's court? Further, Antipater's royal mother Doris was listed by Josephus as something of a retainer to

---

[380] Antiquities XVI 7:3 (194).
[381] Jewish Wars I 29:1 (43-44).
[382] Antiquities XVII 2:4.

the apparently more powerful Alexandra of Perea. Pheroras' wife carried high enough status within the Herodian court to openly battle Herod's daughters. Very strange behavior for a servant girl, don't you think?

The unusual circumstances surrounding Alexandra of Perea only multiply the more one reads Josephus. She was the only Herodian of the royal family known to have had a close relationship with the Pharisee rabbis. First, few Jewish women (especially of common birth) had public association with rabbis. This seemed to be a particular hallmark of the Jesus movement. The Pharisees did not teach the Torah to women and only allowed them limited participation in religious gatherings at the synagogue. The only example of a Jewish royal female acting as patron for the Pharisees was Hasmonean queen Salome Alexandra. Her second husband, King Alexander Jannai, persecuted the Pharisees. However, when she independently reigned as queen upon his death (76-67 BCE), Salome Alexandra favored the Pharisees as her brother was a leading member of their party.[383] The most important passage from Josephus regarding the association of Pheroras' wife with the Pharisees is reproduced below. The Jews as Roman subjects were required to recite a loyalty oath to Caesar but the Pharisees refused on religious grounds.

> [The Pharisees] did not swear, being above six thousand; and when the king imposed a fine upon them, Pheroras' wife paid their fine for them. In order to requite which kindness of hers, since they were believed to have the foreknowledge of things to come by Divine inspiration, they foretold how God had decreed that Herod's government should cease, and his posterity should be deprived of it; but that the kingdom should come to her

---

[383] References from the Talmud indicate Rabbi Simeon ben Shetah was the brother of Queen Salome Alexandra; however, this point is disputed. The Jewish People In The First Century, Volume Two by S. Safrai and M. Stern (Van Gorcum & Fortress Press 1976) at page 621, footnote 6.

<u>and Pheroras</u>, and to their children.[384]
[Emphasis added.]

The Pharisees thought so highly of Pheroras' wife that they gave a prophecy stating that Herod would lose the Jewish throne with it passing to Alexandra of Perea and her children by Pheroras. Again, this seems like quite an honor to be bestowed upon a former servant girl.

Another interesting fact about the wife of Pheroras was the arranged marriages for her children. Josephus records the spouses of three of her children and they were high status individuals within the Herodian clan. Antipater ben Herod, who was crown prince at the time, married his son[385] to the daughter of Pheroras.[386] After Herod's death, Caesar Augustus himself selected husbands for Herod's unmarried daughters—"Caesar granted to Herod's two virgin daughters five hundred thousand drachma of silver, and gave them in marriage to the sons of Pheroras."[387] These clearly were not offspring of a mere servant girl.

The last anomaly in the recorded biography of Alexandra of Perea occurs in the last year of Herod's life after he banished Doris for the last time and charged Antipater with attempted patricide. Thereafter, Josephus records in both <u>Jewish Wars</u> and <u>Antiquities</u> that Herod made friends with Pheroras' women.

> So the king having satisfied himself of the spite which Doris, Antipater's mother, as well as himself, bore to him, took away from her all her fine ornaments, which were worth many talents, and then sent her away, and <u>entered into friendship with Pheroras's women</u>.[388] [Emphasis added.]

---

[384] <u>Antiquities</u> XVII 2:4.

[385] The mother of this son was not recorded by Josephus. Because of this fact, I assume the mother was someone other than Mariamne bat Antigonus.

[386] <u>Antiquities</u> XVII 1:2 (18).

[387] <u>Jewish Wars</u> II 6:3.

[388] <u>Antiquities</u> XVII 4:2; see also, "He also took care of Pheroras's women after their tortures, as being now reconciled to them." <u>Jewish Wars</u> I 30:4.

It's difficult to reconcile this friendship with earlier statements from Josephus that Herod despised Alexandra of Perea for causing trouble with the other women at court and for coming between he and Pheroras. On more than one occasion Herod demanded that Pheroras banish his wife yet he makes friends with her and the other women of her family after the death of Pheroras.[389]

After banishing Doris for the last time, Herod was left without a wife of Jewish royal blood. I believe Herod "entered into friendship" with Pheroras' women at this point because they were of royal Hasmonean blood. It is the only explanation for the strange high status accorded to Alexandra of Perea, her mother, and sister by Pheroras and Herod. Why Hasmonean? Pheroras rejected Herod's oldest Hasmonean daughter in favor of Alexandra of Perea. She must have possessed equal or greater Jewish royal status.

The problem with this solution is two-fold: (a) Herod supposedly executed all the Hasmonean royals and (b) Pheroras' wife was said to be a former servant. How could a woman described as a servant have been of royal Hasmonean descent? One explanation solves both problems. Josephus records Hasmonean king Alexander Jannai possessing a large number of wives and concubines but the exact number is not recorded.[390] The best explanation I can devise for the riddle of Pheroras' wife is that she was the descendant of Alexander Jannai or a son of Jannai by one of his concubines. That makes her of royal Hasmonean blood but far enough down the royal chain to have avoided slaughter when Herod captured Jerusalem in 37 BCE. It also lends some credence to Josephus' defamation of her as a servant girl. Jannai's harem of concubines and their offspring came under the control of Queen Salome Alexandra upon the king's death in 76 BCE. Alexandra of Perea's mother should have been of an age to have lived during the reign of Queen Salome Alexandra and thereby have been influenced by her policy of favoring the

---

[389] Antiquities XVII 3:1.

[390] Having put down a Jewish rebellion, Jannai is said to have crucified 800 of the rebels outside the walls of Jerusalem while he feasted with his concubines in sight of the condemned. Antiquities XIII 14:2.

Pharisees. When Herod decapitated the leadership of the Hasmonean family, those formerly of lower status then rose to the top of the Hasmonean clan. In this way, an illegitimate descendant of King Jannai became an important member of the Herodian family through her rare bloodline.

Things did not end well for Alexandra of Perea. After the death of her husband Pheroras, she was accused of complicity in his death by poisoning. The servants and slaves of her household were tortured (and possibly she herself). Alexandra of Perea attempted to kill herself by jumping off the balcony of Pheroras' palace but only succeeded in badly injuring herself. Josephus reported that she testified against Antipater at his trial before governor Varus. Her injuries prevented her from walking so they carried her into the courtroom on a litter. From there the trail goes cold. We know not what became of Alexandra of Perea or her children.

Chapter 10
Josephus, Jewish Traitor
(Joseph ben Matthias)

In his work <u>Vita</u>, Josephus rambles on about the august standing of his ancestry. He claims descent from Hasmonean kings! How the hell can Josephus claim to descend from Hasmonean royalty after having told us in other works that Herod exterminated all the Hasmonean royals? I find Josephus or his Roman editors to have been masters of deception by omission. Reading his texts very carefully, we can work out the identity of Josephus' father with greater specificity than openly acknowledged. I believe his father was the last high priest (Matthias ben Theophilus) who the zealots executed in the final stages of the great Jewish revolt against Rome. Matthias ben Theophilus was the grandson of the famous high priest Annas ben Seth, who played an important role in the crucifixion of Jesus. Josephus holds a much closer connection to the story of Jesus than acknowledged. In fact, Josephus never directly tells the story of Jesus in his voluminous works.[391] He gives us a few sentences on James the Just but assiduously stays away from Jesus. I believe this was done at the direction of his Roman masters. We shall also

---

[391] I stand with the camp who believe the so-called Testimonium Flavianum found at <u>Antiquities</u> XVIII 3:3 is a forgery that was not part of the original Josephus text.

briefly explore Josephus' career as a supposed Jewish patriot before defecting to the Romans.

Ancestry of Josephus

Josephus describes his family in the opening lines of Vita as being noble and descended from priests. The important portion of this section is reproduced below:

> Now, I am not only sprung from a sacerdotal family in general, but from the first of the twenty-four courses; and as among us there is not only a considerable difference between one family of each course and another, I am of the chief family of that first course also; nay, further, by my mother I am of the royal blood; for the children of Hasmonean, from whom that family was derived, had both the office of the high priesthood, and the dignity of a king, for a long time together. [Emphasis added.]

As previously stated, the claim by Josephus that he descended from Hasmonean kings is problematic given Herod's Gestapo-style extermination campaign executed against the Hasmoneans. Professor Shaye Cohen of Harvard University writes, "In any event, Josephus' Hasmonean ties are probably bogus."[392] I hear you Professor Cohen. Lying is the most logical solution to the opposed facts presented by Josephus but my personal view is that Josephus was indeed of Hasmonean descent however, yet again, obfuscated the facts surrounding how this came to be so. The surviving Hasmoneans acknowledged in the histories of Josephus were all members of Herod's family. None of the Herodian-Hasmonean males of later generations could have qualified for the Temple priesthood as they were not Kohanim. Why? Kohanim status passed from father to son. Only Hasmonean females produced children by intermarriage with the Herodians and they

---

[392] See Josephus in Galilee and Rome: His Vita and Development As a Historian by Shaye J. D. Cohen Brill Academic Publishers 2002) at page 108.

were incapable of conferring Kohanim status. The Hasmonean males were killed by Herod. However, Josephus claimed his **mother** was a descendant of Hasmonean kings. Could the mother of Josephus have been a Hasmonean-Herodian?

It's tempting to jump on this juicy hypothesis and run with it. The theory explains the rapid rise of Josephus within the priestly hierarchy and his close association with the Romans. Although such a marriage would have ingratiated the father of Josephus with King Herod Agrippa II and his Roman overlords, it would have infuriated the Jewish people. Any Kohanim family which intermarried with the Herodians would have been especially despised by the Jewish people. Then again, the first high priest killed by the Jewish mob at the start of the revolt was Annas (who I theorize to have been an ancestor of Josephus).[393] Zealot malice toward Annas was so great that they desecrated his body after killing him and burned down his house. My problem with this line of reasoning is that the works of Josephus were not sympathetic to Herod.[394] In fact, Josephus condemned the progeny of Herod.

> [W]ithin the revolution of a hundred years,
> the posterity of Herod, which were a great
> many in number, were, excepting a few,
> utterly destroyed. One may well apply this for
> the instruction of mankind, and learn thence
> how unhappy they were.[395]

I find it hard to believe Josephus was discussing his own family in this passage but do not entirely discount the possibility.

In the previous chapter, I speculated that offspring of the concubines of Hasmonean kings survived Herod's purge resulting in Pheroras marrying a Jewish woman of royal blood who Josephus described as a servant. By like reasoning, it is highly probable that others of Hasmonean blood but further removed by degree from the royal family of Antigonus survived Herod's holocaust against the Hasmoneans. The Torah permitted Jewish kings up to 18

---

[393] Jewish Wars II 17:9 (441-42).
[394] Jewish Writings of the Second Temple Period by Michael E. Stone (Van Gorcum / Fortress Press 1984) at pages 219-20.
[395] Antiquities XVIII 5:3.

wives. Judging by Alexander Jannai, the Hasmonean kings most likely married at or near their full complement of allowed wives. If a king averages three children by each of his 18 wives, he then sires 54 offspring. If each royal child averages four children of their own, then 216 royal grandchildren are produced. My point is that many thousands of Hasmonean descendants must have existed when Herod captured Jerusalem in 37 BCE. How many generations back from a Hasmonean king did Herod go when filling out his prescription list? Did he stop at grandchildren? Great-grandchildren? In all probability, remnants of Hasmonean royal blood several generations removed from the Jewish throne survived the slaughter by Herod. As this was a priestly family of the highest status, the logical location within Jewish society for surviving Hasmoneans who were somewhat removed from the throne would have been within the Temple priesthood. I believe Josephus is a descendant of Hasmonean priests who survived Herod's purge by pledging allegiance to the new king.

Josephus, the Early Years

Josephus professed as a young man to have undergone training with all three religious orders (Pharisees, Sadducees, and Essenes) but decided to join the Pharisee party. This strikes me as a strange claim for Josephus to make. The high priests of this period are thought to have been Sadducees. Josephus came from a family of high priests. Further, he mixed easily with Romans, which would have been taboo for a Pharisee. At the age of 26 (63 CE) he traveled to Rome seeking freedom for fellow priests then imprisoned by the Romans. During his stay in Rome Josephus inexplicably became acquainted with Nero's wife, Poppea. He not only secured the release of his fellow Jewish priests but, also, received "many presents from Poppea."[396] Josephus, you cad! How does a young Pharisee priest adrift in Rome on his first visit to the big city become friends with the emperor's wife? Josephus gives us the absurd story that a Jewish actor living in Rome made

---

[396] Vita 1:3 (16).

the introduction.[397]   I can fathom only one avenue for a young Jewish priest to obtain entrée into the social circle of the Roman royal family, an introduction from King Herod Agrippa II. The family of Josephus must have been close political allies of Agrippa. The actions of Josephus during the Jewish war make this deduction even more plausible.

Just before the great Jewish revolt against Rome unfolded, Josephus and "two other priests, who were of excellent character" were sent to Galilee to persuade the Galileans <u>not</u> to join the revolt.[398] The peace mission failed and Josephus instead became a leader of the revolutionary forces meant to defend Galilee against Rome. In <u>Vita</u>[399] Josephus refers to himself as a "legate", the Roman term for military general. Later in <u>Vita</u>, Josephus reveals that he was appointed military governor of Galilee "by the community of Jerusalem."[400] That's an impressive resume for a young man who was only 29 years of age when the Jewish revolt commenced in 66 CE and who lacked any military training.

The above facts indicate Josephus was the son of a high level Temple priest, almost assuredly descended from a recent high priest.   The hierarchy of the Temple priesthood was not a meritocracy. Young Jewish priests advanced based on the status and the political power possessed by their families. The only explanation for why Josephus was selected for important positions is the high status of his father who most probably was one of the high priests.   Additional facts discussed below lead to the conclusion that the father of Josephus was not just one of the high priests but THE high priest in office at the commencement of the revolt.   Half of the elected leaders of the rebellion were either former high priests or sons of high priests. The following were

---

[397] Ibid.
[398] Ibid 1:7.
[399] Ibid 1:12 (62).
[400] Ibid 1:64 (341). The word used is "strategos" which is a Greek term that, in this case, is probably best translated as military governor. My copy of the William Whiston translation merely translates it as "governor". See also <u>Jewish Wars</u> II 20:3 (562-568).

listed in Jewish Wars[401] as the elected rebel leaders. Those highlighted are either former high priests or sons of high priests.

- Joseph ben Gorion
- Ananus the high priest
- Eleazar ben Simon
- Jesus ben Sapphias, son of high priest
- Eleazar ben Ananias, son of high priest
- Joseph ben Simon
- Manasseh
- John the Essene
- John ben Matthias
- **Josephus ben Matthias**

Josephus does not acknowledge John ben Matthias as his brother but, at another juncture in Jewish Wars where children of two separate high priests named Matthias were discussed, Josephus differentiated between the different Matthiases.[402] Thus, by the omission of differentiation in this passage, I infer Josephus and John are sons of the same Matthias. They are the only brothers elected as commanders for the coming war, a singular honor. Josephus was given charge of Galilee and Gamala, important territories for entrustment to a 29-year-old priest. These facts suggest but do not prove that the father of Josephus was the sitting high priest at the time the revolt broke out. Coincidentally, Josephus named the serving high priest at this time as Matthias ben Theophilus.[403] The career of Josephus as a military leader is discussed later in this chapter after a discussion of Josephus' father.

The Father of Josephus a/k/a Matthias ben Theophilus

Josephus lauds his father's public reputation but has little to say about his life or employment.

---

[401] Jewish Wars II 20:3 (562-568).
[402] Jewish Wars VI 2:2 (114). Note: in Vita Josephus said his mother was of royal Hasmonean blood yet here he says his father was also noble (meaning of noble blood).
[403] Antiquities XX 9:7.

Now, my father Matthias was not only
eminent on account of his nobility, but had a
higher commendation on account of his
righteousness; and was in great reputation in
Jerusalem.[404]

Josephus mentions his father Matthias one other time stating that,
when the zealots gained control of Jerusalem, they kept "Josephus'
father in prison, and made public proclamation that no citizen
whosoever should speak to him himself."[405] That's the last specific
reference we have to the father of Josephus. Strange that Josephus
does not record the fate of his own father. In any case, the zealots
executed several other high priests but imprisoned the father of
Josephus.[406] The point being that his value as a prisoner must have
been high for the father of Josephus to escape immediate
execution when the zealots gained control of Jerusalem. Further,
the zealots issued a proclamation forbidding the citizens of
Jerusalem from speaking with Matthias (the father of Josephus)
and, still further, the zealots also imprisoned the mother of
Josephus in Jerusalem during the Roman siege.[407] One can only
assume that the father of Josephus did not survive the revolt.
Josephus gave a list of high priests and their children who escaped
through the lines during the siege of Jerusalem but both his own
father and the high priest Matthias ben Theophilus are absent from
the list.[408]

Forgive the pop culture reference but the relation between
Matthias the father of Josephus and high priest Matthias ben
Theophilus strikes me as a Clark Kent / Superman situation. Has
anyone ever seen them together in the same room? Josephus
proclaims he was from a family of high priests. Further, as a young
man, he was given important assignments by the chief priests in
Jerusalem. It appears that his brother was also made a rebel
commander. These facts indicate that the father of Josephus was a

---

[404] Vita 1:2.
[405] Jewish Wars V 13:1 (533).
[406] Ibid (527 & 533).
[407] Ibid 13:3 (544).
[408] Jewish Wars VI 2:2 (113).

very important figure in Jerusalem, certainly a chief priest and perhaps the high priest. When telling the story of the great Jewish revolt in Antiquities, Josephus mentions high priest Matthias ben Theophilus but not his father. When telling the story of the great Jewish revolt in Jewish Wars, Josephus mentions his father but not high priest Matthias ben Theophilus. Neither of these names appears on the list of high priests (and sons of high priests) who survived the war. I reason that high priest Matthias ben Theophilus was mentioned in Antiquities but disappeared from Jewish Wars because he was referred to in that work as "the father of Josephus". All the facts point to the conclusion that they were one in the same person.

Perhaps you have read Vita and demur at this conclusion because Theophilus is not among the ancestors given by Josephus in that work. My examination of Josephus' ancestor list leads me to conclude he intentionally omitted names. Below are the ancestors Josephus acknowledges in Vita with their dates of birth. I've included Josephus in the list to add context.

- Josephus (37 CE)
- Matthias, father of Josephus (6 CE)
- ** Missing ancestor (Theophilus ben Annas)
- Joseph (67 BCE)[409]
- ** Missing ancestor (Annas ben Seth)
- Matthias Curtis (134 BCE)[410]

There appear to be at least two omitted ancestors from the family tree given by Josephus.[411] The first gap involves the father of

---

[409] Joseph was born in born in the ninth year of the reign of Queen Alexandra. Her reign began in 76 BCE making the 9th year 67 BCE.
[410] Matthias Curtis was born the first year of the government of "Hyrcanus". I assume Josephus means king John Hyrcanus I. Hyrcanus II ruled for but one year, 76 BCE, which does not fit the timeline given that he would have to father Joseph as an 9-year-old. The first year of the reign of Hyrcanus I was 134 BCE.
[411] See Historiography and Self-Definition: Josephos, Luke-Acts, and Apologetic Historiography by Gregory E. Sterling (Brill Academic Publishers, 1997) at page 229, footnote 13: "There are missing generations in [Josephus'] genealogical tree."

Josephus. Either Joseph sired Matthias (father of Josephus) at age 72 or we have a missing ancestor between Matthias and Joseph. In all probability Josephus left off the name of an ancestor at this spot on the list. Was his name Theophilus? This is my conclusion. Ancestor lists were extremely important to Kohanim priests. It was the method by which a priest proved descent from Aaron, a prerequisite for position in the upper reaches of the Temple priesthood. There is zero chance Joseph was ignorant regarding the identity of two of his close ancestors. These omissions were intentional.

Josephus tells us he came from a Hasmonean family with high priests in their ancestry. I also reason Theophilus is a family name for the Josephus clan. The ancestor born in 67 BCE named solely as "Joseph" is likely Joseph ben Theophilus (a/k/a Josephus ben Ellamus), the brother of Matthias ben Theophilus who was high priest in 4 BCE. Joseph ben Theophilus served as high priest for one day due his brother's ritual impurity. This Temple priest is the individual I theorize to have been the adoptive father of Mary the mother of Jesus, as discussed in Chapter 4 herein.

Josephus – Annas Connection

There are many implications from my identification of the father of Josephus, if correct. Matthias ben Theophilus (high priest 65-66 CE) was most likely the son of Theophilus ben Annas (high priest 37-41 CE) who was the son of Annas ben Seth (high priest 6-15 CE). Annas ben Seth was the famous high priest whose five sons became high priests. Through omission, Josephus concealed the fact that he was the great grandson of the hated Annas who was complicit in the execution of Jesus. This theory also explains the gushing praise Josephus heaped on Annas, a man despised by his own people.

> I should not mistake if I said that the death of Annas was the beginning of the destruction of the city, and that from that very day may be dated the overthrow of her wall[s] * * * . He was on other accounts also a venerable, and a very just man; and besides

> the grandeur of that nobility, and dignity, and
> honor, of which he possessed, he had been a
> lover of a kind of parity, even with regard to
> the meanest of the people; he was a
> prodigious lover of liberty, an admirer of a
> democracy and government; and did ever
> prefer the public welfare before his own
> advantage, and preferred peace above all
> things.[412]

The foregoing passage strikes me as an odious pile of manure if Josephus refers to Annas ben Seth. Quirinius, Roman governor of Syria, appointed Annas ben Seth high priest in 6 CE after sacking Herod Archelaus as Jewish ruler.[413] Annas was the first Jewish high priest directly appointed by the Romans. Undoubtedly, Annas paid substantial "gifts" to Governor Quirinius in order to secure his position as high priest and, later, retain it for his five sons.

But I find it unlikely Josephus speaks of Annas ben Seth in this passage. He became high priest in 6 CE. It would be extremely unlikely for a priest to ascend to the office of high priest before the age of 40. If so, Annas ben Seth was at least 100 years of age if he still lived in 66 CE. This is highly improbable. In my view, the reproduced quote refers to Theophilus ben Annas (high priest 37-41 BCE) who was the grandfather of Josephus. *Luke* referred to high priests by the second or family name (such as Caiaphas). I believe Josephus used the same convention in this instance, perhaps to cloud the fact that he discussed his own grandfather.

For a critical view of the character of the high priesthood, one need look no further than the Talmud. The high priests and their sons are variously described as using violence to seize more than their due share of skins of sacrifice, beating the people with

---

[412] Jewish Wars IV 5:2 (318-19).

[413] The Syrian governor who appointed Annas high priest was Publius Sulpicius Quirinius. See The Father of the Church (Saint Augustine) translated by John W. Rettig (The Catholic University of America Press 1995) at page 9.

their staves and fists, filling their stomachs with the divine sacrifices, and drinking "three hundred barrels of wine."[414] The high priesthood not only served religious functions but was also a business that generated vast wealth for those who controlled the Temple treasury. The chief priests owned lavish estates derived from regular stipends dispensed from the Temple treasury. This is why the Jewish people rebelled against not only the Romans and Herodians but, also, the families of the high priests with particular animus directed toward Annas.

<u>Implications Upon the *Gospel of Luke*</u>

The *Gospel of Luke* was dedicated to "most excellent Theophilus". Luke the evangelist referred to high priests within the body of his gospel by their paternal name, not the given name.[415] I suggested in an earlier edition of *Herodian Messiah* that "Theophilus" of *Luke* refers to Josephus' father, the high priest Matthias ben Theophilus. I theorized that Luke the Evangelist sent his gospel to the father of Josephus while the later served as high priest. The introductory language of *Luke* forwarding the gospel to Theophilus reads as if the author reports to Theophilus on the Christians (then called the Nazarenes), who were still viewed as a Jewish sect prior to the Great Jewish Revolt.

> [I]t seemed fitting for me as well, having investigated everything carefully from the beginning to write it out for you in consecutive order, most excellent Theophilus.[416]

I've since modified my view of the introduction to Luke's gospel. Although the above-quoted words leave the impression that Luke writes to an important person who is senior to himself, the next sentence found in *Luke* changes that interpretation. It reads, "so

---

[414] Pesachim 57a.

[415] For example, the full name of high priest Caiaphas was Joseph ben Caiaphas. *Luke* 3:2.

[416] *Luke* 1:3.

that you [i.e., Theophilus] might know the exact truth about the things **you have been taught**."[417] Emphasis added.

The salutation "most excellent" surely indicates the high status of the individual in question while the final sentence indicates this individual is studying the Nazarene movement as something of a novice. In his extensive writings, Josephus only applied the phrase "most excellent" as a salutation to two individuals: prominent Romans Marcus Agrippa[418] and Epaphroditus[419]. Marcus Agrippa was the most trusted general of Caesar Augustus. Agrippa was so highly thought of by the Herodians that a grandson of Herod (who later became king of the Jews during the reign of Nero) was named after the Roman general. Epaphroditus is an extremely interesting figure in Christian history as he was also a friend of Paul of Tarsus, see *Philippians* 2:25.[420] Epaphroditus was an important minister in the court of Nero who, depending on your view of history, helped Nero commit suicide or assassinated him. In either case, Epaphroditus survived as a wealthy Roman of status into the reign of Domitian.

Employing Josephus as a measuring gauge for Luke's use of the phrase "most excellent" leads one to conclude that the referenced individual was august possessing political power. The name Theophilus is Greek but was famously attached to a family of Jewish high priests, which I believe to be the family of Josephus. Interestingly, Josephus states in his autobiography (Vita) that he studied all the Jewish sects as a young man. Although he fails to specifically list the Nazarenes, Josephus does mention studying in the desert with an ascetic named Banus, whose lifestyle sounds remarkably like John the Baptist, from age 16 to 19 (or 53 to 56 CE). At this time the Nazarenes were still considered to be a Jewish sect. If I am correct that Josephus comes from the lineage of high priests connected with the name Theophilus, then it is a

---

[417] *Luke* 1:4.

[418] <u>Antiquities</u> XVI 2:3.

[419] <u>Against Apion</u> I:1.

[420] Christian scholars dispute that the Epaphroditus of Jospehus is the same individual who was a friend of Paul of Tarsus.

reasonable (although speculative) conclusion that "Theophilus" of *Luke* is one in the same with Josephus himself. My supposition is that the evangelist Luke, a leading Nazarene, wrote a report about his sect to the son of the high priest using the family's famous name. If true, this explains the similarities scholars have noted between *Luke* and the histories of Josephus.

Josephus As Rebel Commander

The Jewish revolt of 66 CE was as much about class warfare as a bid for national independence. The Jewish upper class consisting almost exclusively of the Herodians and the Temple priesthood who were allied with Rome for a century, during which time they reaped the monetary benefits of that alliance. Only a small fraction of the disgruntled members of those two important Jewish constituencies joined with the vast majority of the Jewish people from the lower classes seeking national independence from Rome. Josephus consistently degrades the rebels as reckless criminals in his histories. Thus, it is strange to find Josephus appointed the rebel commander for the northern portion of the Jewish kingdom. The situation reminds one of a famous quote from Vladimir Lenin, "The best way to control the opposition is to lead it ourselves." Josephus and the chief priests in Jerusalem were advanced political strategist clearly ahead of their time.

Things went badly for General Josephus ben Matthias in mounting his defense of Galilee against the Romans. His war devolved to a last stand at Jotapata. Josephus proclaimed to have "performed a great many glorious and bold actions" personally exposing himself to danger in his last battle.[421] Despite these alleged heroics, Josephus and a number of soldiers under his command hid in a cave after the Romans overran Jotapata. Vespasian (the overall Roman commander and future emperor) sent a tribune named Nicanor who "was one that was well known to Josephus"[422] to extend the right hand of friendship to Josephus promising his life would be spared. One must wonder how a

---

[421] Jewish Wars III 7:5 (151-52).
[422] Ibid 8:2 (346).

Jewish Temple priest became personal friends with a Roman tribune under the command of Vespasian, yet another instance of Josephus omitting facts from his biography. Be that as it may, Josephus wished to give himself up to the Romans but the other Jewish soldiers in the cave prevented him from doing so. The Jews agreed upon a suicide pact and drew lots to determine who was to die whereupon his brothers performed the deed. Lots were to be drawn until all the Jewish soldiers in the cave were dead (with only the last survivor taking his own life). As luck would have it, Josephus drew lots with the others but survived until only two men remained from the entire company. Surrounded by the lifeless bodies of their comrades, Josephus convinced the other survivor that they both should give themselves up to the Romans rather than commit suicide. After capture by the Romans, Josephus famously predicted Vespasian would become Roman emperor. This prophesy by Josephus produced the desired effect on the future emperor. Shortly after his capture Vespasian "bestowed on [Josephus] suits of clothes, and other precious gifts; he treated him also in a very obliging manner."[423]

We are left to wonder whether Josephus fought and commanded his troops to the full extent of his abilities while defending Galilee against the Romans, a war he counseled against and opposing an enemy he later joined. Had Josephus given his allegiance to the Romans even before his capture at Jotapata? The only evidence we have on the subject comes from the writings of Josephus himself. It's difficult to view Josephus as anything but the Jewish Benedict Arnold (a famous American traitor during the war of independence with Britain).

---

[423] Ibid 8:9 (408).

Chapter 11
Paul, Speculative Theories

I separated this material from the chapter devoted to Paul because these theories are farer afield than my central thesis of Chapter 7, that Paul was a Herodian prince. The first issue discussed in this chapter is the three different tales of Paul involved in a physical confrontation at the Temple. I can't help but speculate that they sprang from a common event. The second issue addressed is the surviving letters purporting to be between Paul of Tarsus and the Roman Stoic philosopher Seneca, who was a close advisor to Nero (and Nero's former tutor) and brother of proconsul Gallio who tried Paul in Greece.

<u>Paul At Center of Tumult In Temple (*Acts*)</u>

On Paul's last acknowledged trip to Jerusalem, he was ordered to go undergo a seven-day purification ritual by James the Just upon his arrival in the city. Things turned ugly for Paul when he showed his face at the Temple near the end of his ritual purification. Jews from Asia (where Paul had been preaching) went berserk and incited a Jewish mob to try and kill Paul. Only the intervention of Roman soldiers saved Paul's life.

When the seven days were nearly over, some Jews from the province of Asia saw Paul at the Temple. They stirred up the whole crowd and seized him, shouting, "Men of Israel help us! This is the man who teaches all men everywhere against our people and our law and this place. And besides, he has brought Greeks into the temple area and defiled this holy place." ...

The whole city was aroused, and the people came running from all directions. Seizing Paul, they dragged him from the temple, and immediately the gates were shut. While they were <u>trying to kill him,</u> news reached the commander of the Roman troops that the whole city of Jerusalem was in an uproar.[424] [Emphasis added.]

In *Acts* telling of the affair, Paul's mere appearance sent the Jews into a murderous riot. Paul said nothing to incite the mob. Two other extra-Biblical sources (*Recognitions of Clement* and Josephus) record a riot at the Temple precipitated by "Saul" or "Saulus". In *Recognitions*, it's clear the author refers to Paul of Tarsus. The identification of Paul is less clear in Josephus although Prof. Eisenman opines the Saulus of Josephus to be Paul of Tarsus. Please compare these parallel incidents involving Paul to the above incident recorded in *Acts*.

Tumult Raised by Saul At Temple (*Recognitions*)

The apocryphal work *Recognitions of Clement* relates an incident wherein a figure believed to be Paul of Tarsus raised a tumult during an important meeting of priests and religious leaders at the Temple in Jerusalem. As opposed to *Acts*, Paul was the aggressor here.

Saul's Attack on James the Just

Book I of *Recognitions* has James the Just and other Nazarene leaders of the early church arguing with the high priest Caiaphas, Rabbi Gamaliel, and members of other Jewish religious groups such as the followers of John the Baptist at a meeting in the Temple in Jerusalem. Saul injects himself into the debate at the Temple touching off a riot.

---

[424] *Acts* 21:27-31.

[Chapter LXX -- Tumult Raised by Saul.]

"And when [the deabate between the Nazarenes and competing Jewish facts were almost resolved], some one of our enemies entering the Temple with a few men, began to cry out, and to say, 'What mean ye, O men of Israel? Why are you so easily hurried on? Why are ye led headlong by most miserable men, who are deceived by Simon, a magician? 'While he was thus speaking, and adding more to the same effect, and while James the bishop was refuting him, he began to excite the people and to raise a tumult so that the people might not be able to hear what was said. Therefore he began to drive all into confusion with shouting, and to undo what had been arranged with much labor, and at the same to reproach the priests, and to enrage them with reviling and abuse, and, like a madman, to excite everyone to murder, saying, 'What do you? Why do ye hesitate? Oh sluggish and inert, why do we not lay hands upon them, and pull all these fellows to pieces? 'When he had said this, he first, seizing a strong brand from the alter, set the example of smiting. Then others also, seeing him, were carried away with like readiness. Then ensued a tumult on either side, of the beating and the beaten. Much blood is shed; there is a confused fight, in the midst of which that enemy attacked James, and threw him headlong from the top steps; and supposing him to be dead, he cared not to

inflict further violence upon him."[425]
[Emphasis added.]

In the next sentence, the text tells us the Christians rescued a badly injured James from this murderous assault by Saul and transported James to Jericho for his own safety. A couple of things jump out at the reader from this passage when put in context. First, *Recognitions* presents the Nazarene leaders as members of the Jewish faith arguing Jewish law with other Jewish leaders. The main point of contention seems to be whether or not Jesus was the Messiah. According to *Recognitions*, James and Peter were winning the argument until Saul turned the meeting into a brawl. Second, **Saul tried to kill James the Just.** The New Testament records doctrinal disagreements between James and Paul. *Recognitions* raises the nature of their dispute to an entirely new level.

Recognitions does not use the name Saul (the chapter heading was added by a later editor) but the identity of the "enemy" who started the riot and tried to kill James is clear from the next section of the text.

> Then after three days one of the brethren came to us from Gamaliel, whom we mentioned before, bringing to us secret tidings that **that enemy had received a commission from Caiaphas, the chief priest, that he should arrest all who believed in Jesus, and should go to Damascus with his letters**, and that there also, employing the help of the unbelievers, he should make havoc among the faithful; and that he was hastening to Damascus chiefly on this account, because he believed that Peter had fled thither.[426] [Emphasis added.]

---

[425] The Recognitions of Clement, Book I, Chapter 70 as reprinted by Douglas Hatten in his title of the same name (Lulu 2008) at page 55.
[426] Ibid, *Recognitions*, Book I, Chapter 71. Caiaphas was the only Jewish high priest named in *Recognitions*, Book I. The office of Joseph ben Caiaphas ended in 36 CE. If Jesus was crucified in 36 CE, then this event occurred at a later date.

Recognitions identifies an enemy of the Christians receiving a commission from the high priest to travel to Damascus to arrest Christians. This fact pattern fits exactly the actions of Saul / Paul recorded in *Acts*. Compare for yourself.

> Meanwhile, Saul was still breathing out murderous threats against the Lord's disciples. He went to the high priest and asked him for letters to the synagogues in Damascus, so that if he found any there who belonged to the Way, whether men or women, he might take them as prisoners to Jerusalem.[427]

Saul issued "murderous threats" against the disciples and received a commission from the high priest to arrest Christians in Damascus. The identification of Paul as "that enemy" who attacked James in *Recognitions* is rock solid in my view.[428] Also, further Biblical evidence of Paul's assault upon the Christians is found in his own *Letter to Galatians*, "For you have heard of my former manner of life in Judaism, how I used to persecute the church of God beyond measure and wasted it."[429]

Origins Of Recognitions

Recognitions was first cited by early Christian father Origen at the beginning of the third century CE. On this basis, scholars

---

There is support for the position that Aljoneus who served as high priest from 43-44 CE was the son of Joseph Caiaphas. See "To Bury Caiaphas, Not to Praise Him" by Prof. David Flusser of Hebrew University of Jerusalem posthumously published in *Jerusalem Perspective Online* (01 Jan. 2004): "Thus, two high priests are known who belonged to the Caiaphas family, the earlier one being Joseph (18-36 C.E.). It is even probable that the high priest Elionaeus was the son of Joseph Caiaphas." Thus, this incident from Recognitions, pursuant to the historical markers given in the text, most likely occurred in the 43-44 CE timeframe.

[427] *Acts* 9:1-2.

[428] "Saul is distinctly designated as the 'Enemy'; the mention of the commission to Damascus leaves no room for doubting the identity: this has been admitted from the earliest times." Saul of Tarsus, or, Paul and Swedenbort by Ralph Wornum (Williams and Norgate 1877) at page 110.

[429] *Galatians* 1:13.

appear to unanimously assign *Recognitions* to a period later than the first century CE and, therefore, after the death of Clement of Rome. I note that the contents of *Recognitions* is very problematic for the Roman Catholic Church in that it puts Paul in a bad light[430] and denies the divinity of Jesus. However, the Vatican is perfectly comfortable accepting a supposed letter authored by Clement to the Corinthians (i.e., *First Clement*) although Clement's name appears nowhere on the document[431] and it was potentially written twenty years before Clement served as bishop of Rome.[432] *First Clement* contains useful doctrine for the Vatican yet *Recognitions* does not. Once labeled authoritative or non-authoritative by the Roman Church back in antiquity, it's a steep hill for proponents of a contrary view to climb.

Whoever authored *Recognitions* is not the important point. The work is a known ancient Christian text probably written in the second century CE giving an alternative view of the activities of Saul of Tarsus. This fact alone makes the text worth studying regardless of whether Clement of Rome was the author. *Recognitions* reflects the beliefs of at least one early Christian community, a sect undoubtedly later suppressed by the Roman Catholic Church.[433] In this regard, my thoughts are in agreement

---

[430] *Recognitions* mentions Paul of Tarsus on in Book I where he tries to kill James the Just. Otherwise, the work completely omits Paul, perhaps because the time frame it covers is prior to Paul's conversion to Christianity. Some scholars believe the character Simon Magnus in *Recognitions* is a thinly disguised Paul of Tarsus. I have a hard time agreeing with this hypothesis given that Paul and Simon Magnus both appear together at the Temple in Book I.

[431] The Use of the Old and New Testaments in Clement of Rome by Donald Alfred Hagner (Brill Academic Pub 1997) at 1.

[432] George Edmundson opined that *First Clement* was authored in 70 CE while Clement's term as bishop of Rome dated to approximately 90 CE. The Church in Tome in the First Century by George Edmundson (Longmas, Green and Co 1913), reprinted by BiblioLife, LLC at page 189. Others date *First Clement* to 96 CE yet Eusebius in his *Chronicle* puts Clement's death in 95 CE (i.e., one year before *First Clement* was written). Others date *First Clement* to the second century CE, well after the death of Clement.

[433] Most believe *Recognitions* to be a scripture of a Jewish Christian sect called the Ebionites who denied the divinity of Jesus.

with those expressed by Professor Lynn Thorndike (1882-1965), late of Columbia University.

> [*Recognitions* and *Homilies*] may be mere clever inventions, but there certainly is an atmosphere of verisimilitude about it; and it is rather odd that a later writer should be "very careful to avoid anachronisms," in whose account as it now stands are such glaring chronological confusions as those already noted concerning Clement's voyage to Caesarea and Simon's departure for Rome. But, as in the case of the New Testament Apocrypha, <u>the exact date of the composition makes little difference for our purpose, for which it is enough that the Pseudo-Clementines played an important part in the first thirteen centuries of Christian thought viewed as a whole.</u>[434] [Emphasis added.]

One must acknowledge that *Recognitions* was widely read and venerated by segments of the early Christian Church.

Tumult Raised by Saul At Temple (Josephus)

The passage from *Recognitions* raises the eyebrow even further when placed alongside a parallel passage from Josephus. Prof. Eisenman believes a character named "Saulus" by Josephus was most likely Paul of Tarsus.

> [A] sedition arose between the high priests, with regard to one another; for they got together bodies of the boldest sort of the people, and frequently came, from reproaches, to throwing of stones at each other. But Ananias was too hard for the rest, by his riches, which enabled him to gain

---

[434] <u>A History of magic and experimental science: Volume 4</u> by Lynn Thorndike (Columbia University Press 1964) at page 406.

those that were most ready to receive.
<u>Costobarus also, and Saulus, did themselves</u>
<u>get together a multitude of wicked wretches,</u>
<u>and this because they were of the royal</u>
<u>family</u>; and so they obtained favor among
them, because of their <u>kindred to Agrippa</u>;
but still <u>they [Costobarus and Saulus] used</u>
<u>violence with the people</u>, and were very ready
to plunder those that were weaker than
themselves. And from that time it principally
came to pass that our city was greatly
disordered, and that all <u>things grew worse</u>
<u>and worse among us</u>.[435] [Emphasis added.]

Notice the similarities between the passages from Josephus and
Recognitions. Both describe a meeting of priests and other Jewish
constituencies wherein an argument instigated by Saul escalated to
violence. Unfortunately, the two incidents are historically placed at
least twenty years apart and potentially further.

Josephus states the following after his mention of Saulus,
"about this time it was that king Agrippa built Caesarea Philippi
larger than it was before." The town Caesarea Philippi was located
in the small former tetrarchy of Herod Philip.[436] The "Agrippa"
referenced by Josephus in this passage was Herod Agrippa II
whose reign of Philip's former tetrarchy did not commence until
53 CE. Further in the same paragraph from <u>Antiquities</u> we read,
"And now Jesus, the son of Gamaliel, became the successor of
Jesus, the son of Damneus, in the high priesthood." This change
of high priests occurred in 63 CE.[437] In addition to the parallel
Saul incident from Josephus occurring 20 years apart from its twin
found in *Recognitions*, Josephus has Paul / Saul in Jerusalem doing
battle against Christians in 63 CE!

According to the timeline accepted by most scholars, Paul
converted to the Nazarene movement the 30s of the Common
Era. Further, *Acts* records Paul of Tarsus' arrest by the Romans

---

[435] <u>Antiquities</u> XX 9:4.
[436] This Philip who became tetrarch was Herod's son by Cleopatra.
[437] The names Joshua and Jesus are interchangeable.

during the governorship of Antonius Felix, most likely in 54 CE. He remained under arrest in Palestine for two years before deportation to Rome in 56 CE. History does not mention Paul returning to Judea after his deportation to Rome. If Professor Eisenman correctly identifies the Saulus of Josephus as Paul of Tarsus, it either means Paul returned to Jerusalem AFTER his imprisonment in Rome or Josephus placed this incident in the wrong time period. If Josephus correctly placed this incident in 63 CE, then Paul switched back from the Nazarene movement to the Herodian cause around the time James was executed by the Sanhedrin, perhaps participating in the execution.

Who Was Costobarus?

Josephus' account of the tumult at the Temple includes an individual named "Costobarus" who was of the royal family (i.e., Herod's family) and acted in conjunction with Saulus. The only Costobarus mentioned in Josephus other than the running mate of Saulus was the second husband of Salome, sister of Herod the Great. This Costobarus was executed in 28 BCE. It's a reasonable assumption that the later Costobarus is the grandson or great-grandson of the Costobarus executed by Herod given that we are looking for an important member of Herod's family. Further, given that this individual possessed high status as a member of the Herodian clan yet ruled no territory and Josephus placed him in an important meeting at the Temple, it's a fair conclusion that our Costobarus was Hasmonean. Plotting my hypothesized Costobarus on the Herodian family tree shows him to be a Hasmonean cousin of Phasaelus ben Timius (Paul of Tarsus), a grandchild of Herod's Hasmonean daughter Cypros.

The Costobarus we are looking for was both a member of Herod's family and an individual of considerable importance in Jerusalem. Only one person in the Herodian family tree fits that description—Costobarus ben Antipater, a Hasmonean descendant of Cypros and Antipater ben Costobarus. Under this premise, Costobarus was Paul's cousin of Hasmonean descent. I view the Hasmonean descendants of Herod as having formed a sub-clan

232

within the vast Herodian family. This provides an explanation for the joint action of Saul and Costobarus as reported by Josephus.

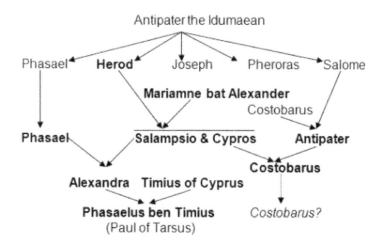

Costobarus ben Antipater may have been too old to be the individual described in Josephus, thus, I added a potential Costobarus as his son. We don't know the names of the children of Costobarus ben Antipater so it's speculation that he had a son also named Costobarus.

Saul & Costobarus, the Terrible Twosome Strike Again

Josephus gives us one last mention of Saul (or Saulus) and Costobarus. The great Jewish revolt against Rome was about to commence and Jewish authorities loyal to Rome attempted to round up local forces to put down the insurgents before Roman legions were called to Judea. Emissaries were sent to Floris and Herod Agrippa II to seek troops.

> [E]ndeavored to save themselves, and sent
> ambassadors; some to Florus [Roman Prefect
> of Judea], the chief of whom was Simon the
> son of Ananias; and others to Agrippa,
> among whom the most eminent were <u>Saul,</u>

<u>and Antipas, and Costobarus</u>, who were of
the king's kindred ... .[438] [Emphasis added.]

After having blown up the reconciliation meeting between
opposing Jewish factions by precipitating a brawl in the Temple,
Josephus reports Saul then aligning himself with the Romans as
war broke out. That is more than problematic if Saul / Saulus of
Josephus was in fact Paul of Tarsus. Church tradition states that
the Romans executed Paul before the Jewish revolt broke out in 66
CE. Further, the Nazarenes fought on the side of the Jewish
nationalists against the Romans during this war. Did Paul go back
to Jerusalem and side with the Romans and Herodians against his
Nazarene brothers in Jerusalem? Thereafter, did the Roman
Church erase this fact from Paul's biography? No conclusions can
be drawn from the reports of Saul contained in *Recognitions* and
Josephus; however, they do raise important questions. I present
these passages merely to spotlight the issue for interested readers.

Paul & Seneca

According to the official biography of Paul of Tarsus (or at
least the accepted biography starting with his official position on
the Sanhedrin), Paul never visited Rome until the final recorded
journey of his life. Yet, we have chapter 16 of his *Letter to the
Romans* that scholars date to 58 CE wherein he greets a laundry list
of people he knows in Rome. Of special interest are Andronicus
and Junia (verse 7) and Herodian (verse 11) who Paul names as
kinsmen. It seems strange that Paul has become closely acquainted
with so many Romans, addressing several as his kinsmen, without
ever having visited the city. This fact has been so troubling to
scholars that they've engaged in mental gymnastics attempting to
excise the entire Chapter 16 from *Romans* on trumped up charges.
Even stranger is Paul's comment found at the tail end of his *Letter
to the Philippians*, "All the saints greet you, <u>especially those of
Caesar's household</u>."[439] Paul had Nazarene acquaintances in the
household of Caesar? Paul was thought to have been imprisoned

---

[438] <u>Jewish Wars</u> II 17:4 (418).
[439] *Philippians* 4:22.

in Rome by the authorities at the time of authorship of this letter yet he sent warm greetings from "the saints" in Caesar's household to the Philippians, very strange.

Perhaps an explanation for Paul's unusual Roman acquaintances including "saints" in Caesar's household lies in the purported letters between he and Seneca. Preserved to the present day are letters in Latin that purport to be correspondence between Paul and the Roman stoic philosopher Seneca the Younger who was tutor, and later minister, to Emperor Nero. In 61 CE (the accepted date for Paul's *Letter to the Philippians*), Seneca resided in Nero's household.

Nature of the Correspondence

Paul and Seneca appear as very close and intimate friends in the correspondence. This point is best exemplified from a line out of a letter from Seneca to Paul dated to 59 CE: "If a person so great, and every way agreeable as you are, become not only a common, but <u>a most intimate friend to me</u>, how happy will be the case of Seneca!"[440] Emphasis added. If Paul and Seneca were such good friends, how did they come to be so? Seneca is known to have traveled widely in the Roman world so one supposition is that Seneca and Paul, both being brilliant minds, became acquainted when their paths crossed during the travels of each. Be that as it may, the letters indicate Paul's prior presence in Rome and attendance at Nero's court. In another undated letter from Seneca to Paul, Seneca writes that he and others at Nero's court await the <u>return</u> of Paul.

> We are very much concerned at your too long absence from us. What is it, or what affairs are they, which obstructs your coming? If you fear the anger of Caesar because you have abandoned your former religion, and made proselytes also of others, you have this to plead, that your acting thus

---

[440] Letter of Seneca to Paul dated the tenth of the calends of April, in the Consulship of Aprianus and Capito (59 CE), translated by William Wake (1657–1737).

proceeded   not   from   inconstancy,   but
judgment.

"Too long of an absence" from Caesar's court means Paul had previously been at court in Rome and, further, his identity was known to Nero. This last point is reinforced by Seneca relating to Paul in another letter that he read Paul's epistles to Nero. Even further, Seneca reports "the emperor is extremely pleased with the sentiments of your Epistles."

It's difficult to fathom how Paul became intimately acquainted with Seneca and Nero unless he lived part of his earlier life in Rome (as many higher ranking Herodian princes did). Further, the relationship testified to in the letters makes perfect sense if Paul, as a young man of noble birth through his mother and wealth through his father, was tutored in Rome by Seneca. The complete text of the surviving letters between Paul and Seneca, translated from the original Latin to English, may be found online.   This link to my blog redirects to the proper URL: jjraymond.com/seneca.

Authenticity Questioned

"No less an authority than the church father , author of the Vulgate Latin version of the Bible, believed the letters [between Paul and Seneca] to be genuine."[441]   In fact, Jerome (347 – 420 CE) named Seneca as one of the early saints of the Roman Church. Despite this stamp of approval from Jerome, scholarly opinion has been decidedly against the authenticity of the letters between Paul and Seneca. My counter-point starts with the basic question behind any investigation of an alleged crime, where is the motive? Who possibly benefited from creating these letters if they were forged? If one argues that opponents of Paul forged the letters, why was he lauded in complimentary language by Seneca in the letters? The letters are short, bland, vanilla (but for the names of the two authors of said correspondence). Any "damage" created by the letters is not to the reputation of Paul but,

---

[441] Paul of Tarsus: a visionary life By Edward Stourton (Paulist Press 2005) at page 190.

236

rather, to the ability of the Roman Church to use the legacy of Paul. Keep in mind that the Roman Catholic Church did not exist when the letters were written. These documents don't look like a hit job against Paul of Tarsus to my eyes. If the letters were written by supporters of Paul to puff up his credentials, why would they pick the chief minister to the emperor Nero as the one to praise Paul? Yes, Seneca was well-respected in the Roman world but other well-respected Romans lacking the taint of the murderous Nero could have been drafted for use by the forger's pen. Further, would a supporter of Paul wishing to inflate his standing tie him to a well-known stoic philosopher?

For an example of an ancient forgery, we need look no further than the interlineations of a testament to Jesus within the works of Josephus. The forged passage inserted into Antiquities has Josephus saying of Jesus, "a wise man, if indeed it is appropriate to call him a man ... performed paradoxical feats, [was] a teacher of the people", was the messiah, and rose from the dead on the third day as foretold by the prophets.[442] No observant Jew would ever imply that a man was God. Further, Josephus famously predicted Vespasian was the messiah[443] so it seems quite odd to have Josephus now telling the world Jesus was the messiah. As the Flavian dynasty founded by Vespasian commissioned the works of Josephus, I doubt the Roman editors assigned to Josephus would have allowed such a slight. The point being that when committing a historical forgery, the perpetrator attempts a significant rewrite of history. It's not worth the effort to plant a small seed of innuendo into the historical record (as was the case with the letters between Paul and Seneca).

Another problem for those opposing the authenticity of these letters is the refusal of proconsul Junius Annaeus Gallio[444], the brother of Seneca, to try Paul when the citizens of Corinth

[442] Antiquities XVIII 3.3.
[443] Jewish Wars VI.
[444] The father of Gallio and Seneca died prematurely. Gallio, originally named Lucius Annaeus Novatus, was adopted by a relative and assumed his name. He went on to serve as Roman consul and, later, proconsul.

hauled Paul into court complaining of his corruption of their religion.

One night the Lord spoke to Paul in a vision: "Do not be afraid; keep on speaking, do not be silent. For I am with you, and no one is going to attack and harm you, because I have many people in this city." So Paul stayed for a year and a half, teaching them the word of God.

While Gallio was proconsul of Achaia, the Jews made a united attack on Paul and brought him into court. "This man," they charged, "is persuading the people to worship God in ways contrary to the law."

Just as Paul was about to speak, Gallio said to the Jews, "If you Jews were making a complaint about some misdemeanor or serious crime, it would be reasonable for me to listen to you. But since it involves questions about words and names and your own law—settle the matter yourselves. I will not be a judge of such things."[445]

Two things jump out from this passage. First, Paul continued preaching in Corinth knowing a) doing so upset the Jews of the city and b) he (Paul) would <u>not</u> be prosecuted by proconsul Junius Gallio. If the proconsul were the older brother of Paul's long and dear friend, then one reasonably understands why Paul did not fear prosecution in Corinth and there was no need to ascribe the incident to divine intervention. Further, notice that a very similar circumstance happened to Paul later in *Acts* when he returned to Jerusalem and entered the Temple. The Jews went bananas intending to do bodily harm to him. To keep the peace, the Romans responded by arresting Paul and later transported him to Rome for trial. Why was Paul set free in Corinth yet held under

---

[445] *Acts* 18:9-15.

arrest in Jerusalem when identical charges were brought by Jews in both cities? It appears Paul received preferential treatment in Corinth from the brother of Seneca.

Even more unusual are the actions of Gallio immediately after he refused to try Paul.

> And he drove them away from the judgment
> seat. And they all took hold of Sosthenes,
> the leader of the synagogue, and began
> beating him in front of the judgment seat.
> <u>And Gallio was not concerned about any of</u>
> <u>these things.</u>[446] [Emphasis added.]

My reading of the events of this passage is as follows. After dismissing the charges against Paul brought by the Jews of the local synagogue, Gallio ordered his lictors to physically drive the Jews prosecuting Paul out of his courtroom. Then supporters of Paul (or perhaps attendants of Gallio) jumped into the fray and beat the Jews in full view of Gallio. The proconsul "was not concerned" by the beating the accusers of Paul received in his courtroom. It is one thing to refuse to hear a case on jurisdictional grounds (i.e., handle this matter in your own courts). It's quite another act to allow (and possibly encourage) others to physically beat the accusers of Paul in your presence. This action shows overt bias by Gallio favoring Paul. Recall that Gallio fled Greece early in his term as proconsul claiming the land made him ill. Could it be that Gallio's beating of leading Jews who accused Paul created such an uproar among the Jewish community that Gallio was force to leave the province? I find this to be a reasonable conclusion from the facts.

Similar Language and Thoughts Found In Paul's Epistles and Writings of Seneca

Seneca was the foremost Roman stoic philosopher of his day. Entire books have been written noting the comparison of Stoic philosophy with Christianity and, in particular, the epistles of Paul. Below are comparative passages from the writings of Paul

---

[446] *Acts* 18:16-17.

and Seneca outside of the disputed correspondence. These items were found during a day of research. Undoubtedly more material exists that I failed to uncover.

Paul	Seneca
All humans are one and should treat each other accordingly.	
"There is no more Jew nor Greek, slave nor free, man nor woman, but you <u>are all one</u> in Christ Jesus. Merely by belonging to Christ, you are Abraham's seed, the heirs he was promised." Galatians 3:38-9 "Here there is no Greek or Jew, circumcised or uncircumcised, barbarian, Scythian, slave or free, but Christ is all, and is in all. Therefore, as God's chosen people, holy and dearly loved, clothe yourselves with compassion, kindness, humility, gentleness and patience. Bear with each other and <u>forgive whatever grievances you may have against one another</u>." Colossians 3:11-13.	"[A]ll that you behold, that which comprises both god and man, is <u>one – we are the parts of one great body</u>. Nature produced us related to one another, since she created us from the same source and to the same end. She engendered in us mutual affection, and made us prone to friendships. She established fairness and justice; according to her ruling, it is more wretched to commit than to suffer injury. ... Let us possess things in common; for birth is ours in common. Our relations with one another are like a stone arch, which would collapse if the stones did not <u>mutually support each other</u>, and which is upheld in this very way." Seneca's Epistle XCV.
Faith in God and Imitation	
"Remember your leaders, who spoke the word of God to you. Consider the outcome of their way of life and <u>imitate their faith</u>. Jesus Christ is the same yesterday and today and forever." Hebrews 13:7.	"The first way to worship the gods is to believe in the gods. ... Then be a good man. Whoever imitates [the Gods], is worshipping them sufficiently." Seneca's Epistle XCV.
God's Children	

"The Spirit himself testifies with our spirit that we are God's children. Now if we are children, then we are heirs— heirs of God." Romans 8:16-17.	"See how unjustly the gifts of heaven are valued even by some who profess themselves philosophers. ... [I]f you rightly appreciate the partiality of nature for you, you cannot but confess yourself to be her spoiled child. So it is; the immortal gods have unto this day always held us most dear, and have bestowed upon us the greatest possible honor, a place nearest to themselves." Seneca *On Benefits*, II.29.
God's spirit dwells with you	
"Don't you know that you yourselves are God's temple and that God's Spirit lives in you?" 1 Corinthians 3:16. "Do you not know that your body is a temple of the Holy Spirit, who is in you, whom you have received from God?" 1 Corinthians 6:19.	"God is near you, he is with you, he is within you. This is what I mean, Lucilius: a holy spirit indwells within us, one who marks our good and bad deeds, and is our guardian." Seneca's Epistle XLI.
Eternal Life	
"But now that you have been set free from sin and have become slaves to God, the benefit you reap leads to holiness, and the result is eternal life." Romans 6:22.	"The day which we fear as our last is but the birthday of eternity." Seneca's Epistle CII. "And when the time shall come for the world to be blotted out in order that it may begin its life anew ... [t]hen also the souls of the blessed, who have partaken of immortality, when it shall seem best to God to create the universe anew ... and shall be

	changed again into our former elements." Seneca *On Consolation* XXVI.[447]
Condemnation of incest between stepson and stepmother.	
"It is actually reported that there is sexual immorality among you, and of a kind that does not occur even among pagans, a man has his father's wife." 1 Corinthians 5:1.	"Then quench the fires of impious love [incest between stepson and stepmother], I pray, and shun a deed which no barbaric land has ever done, neither the Getae, wandering on their plains, nor the inhospitable Taurians, nor scattered Scythians. Drive this hideous purpose from thy chaste mind." Seneca's play *Phaedra*.

The parallels raise an eyebrow but one cannot say more than propose that Paul had been exposed to Stoic philosophy somewhere in his past. There is no smoking gun linking the philosophy of Paul to that of Seneca, although I must admit to being a fan of the theory.

---

[447] The stoic concept of eternal life was quite different than that held by modern Christians. For the stoic, those who have travailed in life until the end of this world live on by having their being broken down into the basic elements of God's creation and, thus, live on symbolically the way a building lives on when it has been torn down and its bricks used to erect a new structure. That said, my personal opinion is that modern Christianity mistakes the letters of Paul for advocating the doctrine of bodily resurrection. The resurrection Paul spoke of was spiritual. See "So will it be with the resurrection of the dead. The body that is sown is perishable, it is raised imperishable; it is sown in dishonor, it is raised in glory; it is sown in weakness, it is raised in power; it is sown a natural body, it is raised a spiritual body." 1 Cor. 15:42-44. Emphasis added. Only a tortured reading of the words renders Paul teaching bodily resurrection.

Chronology

This chronology contains dates for events accepted by scholars and those backed by my own theories.

47 BCE	Herod bar Antipater marries Doris, Idumean princess.
46 BCE	Antipater born to Herod and Doris.
41 BCE	Herod divorces and exiles Doris (along with her son Antipater); betroths Mariamne bat Alexander, Hasmonean princess.
40 BCE	Herod crowned king of the Jews by the Roman senate.
37 BCE	Herod marries Hasmonean princess Mariamne; Jerusalem captured by Herod and Romans; King Antigonus, the last Hasmonean king, executed by Marc Antony at urging of Herod.
36 BCE	Herod appoints his brother-in-law Aristobulus ben Alexander high priest; Herod assassinates Aristobulus (drowned in the palace swimming pool at Jericho).
35 BCE	Marc Antony acquits Herod of the murder of Aristobulus (trial held in Antioch). Herod executes his uncle Joseph, who he left in control of the Jewish kingdom, upon return to Judea.
31 BCE	Herod captures Fortress Hyrcania and executes the members of Antigonus' family besieged there. Battle of Actium.
30 BCE	Herod executes Hyrcanus II, the former high priest and grandfather of his wife Mariamne.

29 BCE	Herod executes Queen Mariamne bat Alexander; Herod recalls and remarries Doris; restores position of his son Antipater.
28 BCE	Herod executes Alexandra, mother of his wife Mariamne and daughter of Hyrcanus II; Herod also executes his brother-in-law, Costobarus, for harboring the Hasmonean sons of Babas.
9 BCE	Herod prosecutes border war with Nabatea; Caesar demotes Herod from "Caesar's Friend" to "Subject King" as punishment for unauthorized Nabatean war; Obadas dies and Aretas IV becomes king of Nabatea.
7 BCE	Herod executes Aristobulus and Alexander, his Hasmonean sons by Mariamne; Herod elevates Antipater to coregent and prime heir; Antipater marries Mariamne bat Aristobulus, the young daughter of his dead Hasmonean brother.
6 BCE	Antipater secretly marries Mariamne bat Antigonus, daughter of the last Hasmonean king.
5 BCE	Antipater sails for Rome as word of his secret marriage to Mariamne bat Antigonus leaks out to his Herodian enemies.
4 BCE (spring)	Pheroras poisoned; Antipater returns to Judea from Rome and is arrest the moment he lands in Caesarea; Antipater tried in Jerusalem before Quinctilius Varus for conspiracy to murder Herod; Varus finds Antipater guilt and sends his verdict to Caesar Augustus for confirmation.
4 BCE (winter)	Antipater conceives a son by Mariamne bat Antigonus while imprisoned; Caesar Augustus confirms Antipater's death sentence but suggests Herod exile Antipater rather than execute him; Herod defies Caesar by executing Antipater, then dies himself five days later; Herod's last will names Archelaus his successor as Jewish king; Herod buried in elaborate ceremony at Herodium.
3 BCE	Archelaus marries his niece Mariamne bat Aristobulus (Mary Magdalene); Archelaus turns his soldiers loose

	on the crowd in Jerusalem at first Passover after death of Herod, then departs for Rome along together with Antipas leaving Herod Philip in charge of kingdom; Varus believes he has suppressed the Jewish revolt touched off by Archelaus and returns to Antioch; Antigonus ben Antipater (aka Jesus Christ) born to Mariamne bat Antigonus at Bethlehem (near Herodium) in late summer; Actions of procurator Sabinus revive Jewish revolt against Rome.
3-1 BCE	Major Jewish revolt rages in the Jewish kingdom eventually suppressed by Roman governor of Syria, Publius Quinctilius Varus; Caesar probates Herod's will naming Archelaus Ethnarch (not king), Antipas and Philip are named tetrarchs.
6 CE	Archelaus divorces Mariamne bat Aristobulus to marry Glaphyra of Cappadocia; Archelaus deposed by Romans and sent into exile in Gaul; Judea, Samaria and Idumea become prefects of Roman province of Syria; Annas ben Seth named high priest by the Romans.
11 CE	Phasaelus ben Timius (aka Paul of Tarsus) born.
26 CE	Pontius Pilate appointed prefect of Judea.
29 CE	Rabbi Yochanan (John the Baptist) begins his public ministry.
31 CE	Sejanus, chief minister to Emperor Tiberius, executed.
32 CE	Emperor Tiberius issues decree throughout the Roman Empire not to mistreat the Jews.
34 CE	Herodias divorces Herod Boethus and marries Herod Antipas. In order to marry Herodias, Herod Antipas divorces Phasaelus, daughter of Nabatean king Aretas IV. Rabbi Yochanan the Baptizer condemns marriage of Antipas to Herodias on religious grounds. Yeshua begins his public ministry—wedding at Cana. Rabbi Yochanan arrested by Herod Antipas and later executed.
35 CE	King Aretas declares war on Antipas; Aretas attacks and defeats the forces of Herod Antipas in battle.

36 CE	Proconsul and president of Syria, Lucius Vitellius, takes several legions into Parthia deposing the Parthian king; Yeshua declared king in Jerusalem just prior to Passover; Yeshua crucified in Jerusalem by Pontius Pilate.
37 CE	Pontius Pilate removed as prefect of Rome by Proconsul Vitellius; Emperor Tiberius dies; Claudius becomes Roman emperor.
38 CE	Stephen stoned to death in Jerusalem by order of the Sanhedrin.
39 CE	Herod Antipas removed by Caligula. Herod Agrippa becomes king of the Jewish kingdom.
41 CE	Caligula assassinated. Herod Agrippa assists Claudius in securing Roman throne. Paul's first trip to Rome to meet Peter and James; begins first missionary journey.
43 CE	Herod Agrippa executes James ben Zebedee.[448]
44 CE	Paul's second trip to Jerusalem. Herod Agrippa dies.
46 CE	Famine starts in Judea.
49-50 CE	Paul goes to Corinth finding Aquila and Priscilla after their expulsion from Rome by Claudius.
51 CE (summer)	Paul hauled before Roman tribunal of proconsul Lucius Junius Gallio Annaeus (brother of Seneca) in Corinth. Paul leaves Greece for Judea.[449]
52 CE	Council of Jerusalem.
54 CE	Arrest of Paul in Jerusalem by Felix; Claudius dies and Nero becomes Roman emperor.
56 CE	Festus succeeds Felix as prefect of Judea and deports Paul to Rome.[450]

---

[448] *Acts* 12:1. I assume this event occurred in the last year of Herod Agrippa's reign as it is related in the text just prior to the death of Agrippa.

[449] *Acts* says Paul sailed for "Syria" but I believe they use the word to indicate the Roman province of Syria (which included Judea), not the modern-day country of Syria. *Acts* 18:18.

[450] We date this event from a change in Roman prefects in Judea. *Acts* tells us Paul was first tried before the Roman prefect Felix and, then, new charges were

57 CE	Paul arrives in Rome after ship wreck in Malta.
59 CE	Paul's two-year Roman house arrest ends.
63 CE	James the Just executed by Sanhedrin.
64 CE	Great fire of Rome blame for which Nero put on the Christians as scapegoats.
65 CE	Nero orders Seneca to commit suicide.
66 CE	Great Jewish revolt against Rome begins.
68 CE	Nero dies, succession unsettled.
69 CE	Four successive emperors reign in Rome until the tumult is ended by the ascension of Vespasian.
70 CE	Romans capture Jerusalem and level the Temple.

brought when Porcius Festus succeed Felix in office. See *Acts*, Ch. 25. We know from external sources that Festus succeeded Felix as prefect of Judea in 59 or 60 CE.

Index of Supplements

250

Supplement 1
From Death of Herod
to End of Revolt, *Antiquities*

<u>**Antiquities XVII, Chapter 8**</u>

1. Salome, sister of Herod, frees leading men of Judea held prisoner at the Hippodrome who Herod had ordered to be killed. Herod's soldiers proclaim Archelaus king.
2. Archelaus puts on elaborate funeral for Herod at Herodium.
3. Seven-day mourning period for Herod's death. Archelaus speaks nicely with the Jewish people. The crowd makes numerous requests to Archelaus and he "contradicted them in nothing."

<u>**Antiquities XVII, Chapter 9**</u>

1. Jewish people lament killing of Matthias, priest who pulled down Herod's golden eagle from Temple gates. They want Jozar replaced as high priest. Archelaus replaces the high priest but refuses to punish others they wish punished.
2. Jewish people upset all their demands are not met.
3. Feast of Unleavened Bread (Passover) occurs. People still lamenting the deaths of the Pharisee priests, Matthias and Judas. They demonstrate at the Temple in Jerusalem and Archelaus turns loose his soldiers on them killing 3000 men. Varus, Roman president of Syria, arrives in Jerusalem and quells the disturbance. Archelaus sails for Rome leaving Philip in control of the government. Varus returns to Antioch thinking the danger has passed. Caesar's

procurator, Sabinus, goes to Jerusalem and seizes Herod's palaces.

4. Antipas also sails for Rome. Salome, sister of Herod, allies herself with Antipas.
5. Archelaus and Antipas each appear before Augustus pleading for the kingdom.
6. Nicolas of Damascus (chief minister to the deceased Herod) speaks for Archelaus.
7. Caesar is moved by the pleas of Nicolas, to uphold Herod's last will that made Archelaus prime heir but Caesar fails to make an immediate ruling on the matter.

Antiquities XVII, Chapter 10

1. Malthace, mother of Archelaus and Antipas, dies in Rome. Letter arrives in Rome informing Caesar that the Jewish revolt has renewed after Archelaus sailed. Varus thinks he has the revolt suppressed. He leaves one legion in Jerusalem and returns to Antioch. Sabinus, Caesar's procurator, is left behind in Jerusalem in charge of the situation.
2. Sabinus uses force while searching for Herod's money. The force used by Sabinus sets off a new revolt during the Jewish festival of Pentecost. The Roman legion left in Jerusalem is partially overrun and forced into a citadel.
3. Sabinus under siege in tower.
4. 2000 of Herod's retired veteran troops join the fight against the Romans.
5. Judas, son of Ezekias, "head of the robbers" (zealots) attacks Sepphoris in Galilee seizing money and weapons.
6. Simon, slave of Herod, declares himself king and burns down the palace at Jericho. Roman forces later execute Simon.
7. Athronges, a shepherd, also sets himself up as king together ruling together with his three brothers and "retained his power a great while". He and his men killed a great many of the Romans and Jewish auxiliary troops. Archelaus (apparently now back in Judea from Rome) takes

the eldest of the brothers prisoner. Later, the last of the brothers of Athronges surrendered to Archelaus.

8. Now Judea was full of "robbers".

9. Varus marches down from Antioch with two Roman legions plus four troops of horsemen and auxiliary forces from allied kings. He stops in Beirut along the way and is given 1500 troops by the citizens of the city. Aretas, king of Nabatea, agrees to attack Galilee at the request of the Romans. Aretas takes Sepphoris, enslaves its citizens, sacks then burns the city. Varus marches on Samaria (aka, the northern Jewish kingdom formerly known as Israel). After laying waste to Samaria, Varus marches on Jerusalem to break the siege of the remaining Romans in that city.

10. After breaking the rebel siege against Sabinus in Jerusalem, Varus sends part of his forces back out into the country to "seek out those that had been the authors of the revolt". He crucifies 2000 and sends others to Rome for trial (which included unidentified relatives of Herod).

Antiquities XVII, Chapter 11

1. Varus secures country (Jewish kingdom) and returns to Rome. Varus gives a party of Jews permission to sail to Rome to petition Caesar for authority to live under their own laws. 8000 Jews resident in Jerusalem join the embassage of Jews from the motherland. Archelaus is also there along with Philip (who is great friends with Varus).

2. Main complaint of Jews is that Archelaus slaughtered 3000 at the Temple triggering revolt.

3. Nicolas, speaking for Archelaus, counters that the Jews killed were insurrectionist who forced Archelaus' hand.

4. Caesar makes final disposition of Herod's former kingdom. Archelaus, Antipas, and Philip become tetrarchs with Archelaus ruling the lion's share of his father's former kingdom.

5. Caesar confirms Salome's inheritance granted in Herod's will.

Supplement 2
Last Days of Herod: Events
Between Eclipse and Passover

Josephus records the following events as occurring after the date a lunar eclipse was visible in Judea but before the Passover. In 4 BCE, there were only 28 days between the lunar eclipse and the Passover for that year. I do not believe the below enumerated events could have occurred within 28 days.

- Herod travels beyond the Jordan to the baths at Callirrhof seeking a cure
- Herod returns to Jericho
- Herod commands all principal men of the country be called to him and placed in the Hippodrome leaving orders for his sister Salome to kill these men upon his own death
- Ambassadors return from Rome with Caesar's verdict against Antipater—Herod can execute Antipater but Caesar prefers exile
- Herod tries to kill himself but his aides prevent him from doing so
- Herod executes Antipater after it is reported Antipater attempted to negotiate his way out of jail
- Herod alters his will yet again naming Archelaus primary heir
- Herod dies
- Salome frees soldiers form the Hippodrome
- Archelaus declared king by Herod's soldiers

- Archelaus brings Herod's body from Jericho and prepares it for burial
- Elaborate burial. Body accompanied by massive procession and laid to rest at Herodium.
- Seven day mourning period for Herod
- Feast for people after mourning period ended[451]
- Archelaus, acting as king in first public meeting with people after Herod's mourning period ends, speaks nicely to the Jews. They make numerous requests and he grants them all.
- Later, the people want the high priest appointed by Herod replaced and persons punished culpable in the execution of priests who tore down Herod's golden eagle from the Temple gates. Archelaus changes high priests but refuses to punish anyone else.
- Later comes the Feast of Unleavened Bread (Passover) and things go terribly wrong. People still mad about the priest getting burned alive by Herod and Archelaus loses his cool. He turns his troops loose on the Jewish people demonstrating at the Temple killing 3000 men.

See Antiquities XVII, 7:4 through 9:3.

---

[451] Jewish Wars II 1:1.

Supplement 3
Governorship of Varus Dated
from Ancient Coins

First, a quick introduction to the historically significant Roman politician and general, Quinctilius Varus. He was of the patrician Quinctilii family, the son of Sextus Quinctilius who fought against Julius Caesar in the civil war. Varus became consul of Rome in 13 BCE and gave the funeral oratory for the famed Marcus Agrippa. Varus and future emperor Tiberius were married to sisters. He was governor of Africa province prior to coming to Syria. His life ended in 9 CE during the Battle of Teutoburg Forest at the hands of an alliance of Germanic tribes. Three Roman legions under Varus' overall command were utterly annihilated by the Germans and took his own life in the battle. His severed head, taken as a trophy by the Germans, eventually found its way to Rome.

Josephus names Sentius Saturninus as the predecessor to Quinctilius Varus as Roman governor of Syria. [452] The academic consensus is that Saturninus held the position from 9-6 BCE. We have archeological proof on the date of Varus' governorship of Syria.

> On the evidence of coins ... it is established that Varus was governor of Syria in the years 25, 26 and 27 of the *aera Actiaca*. Since the Actian era begins on 2 September 31 BC * * *, its 25th year runs from autumn 7 BC to

---

[452] <u>Antiquities</u>, XVII 5:2.

autumn 6 BC. Varus must therefore have
arrived in Syria before autumn 6 BC.[453]

Therefore, the archaeological evidence from the coins gives
a potential range for the Syrian governorship of Varus from
September of 7 BCE to September of 3 BCE.[454] Roman governors
under Augustus generally served for a minimum of three years in
major provinces.[455] Historians say Varus arrived in Syria a poor
man in a rich country and left a rich man in a poor country.[456]
Given this point, I believe Varus served at least the standard three-
year term in Syria. Returning to the coins evidence, the disconnect
between calendar years and Actian years (which begin and end in
September) muddies the waters a bit. The most likely start date for
Varus' term as governor of Syria was during the first half of 6 BCE
with a normally scheduled three-year term ending in the first half
of 3 BCE. Could his governorship have been longer? Yes. We
don't have coins from every year a Roman governor served in Syria
during the first century before the Common Era. Further, under
my timeline, the Jewish revolt against Archelaus started in 3 BCE,
which, if correct, very likely necessitated an extension of Varus'
stay to command the Syrian legions during this conflict. Could
Varus' governorship have been shorter? Unlikely. Not only do we
have the coins showing three specific years but governorships
under Augustus were generally for between three and five years.

On balance, I believe the coin evidence together with the
normal term of Roman governors of proconsul rank under
Augustus makes it highly likely that Varus was still governor of
Syria in 3 BCE when I propose the Jewish revolt commenced.

---

[453] The History of the Jewish People in the Age of Jesus Christ by Emil Schurer,
Fergus Millar, and Geza Vermes (Continuum International 1973) at page 257;
see also Hermeneutical Manual: Or, Introduction to the Exegetical Study of the
Scriptures of the New Testament By Patrick Fairbairn (Smith 1859) at page 526.
[454] The beginning and end of the 25th through 27th years of the Actian era.
[455] The Chronology of the Gospels, The London Quarterly Review, Volume
CXXX (January - April, 1871) at page 268.
[456] Influence of Wealth in Imperial Rome By William S. Davis (Biblo & Tannen
1998) at page 17.

Supplement 4
Antipater ben Herod
as Coregent

The below quotations from the works of Josephus stand as strong evidence that Antipater ben Herod was coregent with his father prior to the former's arrest and trial before Quinctilius Varus, Roman governor of the Syrian province.

- "However, **[Antipater] governed the nation jointly with his father,** being indeed no other than a king already." Antiquities XVII 1:1 (emphasis added).

- "When the affairs of Herod were in the condition I have described, **all the public affairs depended upon Antipater**; and his power was such, that he could do good turns to as many as he pleased, and this by his father's concession * * *." Antiquities XVII 2:4 (emphasis added).

- Speech of Herod: "[What] could equal what I have done to Antipater? To whom I have, in a manner, **yielded up my royalty while I am alive**, and whom I have openly named for the successor to my dominions in my testament * * *." Jewish Wars I 32:2 (emphasis added).

- Speech of Antipater: "And indeed what was there that could possibly provoke me against thee? Could the hope of being king do it? **I was a king already.**" Jewish Wars I 32:3 (emphasis added).

- Josephus also tells us Antipater clothed himself in purple upon returning to the palace in Jerusalem from his trip to Rome. Antiquities, XVII 5:2. Only the king is allowed to wear purple, especially so in the throne room with a Roman governor in attendance.

Topical Index

Made in the USA
Monee, IL
07 March 2021